In your hands is a trove of remarkable queer fiction.

It's contradictory and capacious. When thinking about curating this issue, I decided to seek out work from queer-identified writers of all orientations. I put on my editorial hat and searched for stories that describe a textural, granular, embodied experience of what it's like to be an ever-evolving blob moving about, to and fro, on this wretched planet. After all, a story should rearrange my mind, my genitals. Over the course of a month, I read five hundred stories from the slush pile. Each story showed me something. It was one of the best reading experiences of my life. No joke.

This issue contains seventeen stories of vulnerability, brilliance, and depth. They reckon with queerness and queer states of being from oblique angles. They gesture at the possibility of transformation via language, imagery, description, voice. A personal aside: Sometime during this editorial process, I started taking testosterone. The edges of the world sharpened and clarified; I became impatient for change. Perhaps you could think of the stories in this issue as a trail of polished gems left behind in a forest. Instead of leading you back home, they will help you find your way somewhere new and unexpected. That's my hope for you, and for all of us!

what we've dared imagine for it.[8] *The future of queer fiction is free of binaries and borders, so limitless that it's impossible to contain in one sentence.*[9] *The future of queer fiction is an unapologetic roar.*[10] *The future of queer fiction grows like a weed, like a rhizome: a holy plant splitting concrete patiently, radically, centering each of its shoots, blooming in ways that look strange and grotesque to the pedestrians who try to grind it back into the pavement.*[11] *The future of queer fiction is hysteria, feverish ecstasy that was once diagnosed as mental illness but is now intoxicating joy.*[12] *The future of queer fiction is writing so furiously about queernees that our stories are no longer in need of hiding away.*[13] *The future of queer fiction is boundless; bold, bright, and brilliant.*[14] *The future of queer fiction is something I'd love to see written on a bathroom wall.*[15] *The future of queer fiction is what it's always been—transgressive.*[16]

1. Vi Khi Nao. 2. Bryan Washington. 3. Sarah Gerard. 4. Christopher James Llego. 5. Dennis Norris II. 6. K-Ming Chang. 7. Emma Copley Eisenberg. 8. Kristen N. Arnett. 9. Kayla Kumari Upadhyaya. 10. Juli Delgado Lopera. 11. Bridget Brewer. 12. Venita Blackburn. 13. Timi Odueso. 14. hurmat kazmi. 15. Eileen Myles. 16. Paul Dalla Rosa.

Speaking of hope, during this time of great uncertainty and certain catastrophe, like everyone else, I've been thinking about the future. I asked the writers in this issue to complete the following sentence:

The future of queer fiction is _____ .

Here are their responses: *The future of queer fiction is terminal.*[1] *The future of queer fiction is beyond.*[2] *The future of queer fiction is manifest.*[3] *The future of queer fiction is full of sexy stretch marks, Asian sugar babies, and gushy* **Good morning** *texts.*[4] *The future of queer fiction is the present, and it's here to stay.*[5] *The future of queer fiction is collective liberation and new lineages of love.*[6] *The future of queer fiction is embodied, dirty, sad, funny, brave, introverted, intersectional, shameful, rural, suburban, and international; it looks clear-eyed and with precision at the vast and uncategorizable reality of how queers really live now in this landscape where profound liberation sits right up against profound suffering.*[7] *The future of queer fiction is bigger, broader, bolder than ever before; its shape and significance will continue to expand and grow far past*

I'll leave you with that. Good luck out there.

—PATTY YUMI COTTRELL

GUEST EDITOR
Patty Yumi Cottrell.

EDITOR
Claire Boyle.

EXECUTIVE DIRECTOR
Amanda Uhle.

FOUNDING EDITOR
Dave Eggers.

ART DIRECTOR
Sunra Thompson.

SALES & DISTRIBUTION MANAGER
Dan Weiss.

PUBLISHING ASSOCIATE
Eric Cromie.

WEB DEVELOPMENT
Brian Christian.

COPY EDITOR
Caitlin Van Dusen.

ASSISTED BY
Mehek Boparai, Claudia Brancart, Emma Brewer, Alia DeBurro, Annie Dills, Sophia DuRose,
Kitania Folk, Alexandra Galou, Paz O'Farrell, Finn O'Neil, Emma Theiss, Alvaro Villanueva.

MCSWEENEY'S PUBLISHING BOARD
Natasha Boas, Carol Davis, Brian Dice (president), Isabel Duffy-Pinner (secretary),
Dave Eggers, Caterina Fake, Hilary Kivitz, Jordan Kurland, Nion McEvoy,
Gina Pell, Jeremy Radcliffe, Jed Repko, Julia Slavin, Vendela Vida.

COVER ILLUSTRATION
Angie Wang.

INTERIOR ILLUSTRATIONS
Derek Abella.

TITLE-PAGE & TABLE-OF-CONTENTS ILLUSTRATIONS
Ariel Davis.

PRINTED IN
Canada.

McSWEENEY'S
QUARTERLY
CONCERN

– – –

ISSUE 62

– – –

Edited by
PATTY YUMI COTTRELL

– – –

WINTER 2020

McSWEENEY'S
SAN FRANCISCO

● *Introduction by Patty Yumi Cottrell* 1

● *Letters from RL Goldberg, Amanda Monti, Aarushi Agni, Drew Pham, and Emerson Whitney* ... 10

– – –

DEAR McSWEENEY'S,
Let me start with a joke, because jokes take the pressure off, I find. (I'm not unique in finding that, or in finding that there is often truth in jokes. Freud did that, and no one's done it better since.) Here's the joke:

So Heidegger is on his way to Marburg, Germany, to give a lecture, and, while sitting in the backseat of his car, he tells his driver he's tired of giving lectures. The driver says, "Right so. I look a bit like you." Heidegger says, "Yes, you do." They drive on and Heidegger looks out the window; it is raining. Heidegger watches one big droplet of water slide down the window, greedily swallowing smaller, weaker droplets. This depresses him and he cannot help but complain. Says something like, "I really wish I didn't have to give this lecture." The driver says, "Well, sir, maybe you don't know this about me, but whenever I drive you to your lectures, I sit in the back of the audience and listen. I don't know anything about philosophy, but, frankly, I've heard you give this lecture so many times, I could do it myself." Heidegger is very tired. He says, "This is not a bad idea. Let's trade clothes."

The driver pulls the car over. Heidegger is a bit body-shy and asks the driver to turn around while he takes off his trousers. The driver says, "Well, I've got two sons, and the same parts myself. Nothing I haven't seen before." Heidegger says, "Well, they're called privates. Turn around." The driver

does, chastened, and Heidegger passes him his clothes. They are the same size, so Heidegger's clothes look quite right on the driver. The driver fingers the lapels of the cream-colored jacket and says, "This is a beautiful cream-colored jacket." Heidegger puts on the driver's cap and says, "Toot, toot! I haven't driven in years. Uh-oh!" This does not inspire confidence.

They arrive at the lecture. They were already quite close; Heidegger didn't have to do any tricky maneuvers like a three-point turn or merging into oncoming traffic. The driver, dressed as Heidegger, climbs onto the stage and gives the presentation Heidegger would have given, perfectly mimicking the intonation of Heidegger, the pregnant pauses of Heidegger, the performed aloofness of Heidegger, the self-satisfied grin of Heidegger. In short, he *is* Heidegger, everyone believes. Heidegger-as-driver sits in the back of the lecture hall, enormously tickled.

Finally, an intrepid graduate student stands up, twirling his moustache. This graduate student has nothing against Heidegger per se, but he is intent on proving himself, on stumping Heidegger onstage for all the world to see. He has his career to think about. He asks a difficult question. In the last row, Heidegger catches his breath. Everyone puts their pens down. The room is so quiet, one can almost hear the graduate student sweating, his heart beating like an army goose-stepping. Onstage, the driver, dressed as Heidegger, rests his hands on

— — —

his great belly and says, "My son, this is such a simple question, I will let my driver answer it."

McSweeney's, have you heard this joke before? Perhaps you've heard a different version. Maybe in the version you know it is Spinoza or Einstein, not Heidegger, who gives a lecture. Of course, if the version you know features Spinoza, the joke might have to be adjusted slightly, since Spinoza wouldn't have had a driver—at least, not a car driver. I think we can agree on that.

But the joke isn't the point. The point is: I am not a sexologist. People come to me for advice about things of a sexual nature because I am—or I've been told that I am—irrepressibly genital. It's my pheromones. It takes no additional effort or mental concentration on my part. But I'm no expert. Still, I know all kinds of lurid things. When people ask me the kinds of questions they ask me, I assure them that whatever they tell me I will keep in the strictest confidence. Sometimes the questions make me sad: Why am I not pleasing my girlfriend sexually? What kinds of animals has the human female copulated with? How do I know I'm straight if I've never made love to a straight person? I think the answers I give are good. They're honest, at least. That's one thing I can do. I can listen. Sometimes I answer with a joke. But when people come to me, they're upset. A joke doesn't always take the pressure off. They want answers and they want results.

The things I've been told—wouldn't *you* like to know?

Sincerely,

RL GOLDBERG
SODOM, ME

DEAR McSWEENEY'S,

The last time you wrote, you asked if hands were my favorite part of the body. How did you know?

My mother was a very elegant woman and she had very elegant hands. She took great care of them and lathered each finger with Vaseline and lotion before she went to bed. The only hands more beautiful than my mother's are my own. I am not elegant and sometimes I am not a woman but my fingers are silken and firm, gracious little creatures, separate from the rest of me like golden boots are separate from a Chihuahua or clouds are separate from the sea.

Once, while my mother was on the phone with one of her long-distance lovers, I spent the afternoon looking at hands in magazines. I used tiny nail scissors to cut out my favorites and put them into an envelope labeled HAND, which is German for "hand." I found mostly slim hands with clean manicures, waning moons rising from the cuticles. I particularly like hands with deteriorated skin folding like sand dunes, but those were more difficult to come by in the glossy pages. Eventually, I made a pencil drawing of my own hand and arranged all my cutouts around the drawing like a heavy frame.

– – –

In my last year of high school, my friend's mother cast me as a hand model for a dish soap commercial. Before the shoot I was given a free manicure and travel-sized moisturizer, which was the first and last time I would ever moisturize my hands. On set I was told that my knuckle-to-palm proportions were perfect. I said, "Thank you." Everyone was excited about the illustrious career ahead of me, and my mother's friend became my agent and said my hands would be famous and I said, "Thank you." I met other hand models and all of them wore tragic little gloves to prevent the markings of life from leaking into their skin. I was to work on a look-book and my agent made me interact with various objects, from fine jewelry to the necks of bottles. I was a natural with rings, and the centerpiece of my look-book would be a photograph of my hand fingering a piece of silver.

Water (Aqua), Glycerin, Prunus Amygdalus Dulcis (Sweet Almond) Oil, Stearic Acid, Cetearyl Alcohol, Ceteareth-20, Cocos Nucifera (Coconut) Oil, Macadamia Ternifolia Seed Oil, Citrus Aurantium Bergamia (Bergamot) Fruit Oil, Glyceryl Stearate, PEG-100 Stearate, Phenoxyethanol, Tocopherol, Butyrospermum Parkii (Shea Butter), Glycine Soja (Soybean) Oil, Lactic Acid, Citrus Grandis (Grapefruit) Peel Oil, Fusanus Spicatus Wood Oil, Disodium EDTA, Benzoic Acid, Dehydroacetic Acid, Ethylhexylglycerin, Aloe Barbadensis

Leaf Juice, Daucus Carota Sativa (Carrot) Root Extract, Beta-Carotene, D-Limonene, Linalool, Farnesol.

A week before my third casting, I was making a fruitcake for my mother and the Dutch oven was heavier than expected and I let it slip onto my hand. The smell of burned flesh mingled with that of sweet strawberry. Pain rang up my bone as I called my agent. "Blemishes are unacceptable," she said simply. "What a pity, though. Your hands were special," and maybe I did it by accident and maybe I didn't—I couldn't tell you anymore— but I still have the scar. Sometimes you need a record.

I was with some boy—in those days you were always with some boy—and he introduced me to his friend and the first thing I noticed about her were her hands and in this moment I had a flashback to that first hand drawing and it all seemed to click, but too quickly for me to hear and I went home with the boy and thought of her fingers tracing my thigh as his frail body twisted and turned into tradition.

When I was fifteen, we walked through the city in which my father lived but we didn't meet my father, because he had started another family and he had decided there were only so many hands he wanted to hold. So instead my mother took me to where the fortune-tellers gathered. A big lady wrapped in purple fabric came over and took my hand. "May I?" she asked and I nodded. She opened my

– – –

palm and traced a circle on my skin and refolded my fingers with surprise. "What a shame. I cannot read you." She explained that I was a palm reader, myself. My mother was kind of crying at this point and I was not exactly sure why but for the next four days she stayed in bed while I kept on coming back to the purple lady, and I bought her coffee and cigarettes as she taught me to read palms. On the fifth day she gifted me a necklace with a little plastic hand tied around a white thread. It must've been chopped off a beauty doll or something.

In the candlelight my best friend and I tattooed vague geometric shapes onto the insides of our palms using sewing needles and India ink, and it looked like crap but it was also the most beautiful thing I had ever seen, our rhythmic movements spreading the imperfect ink, like the ocean itself drawing blemishes into sand.

"Use your gifts well," the purple lady told me the last time I saw her. The thread of my necklace is dark now, soaked in juices and dust, but I still have it hanging around my neck and whenever someone asks about it I read their palm. Usually, I am terrible at love but it happens often that I will accidentally seduce the person whose palm I am reading. There was, for example, X., from Paris, who was a real snob until I read his palms and he melted like a puppy and grabbed my shoulders and promised me the whole of the city in this very French

way and we kissed because it felt easy but I am not sure he ever saw me for anything other than seeing his own hands. There was also K., who, after the reading, took me up to her room and threw me onto her mattress and fucked me hard with her fist and four fingers, which I took as a sort of payment for the reading. And there was M., who kept on writing me letters long after the reading but at the time I was so heartbroken that I had lost track of whom or why. The problem with palm readers is that you cannot read your own—the beauty has to find you all by herself.

We were on the fire escape and the moon was waning and she took my chin, looked at my lips, let go of my face, and took my hand, guided two of my fingers into her mouth, and I became weightless. "So soft," she said, sighing, where sky and water meet and I thanked my hands for forgiving me for all the years of neglect and I entered the ocean and watched my fingers glide in and out of the warm tide and her silken rupture spill into the history of my skin.

Dear McSweeney's, these are my hands—will you let me look at yours the next time I see you? In this life so full of sensuous human activity we have everything that is beautiful and everything that is wasted find us through these palms.

Hand-signed with love,

AMANDA MONTI
BROOKLYN, NY

— — —

DEAR McSWEENEY'S,
I have a problem with my lover's pointy
elbows. In March, we fled New York
City to my family's home in Madison,
Wisconsin. And though it's ill-advised
under the circumstances, I frequently
jeopardize our relationship by telling
my lover I would change nothing
about them except for their pointy-ass
elbows. But then I remember they have
knees. Their knees are also very pointy.
Our relationship is healthy, all things
considered, except that when their
elbows graze me, I scream out in pain.
Sometimes I make a joke that they are
"boning" me in my parents' house.

It's mid-May now and we are
still here. I am no longer in physical
proximity to many of my friends and
coworkers. I am privileged enough to
be doing fine despite being immuno-
compromised and having parents who
go to the hospital every day for work.
We have space to move around in my
parents' Midwestern open-plan home,
though there is never the illusion of
privacy. We miss and worry about our
friends, but we make it work. We video-
conference and complain endlessly
about the failures of that medium.

For example, the lag makes it
impossible to sing in unison. I still
perform comedy online to audiences
of a hundred in deafening silence. Our
team works together to figure out how
to write sketches by threading together
videos sourced from different locations.

In work meetings, I joke about how
our rooms all connect through our
screen to make one big sci-fi room. What
Escher-istic shapes that room must be
assuming, with its constantly changing
architecture; our rooms move and
rearrange like the staircases in a magical
British boarding school. Our faces
change size depending on how many of
us are present. We are in a Rubik's cube
we will never see from the outside.

Sometimes things happen in our
real rooms that others cannot see
from our ephemeral collective room.
One time my partner forgot I was in a
meeting and kissed me suddenly on the
mouth, and I hoped no one saw. One
time the computer fell off my stack of
pillows and onto my boobs. Sometimes
I try to whisper something to someone
in my real room while still nodding
attentively at someone answering my
question. There is one clean square
of my bedroom that everyone can
see, and everything else is covered in
Cheetos dust. Kidding, but it would be
dangerous for you to try and prove it.

Sometimes I make a joke like
"Zoom, zoom, zoom, I want you in my
room!" and then we mourn because we
can't be in one another's rooms.

What's really been getting my goat,
McSweeney's, is that I can't know for
sure when anyone is talking to me
unless they say my name. Similarly,
when there is body language, I can't
know for sure if that body language is
directed at me.

I recently developed a crush on one
of my professional correspondents. I
see them in meetings sometimes. They

– – –

live in a little box in New York City. As do I, in Madison, Wisconsin. I imagine that sometimes our little boxes must appear side by side on someone else's computer, and that idea, for whatever reason, is a little romantic. Try as we might, we cannot make eye contact with each other. It's impossible. If I wanted to create the illusion of eye contact, I'd have to look directly into the camera, located above my screen, but in doing so, I could not look at their eyes in their image, the cruel paradox being that in order to make eye contact with someone, you must break eye contact with them. This, of course, ruins the whole game of eye contact, and as far as I am concerned, does not confer the same oxytocin boost that accompanies real-time impassioned gazes.

There are some workarounds, perhaps. I have figured out that when I make a joke and they laugh, some programs will highlight their square, and some programs will put their face on the screen for everyone to see. This is not eye contact, of course, but it *is* a reminder that I am not just screaming into a void, but in fact eliciting a physical reaction from another human being, which, if you think about it, is a little like touching. I do suggest muting yourself if you're going to giddily laugh at the jokes of someone with whom you are supposed to be in a professional working relationship. Or unmute, depending on how daring and direct you want to be. Sometimes you can sing a word and see if someone sings back.

Sometimes you can wear a feather boa, or install a program that lets you put a filter on your face that turns your whole body into an avocado, and see if someone says something about it.

There's a guy on YouTube, Brighton West, who shows you how to use a teleprompter mirror, external monitor, and an external web camera to reflect the image of your friend at the same eye level as your camera. This system costs a fair amount of money that, depending on your profession and your level of loneliness, you might want to just donate to COVID relief or a bail fund.

In any case, I am still getting boned on the regular.

Yours,

AARUSHI AGNI
MADISON, WI

DEAR McSWEENEY'S,
I cried for hours this morning over a cat. She's called Katyusha, named for the Russian folk song–cum–World War II missile launcher. My mother used to whistle the song when I was a child—she remembers it from the American War, when political cadres went from village to village, indoctrinating the people with revolutionary ideas and songs and fervor and, yes, fear. Katyusha wasn't killed by accident, nor did she die at the hands of a novel virus or the police—she's very much alive. If anything, she's healthy and, I hope, happy. I let my ex take her, and because she took her, I spent my morning covered in snot and sobbing on

– – –

the floor of my now-empty apartment. Given the times, my tears feel irrational, selfish, hysterical, even. It's not like I'm a stranger to loss. Dad ran out on me, I lost friends in Afghanistan, and a pair of my kittens died of heart failure. But I can't deny it: I cried for an hour over a cat, and I hope you won't judge me too harshly for this, but losing her felt like losing a daughter.

Before I go on, let's get some things straight (no pun intended) first. I'm a trans woman, and for as long as I can remember, I've wanted children. Maybe I'm looking for a do-over of my own childhood, to revise it in someone else, but I'm already starting to sound like a crazy cat lady with such hysterics. Yet if I am to be truly accepted as a woman, there shouldn't be barriers to my becoming a crazy cat lady, in the same way that I should also experience the indignities of living as a woman: daily street harassment, inequality at work, and the urge to apologize for every slight, even (some would say especially) if I'm not the cause. J. K. Rowling and her kith might go further, say there's more to being a woman. I should bleed monthly. I should have the right downstairs mix-up. I should be able to carry and birth babies. But unlike the present Voldemort of the gender debate, the question isn't whether I am or am not a woman, but rather what it means for me to be a woman. Sadly, in the same way that Rowling lacks empathy for her own gender,

I lack a womb. Instead of bleeding, my time of the month consists of explosive diarrhea. Instead of the "female" reproductive system, I have this outsize clitoris that needs to be tucked between my buttocks when going to the beach. (I don't often go.) And instead of carrying and birthing children, I am a crazy cat lady.

It's not that I think I'd be a good mother. I'd be a bad sequel to my own mother. Rather, the act of mothering is, for me, the ultimate creative act. Much like developing a character, raising a child (or, in my case, a cat) should privilege their agency. Characters should have a life of their own that continues beyond the page, just as children should have lives extending beyond the confines of childhood. Cats are good training for this, as they never fail to remind you that you hold little, if any, sway over them. Cats would make for excellent characters in fiction. But more than agency and desire, our characters need nourishment and growth and love—love, above all else. Especially when they're being little shits.

And while I can't remember a time when I didn't truly want to have children, I also can't remember a time when I wasn't a little shit. In the Vietnamese lunar calendar, I was born in the year of—you guessed it—the cat. Coincidentally, when I was a child, love was always a faraway thing, found only in fragments: Mom breastfeeding my sister, Dad carrying me on his shoulders through the breaking waves, or my

The QUEER
FICTION ISSUE

McSWEENEY'S
QUARTERLY

ISSUE NO.
SIXTY-TWO

– – –

mother's tears and panic when I split my chin on the bed at the age of three. I still have the scar—proof that there was a time when I felt my parents' love. I find that I write often about how my parents passed their traumas on to me and my siblings. I could never understand why a war that'd ended a decade before I was born took up so much space in their lives. It drove me to join the military, to go to war (I usually just tell people I went for the college money, which is also true), as if shared experiences of violence could've brought us all together again.

Obviously, I left the military and became a writer and a teacher instead. Those things, and a crazy cat lady. By the time you read this, more than 150,000 Americans will have died of COVID-19. Protests and occupations of public spaces will go on. Police brutality will, unfortunately, continue being brutal. And women just like me will go on being slaughtered like animals. Humanity is rife with little shits. It's during times like these that we should learn from the oft-maligned cat lady. Perhaps she doesn't do the best job of caring for her feline brood, perhaps their wills are too strong to be controlled, and, yes, perhaps they are also little shits. Yet she loves her cats, and much as she empties fifteen-pound bags of kibble into a room of miniature apex predators, she pours herself into loving them.

What I'm trying to say is that we should consider the cat lady. Consider irrational acts of love. Consider ability and inability and refrain from neat categories that can do only that for which said categories have been designed: separate and organize and ultimately exploit. Maybe that's what we all need in this world—the knowledge that someone, even a woman with diarrhea instead of menstrual blood who refuses to tuck to go to the beach, and who sometimes thinks you're being a little shit, will be there, sobbing on the floor the moment you're gone.

Cheers,

DREW PHAM
BROOKLYN, NY

DEAR McSWEENEY'S,
This March, I flew from LA to Boston on a flight that cost $29.20. At the beginning of this whole thing, I moved into a shed on the east coast. It was part of a community land trust. *What does anyone actually want from proximity?* is something everyone's asking now that all of us live on Zoom.

Earlier today, I found a tick crawling across my palm. I crushed it between my fingernail and my hand. It looked like an adult deer tick. I wondered after I crushed it what would have happened if I'd just carried it outside like I do with spiders or like I cradle the dog.

In the shed, there always seems to be a handful of ladybugs stuck to the window on the door. I try to open it to let them out but all they do is shuffle

– – –

their wings. When I take my jacket off the nail by the door to put it on, handfuls of them emerge from my jacket, sort of sick, they've been flying in and out of my sleeves all day and then crawling into the hole that was made for the cord of the lamp. They die in there, handfuls of them. I don't know where they come from, but they seem to be born in the shed and are motivated to all the windows and doors by heat. They die in droves. Also, it smells like coffee in the shed at night, which is an odd thing, and the ladybug smell mixes with it—a grass smell—because they keep dying in the hot water I make in the five-by-eight place.

Just the other morning, when I turned to the dog, she had a fat deer tick on her forehead. I pulled it out with my fingers in a napkin because I have no tools. Its head popped off and went somewhere, or, more likely, stayed in her. Its legs moved all around in my fingers.

I can't really close anything off, is what I'm saying. Mice come in all the time, they make their bodies dime-sized to join me. I wonder if I've been swallowing ladybugs, they make their way into everything I drink. The fallacy of autonomy is clear.

As one of my last social acts before leaving LA, I went to Isabella Rossellini's show called *Link Link Circus*.

I was excited because my grandmother was a big fan of her mother's. Also, I like Rossellini's series *Green Porno*. In those short films, Rossellini gives a chronology of genitals: ducks

can switch their vaginal canals around if they don't want a mate like that; barnacles can become sperm and impregnate themselves; it's actually endless, these reproductive techniques and their looseness in response to sexuality and gender—this is her point. Humans impose a kind of structural morality on sexuality and gender and use ideas of "naturalness" as a way to reinforce them. We're so wrong about nature, she's saying.

The performance was in Highland Park at the Lodge Room. I was in the back. She had Pan, who looked a little like the dog from *Wishbone*. Pan was dressed up like a chicken and like a handful of other animals, at various points throughout the show, but I couldn't see too well. Apparently, Rossellini was studying animal behavior at Hunter College and that was her inspiration. Like, what was Descartes talking about when he was saying animals aren't sentient? She gave us an explanation of Aristotle's idea of order in nature: the ladder of being, a ranking system of "inanimate things" en route to God:

God > angels > demons > stars > the moon > kings > priests > nobles > commoners > wild animals > domesticated animals > trees > other plants > precious stones > precious metals > other minerals, et cetera…

The point of *Link Link Circus* seems to be that this hierarchy is an absurdity, particularly when Rossellini uses examples of pigeons

– – –

who are able to differentiate between a Picasso and a Monet.

I love Mel Chen's writing about the concept of animacy. They insist that animacy is "political, shaped by what or who counts as human, and what or who does not." They write: "It seems that animacy and its affects are mediated not by whether you are a couch, a piece of metal, a human child, or an animal, but by how holistically you are interpreted and how dynamic you are perceived to be. Stones themselves move, change, degrade over time, but in ways that exceed human scales."

How does our language dehumanize? is Chen's main question. Still, they wonder in their writing about whether shoring up the category of human (as long as it needs another binary, like humanity versus inhumanity, to exist) doesn't do the job.

In *Animacies: Biopolitics, Racial Mattering, and Queer Affect*, Chen constructs an argument about animacy using their experience of mercury poisoning. They've been wracked by its symptoms, and they try to point out that mercury is no less animate than humans, actually—it's alive, it's functioning via their body and making them debilitated.

My grandmother keeps calling our current COVID experience World War III ("We used to run from the Germans and now we run from the germs," she says). Apparently, a "virus" isn't technically "alive"—the adjective definition of *live* is from the root "a light," like burning and glowing.

Actually, everything's on fire.

Yours,

EMERSON WHITNEY
ELLSWORTH, MAINE

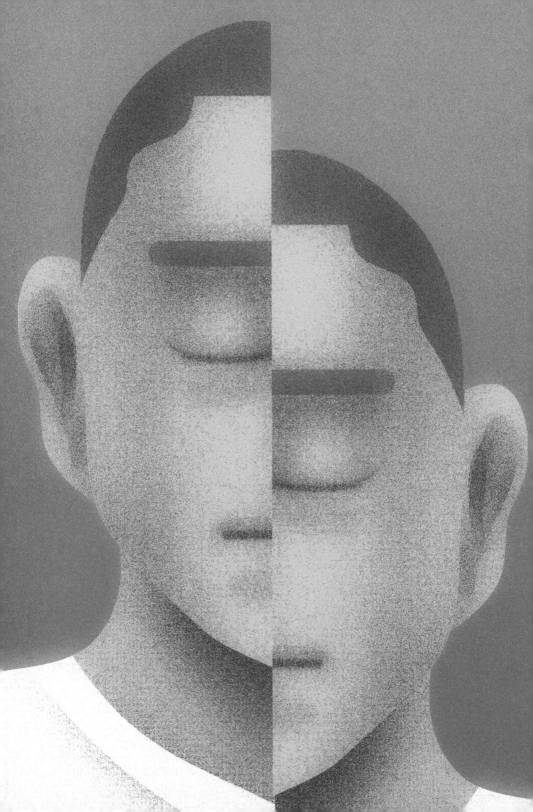

The QUEER
FICTION ISSUE

McSWEENEY'S
QUARTERLY

ISSUE NO.
SIXTY-TWO

TWINS
by
EILEEN
MYLES

I was in Seattle and I wound up visiting this guy who was a twin. He was the one in Seattle. The other brother had stayed in New York where I met them. They were identical twins and actually had never been separated before. I'm sure they had traveled separately but I don't think they had ever lived in different cities. So I was meeting one of them in this new state of separateness and he was both anxious and excited to be like this now. I am about to tell you a small story he, the Seattle brother, shared with mebut as I anticipate this I have a problem I'd like to tell you about that I am beginning to have with all my writing and my being. And my teaching. I suspect we know only so many things and in the middle of a writing class I am teaching I wonder if I have told them this before. And in the middle of my

The QUEER
FICTION ISSUE

TWINS
by EILEEN MYLES

ISSUE NO.
SIXTY-TWO

– – –

writing I wonder if I have written this before. I wrote a short piece
for a magazine which will be included in a book I am writing and
at some point I got an email from them because somebody in the
office wondered if I had written this before. I think I said no but I
had. It was slightly different, the ramping up to the story was not
the same and it was a very good story I think or else I would not
have told it again the ramping up was not the same but the story was
and someone who had read my work knew that and I didn't. Clearly
people who read my work know more about my writing than I do. I
don't know what stories I tell and what stories I have written. I have
an assistant and I am about to give them a very good job. Lots of the
work of working for me is pretty lousy. Taking in my mail, booking
a car to the airport, mailing this book and logging that publication
onto my CV and copying this blurb to put on my website. No it gets
even lousier than that. Find this piece of paper in my apartment.
No worse move my car on alternate parking days and more widely
take my car away for a month when I cannot move it and put my
car entirely someplace else like on a little vacation, a month in the
country for my car when I am away. But now the job I think is getting
really cool. Because when you want to work for a writer you probably
want to do things writerly. Does anyone propose themselves as a writer's assistant without wanting to be a writer themselves. So the job
would be a gateway to the life. A view more or less. The worst actually
is sending copies of my shrink bill to the insurance company. That
is entirely the worst because they would not send us the reimbursal
in fact they claimed not to have received the forms. This went on
and on. And the assistant had to keep calling them and there was
even a request to send a form or record a statement that they could
speak for me, essentially be my double in insurance matters. We
did this once, at least once, and then they claimed that it had never
happened. And then we had to do it again. Finally the check came,

and another and even a third. I have never told my assistant about
all three. Only that it came once.

The great job is looking at my books, only the prose I believe,
poetry can repeat itself all it wants, but poetry hardly ever tells
stories so I don't think it has this problem. Looking at my books
and making a list of the stories I have told, chapter by chapter, the
whole thing. I am thinking of four books. I figured we would pick
a sample chapter and I would make a list and they would make a
list and we would compare to see if we had the same idea of what
a story is. Because it's like this. I am not so much a storyteller as a
story wanderer so I might be on my way to tell this and this reminds
me of and I go there and then that opens up onto another and then
one after that. So any "story" might have so many tiny shelves and
episodes and those are the ways I get fucked up now. Those little
tiny stories are easy to repeat. So which ones are in my mind, always
available to be trotted out when I'm talking or teaching and which
ones have already wound up in my work, my writing. Not to femi-
nize myself but I think of it, my work, as the egg I have laid. I could
probably say a lot about memory since that is the real subject of this
thought I'm on now, that my memory is much looser, baggier than
ever before. I'm not sure I'm losing my memory but it might be losing
me. I have to be reeled back in to the story I began here for instance
about the brothers because I could easily never return. My memory is
like a land that is erasing as it goes. Why? Because there is too much?
Or because I am a victim of trauma. Because alcohol and drugs have
irretrievably ruined me, the damage coming slow, but there in the
substrata of my brain is a certain date and then it is beginning to
erase which is now. So the story about the brothers in Seattle, or the
one brother, is so good that I can't imagine I haven't told it before,
but here goes. And most weirdly it's *not the point* of this story but a
ramping up to the real story which is slight but daily like a bug and I

need to leave it here while not entirely understanding its connection to love which the book I write is about.

The brother when explaining the shock of his new single condition (being reduced to the state of aloneness which is particular to everyone who is not born of the same egg as a sibling) told me about going into a department store in Seattle one day and coming around a corner he almost walked into a full-length mirror which everyone has done and rather than thinking, Who's that, or, That's a hot person, or, I like that shirt, or, Fuck I'm getting old, he instead thought excitedly: It's my brother!

That's it. And then he shared with me one of the things he liked about Seattle. Seattle is on water, I guess Puget Sound, and there's a lively (or there was in the '90s, when this story occurred) houseboat scene in the harbor. In one of the houseboats lived a psychic masseuse, one who was really cute, straight I believe but still a crush of the brother I visited who was now alone in the world for the first time. This psychic masseuse was so marvelous and my friend, the brother, told me he wanted to give me a gift. Because I was from New York and I reminded him of home and he knew like anyone who knew me would know that I would never pay for something so frivolous as a psychic massage. Who would. I mean these days in the present when I am no longer broke I would probably pay for anything including sex. I love to spend money and pick up the check etc. I'm like the worst nouveau riche. These brothers came from the Upper East Side of Manhattan. They had an air of wealth and were in the club scene in high school and were a little bit famous as they were cute and were identical twins. There's even a famous photograph of them in some stupendous outfit. A long drapey thing all cut out. Their skinny little backs and the two identical brothers looking back flirtatiously. They had amazing style I think and designed their own clothes and who doesn't look great in everything when you're young. And they grew up in New York City,

The QUEER
FICTION ISSUE

McSWEENEY'S
QUARTERLY

ISSUE NO.
SIXTY-TWO

– – –

went to prep schools I think and were cool. As fourteen-year-olds in the nightclub scene would have to be.

I'm in Bergen. I'm in a Kunsthall across from a lake and all of us are silently writing. It's a gig. I love just being in a place and not exploring so much but allowing it to be there just like it is allowing me. Perfect.

So the brother says I want to give you a gift. And he's younger than me. I'm probably in my forties. I've got a career but I'm kind of poor. I practically write about it. Someone said once This is Eileen. She is famous for being poor. I think I've written that. Somewhere. So this guy's twenty years younger than me and he wants me to get a psychic massage from the boy he likes. This is a gift to me and I am a way for him to contact the boy. X sent me I say. I can't imagine how he would have paid. Maybe it was free? Maybe there was an envelope with a note. Right? When I look back on the first oh even thirty years of my life in New York and in the world as a writer I had only these kinds of experiences: horoscopes, sensory deprivation tanks, massages period, bodywork, rebirthing if somebody else paid. Even restaurants. I never went out publicly for food. It was a no-frills kind of living. I think sometimes I remember the masseuse's name. He was cute. Began with a B. He was a brown-haired hippie boy. His hair was longish, curly, I think he was probably shirtless and I just lay down on his table on the houseboat on a beautiful day in Seattle on Puget Sound and he oiled and relaxed me and may have asked me a few questions about myself. Writer, oh that's cool. Is there a way for me to read your writing. I have books. Oh, can I find them. I mean you can go to such-and-such a bookstore but if you give me your address I'll send you one. I'm sorry I don't have one on me. Oh no I will buy it. I love to support artists. I make art, mainly music. And he indicated a keyboard across the room. I don't spend as much time on my music as I'd like. Okay I'm getting some feelings from you. Have you been… I don't want to get anywhere where you aren't inviting me. Your space is your own. Thank

— — —

you I said. But is there some kind of violence you have experienced in your life... possibly around your sex, yes, I think... you don't have to tell me the details.

And of course I did tell him. The water glittered and the sky was clear as I told him about being sexually assaulted on Cape Cod when I was young and drunk. He nodded as he rubbed my arms and my back. He was silent as his whole body absorbed my pain it seemed and he muttered I get it, I get it. That's very very hard.

And then he said it. When he got to my foot. He lifted my foot and he said this little foot feels very uncared-for. You have a high arch and it's very very tense. He was touching it then. Did you ever do dance. That would be good for you. Yes I did ballet when I was a kid. Not for long. But I liked it and I was good...

He said a lot of your energy, a lot of your pain is stored right here. When you have a shower, here's what I want you to do. Just lift your foot, one foot at a time, it's both but your right foot is worse, give the bottom of your foot a little rub and say, this might sound silly but I think it will help. I must heal my anger at men. I must heal my anger at men. Do that. It will help you, I'm sure. It's just a feeling I get, but that's what I'd do. I'm not... trying to get into your space at all but these little feet, he held them then, are calling out for it. Give the bottoms of your feet a little love and push that anger out, just a little rub...

You know I don't even have a shower at my home. I've got a tub. So it's not every day of my life. But I'm standing at the gym, many days, most days, water pours down my back, I'm lifting my arms and I'm making foam with soap in my pits, I'm standing on one leg and I rarely take a shower without touching my foot and thinking about him:

I must heal my anger toward men.
I must heal my anger toward men.

The QUEER
FICTION ISSUE

McSWEENEY'S
QUARTERLY

ISSUE NO.
SIXTY-TWO

– – –

and you know rape victims always spend hours in the shower. It's just a fact. And the houseboat rocked. And the little foot screamed and cried.

How did you like him.

I mean, it was good.

Weird?

Well yes of course.

But it definitely will stay with me.

Good. Well tell my brother I said hello when you see him.

He laughed.

Ha. I will. And I do see him, I said, closing the door.

The QUEER
FICTION ISSUE

McSWEENEY'S
QUARTERLY

ISSUE NO.
SIXTY-TWO

PALAVER
by
BRYAN
WASHINGTON

He made his mother a deal: for every story he told, she'd give him one of her own.

That's hardly fair, she said.

Bullshit, he said.

It was the first time he'd used the word with her. And she let it slide, the first of many firsts between them.

He'd been living in Shin-Ōkubo for the better part of three years. She'd flown from Houston to Los Angeles to Taipei to Tokyo to see him. Or at least that's what she'd said on the phone. He knew that she and his father were going through it. This was one of the reasons he'd left, although he hadn't thought about that at the time.

Now his mom sat on the sofa, snacking on a bag of chips, holding a magazine neither of them could read. Her son stood beside a broom.

The QUEER
FICTION ISSUE

PALAVER
by BRYAN WASHINGTON

ISSUE NO.
SIXTY-TWO

– – –

His place was mostly plants and some shoes. He had this balcony over-looking a bus stop, next to a convenience store and a stairwell for the train station.

You go first, said the son.

Absolutely not, said his mother.

Fine. I'll start.

Jesus.

Once upon a time, said the son, I fell in love with a married man.

I don't need to hear this, said his mother.

We met in a bar one night, said the son. He bought me a drink. Then he asked me to come home with him.

The mother looked at her son's face before she turned to the wall, and then to the window beside them. The one thing his apartment had going for it was the view. It'd drizzled her first morning in the country, and she'd watched sheets of rain paint a gaggle of grade schoolers by the stoplight.

You're serious, she asked.

No joke.

You aren't serious.

Why would I lie now?

Unbelievable. Were you safe?

I'll only tell if you play.

This isn't a fucking game.

Is that a yes?

God, said his mother.

Good, said her son, sweeping in what passed for his kitchen. We were safe. We're safe.

Is this a thing that's still happening, asked his mother. Are you still seeing him?

It's your turn, said the son. You give me one of yours first.

* * *

The QUEER
FICTION ISSUE

McSWEENEY'S
QUARTERLY

ISSUE NO.
SIXTY-TWO

– – –

I'll make it easy for you, said the son a little later. Just tell me how you met Dad.

It was his day off. His mother sat beside him on a bench in the train station. They were waiting for the local line, just after rush hour, and he figured they must've made a funny picture, as his mom groaned with her arms crossed and he tapped away at his phone, leaping between a volley of apps.

Who the hell are you talking to? his mother said. How long were you living here before you lost your mind?

I only asked a question.

You're being fucking disrespectful.

Hardly.

Who are you texting?

My students.

Is that appropriate here? asked the mother.

It's fine, said the son. And it's your turn.

Gradually, the platform filled beside them. Every other occupant was a businessman of some sort. Every now and again, they'd chance a glance at the mother and her son, but at some point a lady rolled two twins in a stroller onto the platform.

The kids wouldn't stop crying. Everyone turned to glare at them. Eventually, gradually, the children settled down.

When the train arrived, tinkling a three-tone melody, the son and his mother waited a moment. Then they both stood, trailing the woman with the stroller, leaning into a pair of seats by the conductor's booth.

The woman with the twins turned their way, sighing. Both of her kids waved. So the mother and her son waved back.

Once upon a time, the mother didn't tell her son, I thought I'd take you back to Toronto. We'd live with my sister. The two of us would leave

The QUEER
FICTION ISSUE

PALAVER
by BRYAN WASHINGTON

ISSUE NO.
SIXTY-TWO

– – –

Texas, in the middle of the night. We wouldn't say a word to your father and we'd never come back.

Once upon a time, the mother didn't tell her son, I thought I'd become an opera singer.

Once upon a time, the mother didn't tell her son, I wrote poetry. I scribbled the words in a notebook and hid it in the guest room. But one day—you wouldn't remember this—I found you crying underneath the bed, and the pages were spread open, right at your feet. I think you were nine. I never wrote a poem again.

The son taught English at a juvenile detention center in Yanaka. His pay could've been better, but it was more than enough to live on. Most of his students would never have a reason to use the language, or at least that's what the son told his mom, but the teens still let him teach them, falling asleep only occasionally. They thought he was interesting. Every hour or so, he gave them breaks to use their phones.

That sounds depressing, said the mother.

Sometimes it is, said her son. But I like it.

You couldn't just have been depressed in Texas?

I was.

And whose fault is that?

The son opened his mouth, and then he closed it.

My students are funny, said the son. And they don't take any shit.

Impossible, said his mother.

How so?

They put up with *you.*

That isn't cute, said the son.

Anyway, said the mother. I thought you were an accountant or something.

Thanks for caring, said her son.

– – –

Don't act like you've ever kept me in the loop.

Whatever, said the son. I had another job the first few months.

And how'd that go?

It was fine. But one of the clients complained.

Because you're Black, said his mother.

No, said the son, but then he didn't say anything else.

Some nights, the son stayed out a bit later. His mother would walk to the convenience store for dinner, nodding at the cashier when he bowed. Sometimes her husband texted her, and she'd think about how to reply. But she never sent anything. It was enough, for now, for him to know she'd read it.

Then one evening, smoking on her son's balcony, the mother found, folded under her chair's leg, a crumpled Polaroid of two men. One of the men was her son. The other guy looked a little older. They both smiled, holding inflatable numbers on each other's shoulders, and the mother thought, briefly, that her son looked better unshaven, after all.

So she took a photo of the photo with her phone, and then she refolded it, slipping it under the seat. The mother started to light another cigarette, but then she thought better of it, and she stepped inside instead, kicking off her son's flip-flops, leaving a window open for the breeze.

The next evening, the son and his mother sat in a bar, one of the tiny enclaves lining the alleys of Ni-chōme. Posters and flyers showing men fucking in various positions were splayed across the walls, while a pulsing techno track thrummed from above. The son watched his mother eye each picture, and he winced at her, just a bit. But she didn't say anything about them.

The room was mostly empty. Two dudes fingered their drinks in the

– – –

corner, whispering in each other's ears. The bartender, a bearish man, napped by the register. The son drank a frothy beer, calling out for a second, and his mother shocked him by raising her finger for one too.

The bartender said something in Japanese. It made the son laugh. He replied with something that made the bartender shake his head.

He thinks I'm charging you, said the son.

Don't lie, said the mother. I know where we are.

You didn't say anything.

It didn't need to be said.

Is this your first time in a gay bar?

Tell me about your married man, said the mother.

This made the son wince again. He fidgeted in his seat.

Once upon a time, he said, a boy met a man.

Here we go, said the mother.

The man promised this boy a kingdom, said the son. Or at least a house in the suburbs. And the boy thought this man was lying, but he wasn't. Which made the boy happy. Except the man maybe hadn't told the entire truth.

That he had a wife, said the mother.

And a child, said the son.

Jesus.

On the way.

That doesn't make a difference!

She hadn't meant to raise her voice. The son and his mother looked around the bar. But the two men in the corner only grinned, raising their beers.

I know you don't have any morals, said the mother, but do you think home-wrecking is a game?

You're asking the wrong question, said her son.

Does his wife know?

It's your turn, said the son, sipping his beer.

– – –

*   *   *

A little later, on the train home, the mother exhaled in her seat. Their car was packed with drunken businessmen patting one another's backs, and couples nosing each other's ears, and stragglers tapping at screens.

Fine, she said. Your father stole me from a tower.

We can't talk on here, said the son.

You asked me a question and this is your answer.

The game's no fun if you lie.

Your father plucked me from the top floor, said the mother. Carried me all the way down. Slayed a dragon and all of the townspeople.

You're being sore, said the son. You didn't fly all this way to be sore.

I didn't fucking fly all this way to play games with you, said the mother. And how would you know, anyway?

Dad's not that kind of guy, said the son, and his mother started to say something else, but the train slowed to a stop, and his mom shifted in her seat, and he reached for the rail, steadying them both.

Most days, the son went to work. The mother followed him to the train station, where they diverged—and she rode from Shinjuku to Akihabara to Shibuya, funneling change into vending machines, walking in and out of shops, snapping photo after photo in Yoyogi Park. In front of the park's shrine, some women asked the mother to take their photo, so she did. When they asked the mother if she wanted one of herself, she smiled as they snapped about forty.

Some evenings, when the mother knew her son was finally asleep, she slipped on her sneakers, hopped down the stairs, and walked the strip lining the road by the station. Even on weeknights, the streetlights were always on. Traffic slowed to a trickle. The mother made bets with

– – –

herself—she'd walk to the next intersection, and then she'd turn right back around, but when she actually reached said intersection, it became the *next* intersection, and *that* one became the intersection that *followed*.

When the mother made it back to the apartment, she'd stand in the doorway, waiting to hear her son's snores. Once they returned, the mother settled back into bed, flipping her phone onto its side. There was a night when her husband texted her a single emoji, and she responded immediately, without even thinking about it, just as a reaction. She thought about how there are some things we simply can't shake.

Once upon a time, said the son, I spent the night on a bench in Montrose.

Once upon a time, said the son, I woke up in an entirely different part of Houston, in someone else's clothes.

Once upon a time, said the son, I brought a boy to the house. In high school, I think.

You didn't, said the mother.

This is a thing that happened.

Liar. When?

You were at work. Or something.

What? Where did he come from?

Who?

This boy.

Where they all come from. We met on an app.

Did you have sex? In the house?

Shit, said the son. Are you really asking me that?

You're the one who brought this up, said his mother. I'm asking because I'm worried about you.

You weren't worried then, detective.

I said I *am* worried, said the mother, you little shit.

– – –

Then don't be, said her son.

And anyway, said the son, Dad caught us. He told the guy to go home.

This made the mother open her mouth, but she didn't say anything. Her son waited for the words, but they just didn't come. So they both moved on.

Once upon a time, the mother didn't tell her son, my own mother tried to marry me off.

Once upon a time, the mother didn't tell her son, I couldn't have possibly made her life any more difficult: I broke every rule she ever put in front of me.

Once upon a time, the mother didn't tell her son, I introduced your grandmother to your father, and she told me she'd never approve. I laughed right in her face. And once I started, I simply never stopped. I laughed for weeks and weeks and weeks, until I ran out of breath, and then I started again.

Sometimes, in the evenings, they walked—usually in silence. They let the city do the talking between them. But this night was dimmer than most, and they'd chosen another club in Ni-chōme, and jazz drifted from the speakers, and the son looked entirely too distracted, flipping his phone on the bar counter.

Eventually, the soundtrack changed. When the mother said the singer's name aloud, her son made a face.

What, she asked.

Nothing, said the son. You're just full of surprises. Flying here. Listening to city pop.

Children are the least surprising parts of their parents' lives.

Also, said the mother, does your married man have a name?

– – –

This again, said the son.

You brought it up.

He does, said the son.

You don't have to tell me what it is, said the mother.

I wasn't going to.

What do you even do together?

Do I need to spell it out?

You know exactly what I'm asking you.

Well, said the son, once upon a time—

Enough with that.

He takes me to baseball games, said the son. He likes baseball. And we go for walks.

That's it?

Are you saying there should be more? Do you think we're aliens?

No, said the mother, but her son couldn't read her tone—it had a tenor he'd never heard her use before.

The son picked up his phone again. He tossed it back onto the counter.

Fine, said the mother. Then tell me a story about your students.

You don't want to hear about them, said the son.

Of course I do. And you clearly need something else to talk about.

They don't take me seriously, he said. It's like they know the whole thing's just an act. But they've taught me a lot.

The mother was about to ask what, specifically, the teens had taught him—but the son raised a finger, grabbing at his cell.

He spoke quickly and quietly. His tone reminded her of his father's. And then the son stepped across the room, down the stairs, and out of sight, whispering into his phone, leaving his mother alone.

He didn't come back for a while. Eventually, the mother realized that the bartender had been watching her. They made eye contact, and the bartender nodded, reaching for another glass.

The QUEER
FICTION ISSUE

McSWEENEY'S
QUARTERLY

ISSUE NO.
SIXTY-TWO

– – –

*   *   *

That night, they walked back to the apartment in silence, and they'd nearly made it to the complex when the son sat on the bench out front, hiding his head in his hands. The mother eyed him, blinking. She thought about rubbing his back. She wasn't sure if she should.

Listen, said the mother. I won't claim to know what it's like. But I do know that disrupting a marriage could be the death of you. You have to trust me.

Is that why you flew here, asked the son. To lecture me?

I'm only telling you what I see. You have to take care of yourself.

You don't know anything about it.

I know that it's eating you up.

You don't know shit.

I know that it's got you crying at midnight halfway across the world.

What if I told you that everyone knows, said the son. Him and his wife? What if I told you that she doesn't mind? That she's got her own thing going on too? What if I told you that that's just the way it is, and I'm fine with that?

The son found himself breathing heavily, and the mother took a second to catch her own breath. A group of guys walked around them, smoking, and one of them looked their way, whistling. When the son stood up, the mother put her palm on his shoulder. He sat back down.

Maybe I should just go back, said his mother.

Maybe you should, said the son.

I left because you made me, he said.

No one made you do anything, said his mother.

No, said the son, you made me. I would've died. So you made me.

The mother wasn't sure if they were talking about the same thing, and before she could ask, the son shook his head. He stepped into the complex alone.

The QUEER
FICTION ISSUE

PALAVER
by BRYAN WASHINGTON

ISSUE NO.
SIXTY-TWO

– – –

*   *   *

Once upon a time, the mother didn't tell her son, I caught you with a boy. You never knew that I knew.

Once upon a time, the mother didn't tell her son, I watched the way you looked out the window afterward, and I thought about cupping your cheeks in my palm, telling you to go where you wanted.

Once upon a time, the mother told her son, I flew halfway around the world to find you, and you were doing mostly fine. Or as fine as could be expected. I didn't know if I preferred that to finding you in a mess. I didn't know if one was better than the other. Wasn't sure if I should stay to find out.

His mother had planned to stay a week, but on her last morning she extended her ticket.

The airline didn't give her a hard time. Her son didn't say anything about it either. That evening, he didn't come back to the apartment, and she walked up the road to sit in a bar by herself. She ordered a glass of wine, watching the couples sitting across from each other. Another woman sitting alone made eye contact, and the mother nodded, and she nodded too.

The next morning, the son returned. He was brighter than when he'd left.

You weren't wearing those clothes yesterday, said the mother.

Another case closed, said the son.

I just don't think it's right.

Which part of it?

You know what I mean.

I don't think I do.

– – –

Then that's your problem, said the mother. It's your problem for not trusting me. It's your life. But you have to trust me to know that, at least.

And before her son could say anything else, the mother added, It wasn't my first time.

Your first time what, said the son, wiping at his face.

At one of those bars. At a bar like that.

Oh.

I'd been with my sister.

Oh.

She took me a few times, said the mother. Once, she took me and your father. We had a nice time.

The mother and her son stood across from each other. She glanced outside, through the window, at some kids hopscotching on the sidewalk.

Okay, said the son.

Okay, said the mother.

Well, said the son. That would've been nice to know. Before, I mean.

The son was still standing in the doorway, and when a man in the hallway passed behind him, he turned around, nodding and saying something his mother couldn't understand. Then the son turned to his mother. He stepped back outside and closed the door.

On the weekend, they went to the park. The mother watched her son pick up snack after snack in the convenience store, tossing them into his basket, bantering with the man behind the register. Neither of them said much as they took one train, and then another, filtering from her son's part of Tokyo, before walking through a handful of alleys that sprawled into an open field. A soccer game went on to their right, while a group of students danced to hip-hop in the foreground. What looked like the beginnings of a wedding photo session played out just beside the blanket they'd unfolded onto the grass.

The QUEER
FICTION ISSUE

PALAVER
by BRYAN WASHINGTON

ISSUE NO.
SIXTY-TWO

— — —

The son spread the food across their blanket, opening boxes and shuffling silverware.

I forgot to bring a fork, he said.

I'll be fine, said the mother.

I meant for me.

Of course you did.

So, said the mother. What do you and your boyfriend eat together?

This was enough for the son to look up.

I've never heard you use that word, he said.

Well, said the mother.

The son grinned. His mother didn't.

He has a name, though, said the son. You can call him that.

Baby steps, said the mother.

The son watched the students as they made their way through their dance.

We go to bars, he said. We eat at stalls. Sometimes he cooks for me.

Do you ever cook for him?

Sure.

Often?

Often enough.

You should cook for the ones you love, said the mother.

Is there a story behind that?

The mother looked at her son, squinting. For the longest time, she'd thought he looked like his father, before deciding that she wasn't exactly sure *whom* he looked like. It would be a few years before she decided this was because of their own similarities.

Once upon a time, said the mother, I met your father in a library. He loved poetry. That was his thing. He saw that I loved it too. And that's when I knew—him seeing what I saw. That's what tipped me off.

Listen, said the mother. If you're ever in a relationship as long as the one I've been in with your father, you'll know what to look for.

– – –

And you should trust yourself to know. Whatever that means to you. Whatever that looks like.

The son turned away from his mother. He wiped at his face. The married couple beside them stumbled around in front of the photographer.

That sounds sentimental, he said.

I didn't say it wasn't.

His mother looked over the top of his head at the newlyweds taking photos. When the woman looked up, they made eye contact. The mother smiled at her, and the woman smiled back.

Anyway, said the mother. I thought we were taking turns.

So now you want to play?

The son looked at his mother and then at the group of students, chanting and dancing. It felt like the temperature had fallen just a bit. The song sounded a little like one the mother knew, some tune she hadn't heard in a very long time, but as soon as the thought occurred to her, she cast it away, and she knew it couldn't have been possible.

Hey, he said. I'm sorry.

Yeah, she said. You should be.

No, he said. I meant for the other thing. For everything. You probably think I'm an idiot.

The teens in front of them slowed their dancing, falling all over one another. It was enough for the mother to grin despite herself. The world was bigger than anyone could ever know. Maybe that was hardly a bad thing.

You are an idiot, she said.

Thanks, said the son.

You're welcome.

Maybe you *should* leave, after all.

I don't think so, said his mother, grabbing another rice roll from the basket. Tell me something else.

The QUEER
FICTION ISSUE

McSWEENEY'S
QUARTERLY

ISSUE NO.
SIXTY-TWO

SWIFFER
GIRL
by
EMMA
COPLEY
EISENBERG

Do you remember Swiffer Girl? I barely remember her, but I do remember her. I remember that she existed years ago, back before I felt every man I passed in the sunshine like a mortal enemy, back before college, before moving to six cities in six years, before good sex and good love, before *misogyny* and *intersectionality* and all the other language I've learned to describe experience. I never "got sober" the way other people did, just met a person who has a rare condition that makes her allergic to alcohol and married her. There was no dramatic quitting, no taking out a trash bag heavy with clear glass bottles, no standing up at meetings to repeat the same confession, just a gradual secretion via perspiration and rehydration. Slowly, the booze left my bloodstream and was replaced by other

– – –

liquids—Lemon Zinger tea, chocolate milk. I forgot Swiffer Girl for
years. Then I didn't.

She could have happened only where she happened and only in the
Manhattan of the early 2000s, when my block still had the gay porn
video store, and the man with the parrot still spent all day in the sun
on a metal folding chair; before the Pinkberry moved in with its many
handles of soft serve, but after the pottery studio came and hung its
red sign.

Technically, she was the Bronx, since she originated there, on the
strange green campus of one of its ritzy private schools. She was not
Brooklyn: the place my father had come from and to which he vowed
never to return. It's possible that she reached Queens.

Each morning I rode three trains to get to school, and on each train
I could expect at least one penis—here, a flaccid one reclining crook-
edly through a half-zippered fly, there, an erect one framed neatly
by the two lapels of a sport coat. On each train I could also expect
at least one person in visible emotional or physical distress. A very
thin woman in very expensive shoes would be crying, and the woman
standing above her in a sweatshirt and enormous running shoes would
be trying not to notice. In the passageway where people ran toward
the number 7 train, a man with plastic bags wrapped around his feet
would be asking for mercy. *There is no time for his mercy*, the running
people said, their hair flopping or streaming behind them, no space
in their bodies for what such mercy would require. If you cracked
yourself open a smidgen, went the thinking, there was no telling what
might come leaking out.

My freshman-year history teacher was a fat dyke—or so I had heard—
who wore a New York Mets cap. Her hair was so dark brown it looked
black. She felt like my sister, or my mom, or some other vital organ.

Lazy, she would say of my essay. Facile, reductive. That's not how
it happened at all.

– – –

But she loved me back. Oh, how she loved me. She let me stay in the teachers' lounge all through lunch and sometimes into the next period, saying nothing as I watched her read the newspaper and tear through her roast beef sandwich—kaiser roll, mustard, lettuce, no tomato. She ate that sandwich. I ate her.

My sister was a few grades ahead of me at our school, but her classes were on the eighth floor, whereas mine were on the sixth, a distance too great to cross.

Head up, shoulders back, don't scuff your feet, she told me, when our lines passed each other during a fire drill. She had a boyfriend, a tall boy with the world's biggest backpack and a crown of Jewish curls, who trotted the halls with the entitlement of a prizewinning dog. My sister stayed most weekends at his house.

What's wrong with our house? my mother often asked.

No one is ever here, my sister said.

Except me, I said.

Except you, she said.

You would think, from your perspective, that that would be a good thing, my mother said.

You would think that, my sister said, but you would be wrong.

I watched the video of Swiffer Girl after school one day, during that swath of unsupervised afternoon when my parents were still at work and my sister was at Model United Nations Club, rhetorically murdering the less intellectually fortunate.

I watched Swiffer Girl alone in the small office next to my bedroom. The room contained only a couch, a big double window, stacked vertically, that looked out onto the roof of the Irish bar next door, and a garishly colored computer with a back made of clear plastic so you could see the machine's workings. This was before there were

– – –

smartphones for the masses but after there was AOL, in that brief sliver of years when we knew what the internet was but did not yet know what it meant.

Who sent me her video? I recall an email with many, many, names, one of those emails you forward on lest you have bad luck for seven years. Though that can't be right—who would have been rooting so actively for Swiffer Girl's demise that they would spend that kind of time composing it? Anyone, I know now. Anyone at all.

What happened to Swiffer Girl? I have heard she moved to Texas. I have heard she opened a club with Jell-O wrestling, that she has a brother who works in Silicon Valley and who pays for her shoe and coke habits, that she went bonkers and ended up in a mental institution. I have heard she died.

My wife's work has a private investigator on retainer, and she has offered me his number more than once for other matters, but I'm not sure I want to know. Plus, there must be about a thousand Amy Cohens in America, which is perhaps the only kindness in this whole situation.

I watched the video of Swiffer Girl several times that afternoon but came to no conclusion about the ending which seemed to cut off strangely, about the beginning (what led her to make this video in the first place?) or about the middle, a.k.a. what she might have been feeling as she did it. I paused the video several times and brought my face close to the screen to examine the texture of the Swiffer's handle near the top. It looked plastic, rough, almost corrugated. But in a good way?

Didn't know.

Swiffer Girl was a freshman, too, a student at that Bronx school, like my school but ritzier still. She did it for a guy, went the word at school, just some guy, and then instead of keeping the video for himself he'd sent it to all his friends. The guy faded immediately from view. She was a "crazy whore," went the comments at school, analog only, for YouTube hadn't yet been invented. It was she, Swiffer Girl herself, who was "fucking crazy, fucking bitch, whoring bitch, crazy bitch, crazy, crazy, crazy."

That afternoon, though, I pushed back the wheelie office chair and took the elevator down to the lobby. Someone had scratched the initials "KR" into the elevator panel just below the emergency button, and the whole car smelled of sweet Cuban cigars from the man in 7G. His wife wouldn't let him light up in the apartment, so he rode the elevator up and down, sometimes all night, pressing elevator buttons and smoking.

Every pump at the gas station across the avenue was full, cab drivers shouting greetings at one another over the hoods of their cars. I was a child and I had no parents and no sister and no best friend but I had my own set of keys to our apartment and I had these cab drivers and the cold sun on my neck beneath my ponytail. I had this city. There was still garbage in every gutter and the streets still had room for me.

At the deli, I perused the slices of cut melon in clear plastic containers rubber-banded closed and stamped $1.99, as well as the pieces of cake in Saran wrap piled in the plastic basket by the register—$2.99. I ran my hand over the twenty-four-hour energy drinks, the penis-enlargement pills, the discounted bagels with butter.

How was school? Anna asked. Her shiny black hair was piled on her head using an elaborate system of large bobby pins.

We learned about Buddhism, I said. About being a bodhisattva, which means you are a spiritual leader and also, I think, that you come back in the next life in a different form. A horse, for example, then a pig.

– – –

Sounds interesting, Anna said.

It was, I said. But I don't believe it.

No, Anna said. You don't believe in anything.

It was true. In my house there was no God, no astrology, no tarot; even science fiction books were suspect. We believed only in the mind, in science, in experiments, only in things that could be empirically verified, only in touch, taste, and smell, but sometimes not even in these. I did not believe in my body, for example.

From the deli, I could go anywhere. I could go to the pier and eat my carrot cake on a bench while watching the pigeons, or I could go to the courts where the boys played basketball, or I could go to the gay bookstore, where they sold crystals to change your body's energy.

In the gay bookstore, I found one decent book on Buddhism. This book gave a different definition of *bodhisattva* from the one I'd learned in school. It said instead that the term meant a person who has already reached enlightenment but deferred their arrival at nirvana in order to stay on earth and help other people. It was noncommittal on the subject of whether bodhisattvas came back to life over and over again.

Over cups of coffee as big as bowls, two men in muscle tees stared deeply into each other's eyes.

My mother was an actress, one of them said. Very glamorous, huge tits, huge hair. I'd watch her getting ready to go out.

I wonder if I watched her on TV, said the second one. When I was a kid, I watched TV all the time. Wake up, TV. Go to sleep, TV.

I wondered if this was how it was accomplished—sex, and maybe even love—and if these two men would end up together forever. I knew about gay men and saw them all the time, growing up in New York City, but I wouldn't learn the word *lesbian* until decades later. Perhaps

– – –

I heard it as a child—anything is possible—but I never saw it, and certainly never knew it.

No, the first man said. You probably never saw her, because she was only ever in movies. Never on TV.

Oh.

It seemed like they might fall in love forever, these two. It seemed like they had as good a chance as anyone.

I walked the blocks back to the deli to tell Anna what I'd learned, but on the way there I passed the Cup of Joe with the big plate glass window. There was a woman sitting alone at a table shoved right up against the window and she was sipping coffee from a much smaller mug than the men had been using, a mug that was meant to be refilled over and over. She looked at me and I looked at her.

So what do you believe? I asked Anna, after paying for a slice of lemon cake with vanilla icing.

I don't know, Anna said. She turned toward me and rested her hands on two corn muffins, Saran wrapped and sitting side by side.

Happy is dying, she said. That's my son. But he calls me still. He does call.

What's he dying of?

Who knows, Anna said. He won't tell me. I think it has something to do with his liver. Or his kidneys. It could be either one. It is one or it is the other.

If it's his liver, he could be an alcoholic, I said.

How do you know that?

I listen, I said. I know things.

I unwrapped the piece of cake and bit into it. I believed in taste, in its power to give and to take away, to fill my senses for a while and then, when it was gone, to leave me wanting.

– – –

Well, Anna said, I believe that when people die they stay dead. None of this returning afterward to haunt us until the end of eternity. No Jesus rising from behind the boulder as a bunny rabbit. Happy says he has felt haunted all his life. Once he even said there was a ghost here, in this deli.

The ghost of who?

The ghost of me, Anna said. Which made no sense, which I told him, since I was still me, an alive and living person. But even that didn't change his mind. He said, "You're here, Ma, young you who went to typists' school before you married Dad. You're in that box of Cheerios. You're over there behind the deli counter." He's a very sick boy, you see, and always has been, to some degree.

I thanked Anna for her input, and said I'd keep it in mind. At home, our apartment felt large and kind. I was grateful, as in relieved, to be alone, but also tired of being alone. If you have a feeling, or a transformation, but no one is there to witness it, does it count? I wondered if there would be consequences later for this much aloneness, as if by liking the state so much now, I would close off further opportunities later. My sister was uptown, her fingers exploring those masculine curls, and my mother was in some library or other, alphabetizing its books according to a system I did not understand. My father was home, maybe. The entryway smelled like him, and his coat was hung neatly on a wooden hanger. I took the coat down and put it on and looked at myself in the mirror. I could have been a businessman on my way to work. I could have been any stranger, turning a corner.

Swiffer Girl's face on the screen is not exactly like a face but more like the back of a china plate, smooth and white and full of light, yet somehow turned away. She has the good sense not to be completely naked, but to keep her bra on, one of those small, stretchy lace affairs

The QUEER
FICTION ISSUE

McSWEENEY'S
QUARTERLY

ISSUE NO.
SIXTY-TWO

– – –

with a hole in the center, the breast cups connected only by two strings. But when the camera zooms out, you can see her whole stomach, very pale, and then the vagina area, boring with its few wisps. She holds up the butt of the Swiffer pole and fellates it in a perfunctory way for several minutes, then gets on all fours and inserts it. She keeps her right palm down on the bedsheets (gray, cotton, no pattern) and keeps the pole steady with her left hand. She keeps bringing her body onto it; the Swiffer handle keeps going in and out. She looks at the camera. Her eyes stay open. Her mouth stays closed. The only sound is the sound of the actual Swiffer part, the part you would use to clean, flopping around on the bed behind her. It hits the sheet with its wide, almost sharp side—she has not added the pad.

Had the camera stopped filming by some sort of accident? Had she kept going to orgasm but edited that part out, wanting to keep that part for herself? And who had been standing there behind the camera—a friend? Some other boy, a "nice guy" she didn't love like she loved the one for whom she'd made the video?

Later, at a college party in a town where there are no seasons but people speak many languages, I'd find out that no one had filmed it, that the camera had a remote control and that she'd been there alone. Just her. Looking at me. But I didn't like that answer; it felt too sad. To be in a room all alone in that moment was the saddest thing I could imagine.

So when I told the story of Swiffer Girl at parties, which I did several times a year in college and for a few years after until I stopped, I added a sister.

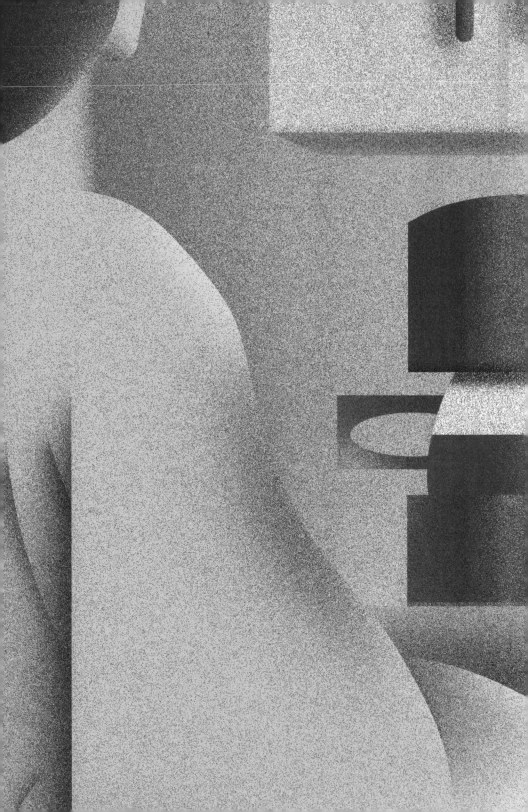

The QUEER
FICTION ISSUE

McSWEENEY'S
QUARTERLY

ISSUE NO.
SIXTY-TWO

DOCILE
BODIES
by
CHRISTOPHER
JAMES
LLEGO

I'm lactose intolerant, but he was my daddy and he wanted to watch me drink from the cow's teat. I got on my knees, spotted a brown patch on the cow's udder, and sucked, moaning because that would get Nicholas hard. The cow mooed, and I knew I had seconds before it kicked. I wanted my face to stay intact. With an Asian penis and a slow metabolism, my curved nose and high cheekbones were all I had to offer.

"Baby," Nicholas said as we walked back to the farmhouse, "you make me hot all over."

"Thank you, sir."

"Feel it," he said, so I felt it, and it was throbbing.

I woke up with a toothache and a bruised ass. In the kitchen, Nicholas tried to figure out how to operate the coffee machine. The

– – –

Airbnb had advertised modern appliances, but these farm folks thought refrigerators with ice dispensers were innovative. The Wi-Fi was slow. The microwave barely heated. Steam radiators clanged at three in the morning, and the TV in the living room still wore antennas. Nicholas poured water into the coffee machine's reservoir, then slapped its side until he gave up and threatened to sue.

"You lift the nozzle," I said, recognizing the machine from my dad's house. I wiped crust from my eyes and drank water straight from the tap. It had a metallic flavor that might've been caused by the rusted faucet. My tongue tasted stale.

"Why don't they have an espresso machine?" Nicholas asked.

"You're the one who wanted a rural weekend."

"Don't test me."

"Sorry, sir." I hugged him from behind, my wet lips kissing the acne on his shoulder. He was taller than me, his hands as big as my face. I liked how calloused his fingers were from playing the guitar, even though he sang when he played, and his baritone cracked when he attempted low notes. On our second date, he made me shut my eyes while he pretended to audition for *The Voice*. I thought of our takeout growing cold as he fumbled through a ballad I didn't recognize. Afterward, he asked me why I hadn't pressed the buzzer, and I said there was no buzzer to press. He said I could've poked his chest, which excused me from having to tell him he lacked talent.

"You make the coffee," he said, then went to the bathroom to pee, his stream as heavy as his penis. I tried to jerk off and forgot to press the START button, so when he came back asking why the coffee wasn't brewing, I lied and said the machine was broken. He noticed my erection and lifted me up onto the counter, which was too cold to be pleasant. My butt still hurt, and I didn't have it in me for a round this early, so I told him I loved him. He backed off.

"I love you," I repeated, and watched as he walked out the door

The QUEER
FICTION ISSUE

McSWEENEY'S
QUARTERLY

ISSUE NO.
SIXTY-TWO

– – –

wearing nothing but his wrinkled green boxers, carrying a pack of Marlboro Lights he'd chain-smoke until his thoughts were back in order.

The coffee started brewing once I pressed START. The machine gurgled until it hissed, and I found two novelty mugs in the cabinet above the microwave. One had an I ♥ NY logo, which felt wrong upstate. I drank from the yellow mug patterned with purple Labradors and stared at Nicholas through the window. My fingernail scratches had scarred his back, meaning that, for this weekend, he was mine. The first sips of coffee made my stomach rumble, and I thought of the pain in my ass, meaning I was his.

When he came back inside, he asked me how I'd fixed the machine.

"I just did," I said.

"Genius," he said, then kissed me while his hands cupped my ass cheeks. I wanted to chew on his smoker's breath. "I love you too," he said, grabbing his milk jug from the fridge and pouring whole milk into his novelty mug. "There's a lot of love in this house."

We went for a hike after eating tofu scramble. I'd wanted more—a banana, an apple, a bowl of cinnamon oats—but he had a rule about me asking for seconds.

I was wary of ticks because my mom was bitten during a trip to the Philippines and spent two weeks certain she'd contracted Lyme disease before her doctor informed her she just had lung cancer. Our family physician was my godfather, and the last time I'd gone in for a checkup I'd weighed only 190 pounds. No need to see my new stats.

"This is a long trail," I said, trying not to breathe like an asthmatic. My boots hadn't been broken in yet. I felt them rub up against the backs of my ankles. I'd have to tear off the blisters during tonight's bubble bath. I hated when dead skin floated in the water.

The QUEER
FICTION ISSUE

DOCILE BODIES
by CHRISTOPHER JAMES LLEGO

ISSUE NO.
SIXTY-TWO

– – –

I swatted a fly buzzing beside my ear. Nicholas was a few steps ahead of me, his head tilted up at the sky. "There's no smog outside the city," he said. "You inhale and you breathe in clean air."

It smelled like manure, but I nodded along while he examined the bark of a fallen tree. He wore shorts even though it was autumn. His leg hair grew in patches, his calves were smooth. His thighs were so meaty that I wondered why he wanted me. At a bar, he could smile and the bartender would offer him free whiskey. I felt the heaviness of my gut from my one plate of breakfast.

"If you think about it," Nicholas said, "bark is the one thing protecting trees from violation."

He liked making statements that he thought were philosophical. He expected praise, so I grabbed his hand and kissed each knuckle. "I used to scratch off bark with my keys," I said.

"Why?"

"I'm an only child."

He made me kiss his other hand, then told me to unbutton my pants and bend over against the fallen tree, so I did, and when he said he hadn't brought lube, I said spit was all I needed. I watched a trail of ants crawling along a leafless branch while he moaned behind me, his hands gripping my hips, his thumbs pressing down on my bruises. I bit the insides of my cheeks. Shards of chipping tree bark pricked my palms.

"Baby, tell me you love me," he said.

"You are my life, sir."

"Tell me you'd do anything for me."

"You can do anything you want to me, sir."

When he finished, he told me to lick him clean. He tasted like rubber and I wanted to spit him out, but he said he loved me, so I swallowed and got back up. He kissed my forehead and traced his thumb across my chapped lips. I smiled, knowing that we had only a few more

The QUEER
FICTION ISSUE

McSWEENEY'S
QUARTERLY

ISSUE NO.
SIXTY-TWO

– – –

hours. He shoved his thumb into my mouth and said I was the love of his life. I sucked until he got bored.

We continued down the path and were met by a small gorge. Dead leaves floated on the surface of the murky water. A fat frog hopped away once it noticed us. A tailless squirrel climbed up a short tree, as if in search of its missing appendage. Nicholas removed his clothes and jumped in, expecting the water to be deep, but it was a toddler's height. He pretended not to be injured as he limped toward the stream.

"Get in," he said.

"Are your legs okay?" I called out.

"Yeah, the water's okay," he shouted back.

In the cold water, my penis shriveled. Floating leaves touched my hips, and I kept thinking they were bugs. I wanted to be back in my dorm room.

"We didn't bring towels," I said once I reached him by the stream. He said we were free to roam naked, which I didn't want to do. A tree branch would prick me, an ant would bite. A pervert with a camera could flash a photo from the bushes. Above us, gray clouds gathered. It would rain soon, and we'd be stuck indoors for our last evening.

"You don't like swimming?" he said.

"We're standing."

"Squat."

We squatted and lingered in the water. My nipples were solid. I wanted to ask him to lick them, but I never initiated. I stared at his face while he meditated. His scruff was sexy. His hair still existed. He had lips that I enjoyed kissing, but he liked using his tongue, which too often tasted like pepperoni. He liked biting my chin until it bled, and I had to moan and say I liked it.

I peed in the water, expecting warmth, but all I felt was dirty. I

The QUEER
FICTION ISSUE

DOCILE BODIES
by CHRISTOPHER JAMES LLEGO

ISSUE NO.
SIXTY-TWO

- - -

moved closer to Nicholas and removed a wet leaf from his chest. I kissed him and asked if he was ready to go back. He opened his eyes and asked if that was what I wanted. I told him I'd do anything he wanted.

Nicholas had a hard time getting up, his age visible as his knees popped. "You're so short," he said.

"You're towering over me." I stood up, my eyes reaching his chest. He bent down to kiss my eyebrow and told me to hold his hand while we walked back to our clothes. "It's going to rain," I said, using my shirt to dry off. Nicholas returned to the trail, his clothes balled in his hand. He shook to get rid of the water, his penis flopping. I hated his foreskin.

We walked barefoot along the trail. I followed behind, hoping he knew where he was going. I wanted to smoke a cigarette, but he hated seeing me smoke, which felt hypocritical. Twigs cut the soles of my feet, and I worried that a mosquito would land on my exposed penis. The cold air bit my nipples.

"My dad used to take me camping," I said, unnerved by the sound of my own breathing. Nicholas didn't look back. "He said the mark of a true man was being able to make a fire using sticks and rocks, but I always failed. And then my mom died."

"I think this is it," Nicholas said. He'd found the fallen tree where we'd fucked.

I'd been following a lost man.

I lasted two minutes in the shower before my shivering body made Nicholas go limp.

"Cold showers are about discipline, which you lack," he lectured as he slid open the curtain, his other hand cupping my bruised cheeks. I stepped out of the tub and nearly slipped on the tiles. "You need to grow up at some point," he said, and I nodded, shaking as I reached for the beach towel hanging behind the door. "That's mine," he shouted, cold water sprinkling out from the still-open curtain. "Use the cum rag in the bedroom."

"There are extra towels in the closet," I said, his towel in hand. "I'll grab you one."

"No," he said. "I want your body to smell like my babies."

"Yes, sir." I hung the towel back on the hook, then dried off in the bedroom using the short towel beside the broken radiator, grossed out by the cold air and the feeling of semen rubbing around my wet body. Wanting a small victory, I dug into my backpack and pulled out my phone, which I always put away when Nicholas took me out on dates. Our first time together, when he brought me to his apartment after dinner at Jean-Georges, he'd swiped my phone from my hands, said it was impolite not to provide my full attention, and tucked it into his back pocket. His stained veneers made him look like a creep, but he'd shown me old photos of him and his baby nephew, and babies rarely smile at murderers.

Nicholas turned off the faucet in the bathroom. I had a text from my boyfriend. I listened for the sound of Nicholas's electric toothbrush as I opened my messages.

How's Brooklyn? Brendan had texted an hour earlier.

My dad's cough has gotten worse, I lied, though maybe it was true.

He texted back immediately, which meant he was horny. **Sorry,** he wrote, which didn't make me feel any better. I pictured him having a hard time typing with his left hand. **You get back tonight, right?** he added.

Late, yeah, I texted back, worried he expected something tonight. He'd see my bruises and ask how I'd gotten them, and I'd say my dad had hit me, which used to be true, and he'd say my dad deserved to die, and I wouldn't react, because I didn't want to blame myself if it came true.

– – –

The Foucault reading is dense, just fyi.

I figured he'd stopped masturbating, which made me smile. I imagined the Asian twink in his video, paused on all fours, begging to be played. But Brendan had picked me.

I'll be up all night, I texted, expecting him to ask if he could join me, which I'd reject, and then he'd beg, and I'd finally cave. I liked when he got desperate. I liked being yearned for. The other night, I'd nearly replied **No** to Nicholas's offer, but there was something about receiving his emails that made me want to open them again. It was the way he signed off: **Grateful for you.** I liked the idea of an older man thinking he was lucky to be alive at the same time as I was.

I'll buy us coffee, Brendan texted, then sent a heart emoji, which killed my script.

Before I could respond, Nicholas walked into the room, cleaning his ears with a Q-tip, and said, "Who are you texting?"

"My dad."

He checked the earwax on his Q-tip and tossed it into the wastebasket. "I don't like thinking of you as someone's son."

"Sorry, sir," I said, tossing my phone back into my bag. "I don't talk to him often, if that helps."

"I want to be your only daddy," he said. I thought he was flirting, so I placed my hands on his waist, but he pushed me back and said to dry off before I got the hardwood wet.

"Sorry," I said again, annoyed that I was here. Life went on in the city, and up here we sat in dirty water and stared out windows. I thought of tipping cows. I shut my eyes, trying to meditate like Nicholas had in the gorge, but he said to quit mocking him, so I stopped.

He went to the kitchen to start cooking dinner while I shaved my nipple hair in the bathtub. I considered running a bath for my blisters, but I didn't want to reuse the cum rag. Nicholas yelled that he was cooking chicken for dinner.

"I'm vegan," I said, joining him as he sautéed chicken breasts in an old ceramic pan. The fire alarms looked inoperative, so I opened one of the windows in the living room just in case, then noticed the rain. I thought of the cow who'd given me her milk, hoping she'd found shelter.

"You need more meat in you," he said.

Nicholas was a chubby chaser, and I should've been more appreciative that he kissed my stretch marks when he rimmed my ass. Freshman year, a guy had asked me if they were tattoos, so I turned off the lights while he took my virginity. Diet pills only made them worse.

We attempted doggy one final time, but dinner had made my stomach gurgle, and I found myself in the bathroom while Nicholas strummed random chords to hide the noise. The bedroom was too close to the bathroom, so I yelled for him to go outside and smoke, but he said he didn't take orders. I ran the faucet.

I flushed the toilet twice, thinking a second flush would capture some of the smell. There were usually candles or air fresheners at Airbnbs, but this bathroom didn't even have a plunger. In the cabinet underneath the sink, I found an unopened twelve-pack of single-ply toilet paper and a pile of browned magazines from 2001. I washed my hands under cold water and told my reflection that he was disciplined. I turned to the door in search of the towel, then remembered that Nicholas had left it in the bedroom. I listened to the strumming continue.

"The meat got to me," I said, hoping for an apology, but he didn't look up from his guitar. I watched his thick fingers trying to line themselves up along the strings. He stopped strumming when he couldn't figure out a chord, then asked me why I was still standing. Cold water dripped from my fingertips. I wanted to flick it at him.

The QUEER
FICTION ISSUE
DOCILE BODIES
by CHRISTOPHER JAMES LLEGO
ISSUE NO.
SIXTY-TWO

– – –

He attempted another chord that didn't sound right, then cussed and placed the guitar on the pillow where he'd pushed down my face not ten minutes ago. He stared at my hairless nipples and told me to lie in bed with him.

We cuddled underneath the thin blankets. His chin stubble brushed my earlobe. His limp penis pressed against my bruised ass. I enjoyed being the little spoon because I didn't have to do anything. Light rain patted the windows.

"My knees are killing me," he said.

"Drink milk," I said, imagining him on his swollen knees, sucking on a cow's teat. It would try to escape, so he'd bite down until the cow knew who belonged to whom.

He said he wished he were nineteen again. I said it sucked not being allowed into bars. He told me it was a good thing because it meant fewer temptations. I wanted to tell him that being told no made me want the thing more, but I agreed with him instead. "You always agree with me," he said, then sat up to play the guitar.

"Could you play me a song?"

"No."

I watched him strum two chords, then placed my hand on his knee. "Did I do something wrong?" I asked.

He didn't say anything.

"Because if I did something wrong, I'm sorry."

He brushed my hand off and said, "You should call your dad more often."

"I thought you didn't like it when I talked about my dad."

"*I'm* the one talking about him," he said. He turned to the window and stared at the rain. I wasn't sure if I should touch him, so I kept my hands underneath my pillow while Nicholas scratched the skin tag on his neck. I wanted to see his face, brace myself if he intended to yell. He turned back to me and said, "My nephew died last September."

"How'd it happen?" I asked, still unsure if I should touch him. I cracked my knuckles underneath my pillow.

"That's personal."

I felt bad for him in the same way I felt bad about getting an F on a plagiarized paper, so I told him he made me happy, and asked if he wanted to talk about it, but he said he'd rather teach me chords. I let him use my fingers on the strings while he shared a story about stealing his first guitar from band class in junior high. I tried to imagine him as a teenager, but I felt like a pervert, so I thought about his dead nephew instead. I wanted to ask a question, but I needed Nicholas to remain a mystery—otherwise, I'd have no reason to come back for more.

"I don't want our weekend to end," he said, puppeteering my fingers into a G major chord.

I noticed a hangnail on my thumb and asked him to stop playing with my fingers, then felt useless when he let go of my hands. I wanted to peel an orange and wince from the burn.

"You have work tomorrow," I said. "And I have class."

"Drop out and move in with me."

"Nicholas."

"I'm sorry," he said.

The drive home took two hours. I wanted him to drive over the speed limit, but the rain made Nicholas careful. What was the point of a luxury car if he drove his age? The air conditioner was on. My legs kept falling asleep. We listened to jazz for an hour, then he talked about his goals on the last stretch of highway. He said he had played the clarinet until his older brother used it to bat Nicholas on the back of his head and bent the keys. Then he grew up and earned an engineering degree. He turned to me while we tailgated a truck.

The QUEER
FICTION ISSUE

DOCILE BODIES
by CHRISTOPHER JAMES LLEGO

ISSUE NO.
SIXTY-TWO

– – –

"I can't wait for you to grow up," he said, then rested a hand on my thigh.

When we reached campus, two night guards were patrolling the quad in neon jackets and oversize sunglasses. One of them walked around without an umbrella, trying to appear macho. I'd have to run to the dorms if I didn't want to get drenched. I considered asking Nicholas if he had an umbrella I could borrow, but I didn't want to hold on to anything of his. The weekend was over.

"When can I see you again?" he asked.

"Email me."

He reached into his pocket and pulled out ten hundred-dollar bills. "Add it to what I've already given you."

"Thanks, sir." I tucked the money into the small pocket of my backpack.

"Call me Nicholas, please," he said.

"Okay." I unlocked the door and stepped outside.

"It's been two months," he called out from his rolled-down window. "I still don't know your real name."

"Do you want to?" I asked.

He lit a cigarette. "I don't know."

I crossed the street and passed the front gates, knowing Nicholas would watch until I was too far down the quad. He'd email me in a few days. He needed me.

Brendan was eating a burrito bowl on the floor while his roommate watched a ten-minute washboard-abs YouTube tutorial. I took a seat beside Brendan, leaning against their shared mini-fridge, and told him I'd missed him. He swallowed a mouthful of steak cubes and kissed me, his mouth tasting like meat and gingivitis. His roommate asked if we wanted the room, and I hoped Brendan would say yes so I could

The QUEER
FICTION ISSUE

McSWEENEY'S
QUARTERLY

ISSUE NO.
SIXTY-TWO

– – –

blow him, but he told his roommate to stay because we wouldn't do anything silly. I took it as a sign, wondering if what I had intended to do was silly.

I climbed onto Brendan's bed. "Did you grab me any coffee?"

"Shoot," he said.

"You had time to buy Chipotle."

"There's Mountain Dew in the fridge. Want one?"

"Soda me," I said, then laughed at my own pun. Brendan didn't catch it.

He opened two cans and joined me on his hard mattress. He clinked my can in celebration—maybe he knew he'd just dodged a breakup. I wasn't sure how long I'd stay with him. His birthday was coming up, which meant I needed a gift, but I didn't want to spend any money on him. I didn't want to spend money even on myself. I played with the tab of my can. The carbonation would upset my stomach, but we weren't going to do anything silly, so I took two large gulps and burped in his face.

"Tasty," he said, then crinkled his nose in a way I always found cute. There's something about beautiful faces acting ugly that I find endearing, like when a valedictorian smokes a cigarette, or a father changes his baby's diapers. "You're wet," Brendan said, noticing only because my clothes were soiling his bedsheets. He asked me if I wanted a towel, and I took it as an exit sign, telling him I needed a hot shower. Not wanting to lead Brendan on, I said I needed to call my dad first.

"Weren't you just with him?" Brendan asked.

"I can't check up on him?"

"You can."

"Thanks," I said. "Pray that I get my reading done before I pass out."

Brendan said God was a lie.

"So was that coffee."

The QUEER
FICTION ISSUE

DOCILE BODIES
by CHRISTOPHER JAMES LLEGO

ISSUE NO.
SIXTY-TWO

– – –

I walked down the hall. I shared my room with a junior who had an older girlfriend that lived in the Bronx, so he was never around, leaving me with a home that didn't feel lived-in. The walls needed posters. The desks needed plants. I'd once thought owning a turtle might be pleasant, but then I'd have to feed it and call it by a name, which felt too intimate.

I called my dad to see if he was alive, not sure which answer I wanted.

"You're still awake?" my dad asked, phlegm in his throat. In the background, a news anchor reported a missing teen from Flatbush. I wondered if my dad had remembered to lock the front door. His heavy breathing made my ear itch, so I put him on speaker and placed my phone on my bed while I counted my cash.

"It's barely eleven o'clock," I said, stacking the bills into piles of ten. My dad was chewing on something for too long. I turned off the speaker and pressed the phone back to my ear, listening to the sound of his molars mushing. "I'll wire another thousand to your bank," I said.

"I'm really sorry," he said after swallowing.

"Don't apologize, Roger. You need to pay for chemo." I pulled the hangnail on my thumb until it bled, then muted my phone and screamed into my pillow, which smelled like dandruff. I thought of the money he could've saved if he had health insurance, but I couldn't blame him. I unmuted.

I heard the news switch to a profile of a football team's winning streak. My dad flipped to another news channel, where the anchors were discussing politics. He turned off the television and coughed into his phone.

"I cooked chicken adobo for dinner," he said. "I took a photo of it. I'll text it to you." He'd been taking too many pictures since he upgraded his phone. Dogs in the neighborhood, his Mexican coworkers, a male nurse with a panda neck tattoo. One night he sent a photo of a paper

The QUEER
FICTION ISSUE

McSWEENEY'S
QUARTERLY

ISSUE NO.
SIXTY-TWO

– – –

cut, then a second text explaining how he'd gotten it. He said it was from paper. I wondered if anyone still listened to him.

"I ate chicken today too," I said, then checked the photo he'd messaged. Blurry, his head casting a shadow. The chicken looked dry. He'd added too much black pepper.

"My chicken was perfect," he said. "Your mom would be proud."

"Yeah," I said. "She would be."

The QUEER
FICTION ISSUE

McSWEENEY'S
QUARTERLY

ISSUE NO.
SIXTY-TWO

THE
CHORUS
OF DEAD
COUSINS
by
K-MING
CHANG

I warned my wife about them. They volunteered as our bridesmaids and came dressed in nets, fishhooks in their eyes, alive. They glued thorns into all the bouquets and stepped on my wife's dress until it tore, baring her ass, and then they used the veil to run around outside and catch hairy moths in its gauze. They knotted my tie into a noose and hung it from the church ceiling like a chandelier, but I didn't know how to kick them out once they were there. They brought gifts, fistfuls of worms and a downed telephone pole. They ate the cake and told us it was dry and asphalt-like. They farted in the minister's face and shattered a stained-glass window depicting a nativity scene and said it was our fault that Mary was beheaded and baby Jesus was powdered into an anthill of sand. When the ceremony moved outside, some of them attempted to straddle clouds and deliver a speech, but then it started to rain, a rain that fell thick as unpinned hair let down by my hands and tangling everywhere. My wife said she'd never known I had so many dead family members, that when I'd mentioned my cousins she'd thought I meant a few, and I said, "You should see how many are still living." My mother always used to joke: "In this family, it's one in the ground and a dozen more dangling from the trees, waiting to be plucked. It's one buried and a hundred more begging to be born."

It was only a week after our wedding that my wife threatened to leave me, saying that the chorus of dead cousins was straining her sleep, dicing her dreams fine with their fingers like pocketknives. It was true they were intrusive, carving out our windows and replacing them with panes of molten sugar that the raccoons came to lick at night, waking us with the drumbeat of their tongues. It was true they liked to get into bed with us, six of their bodies sardined between us, and that most of my cousins kicked under the sheets as if trying to surface from sleep. We woke with black shins and rubber ribs. But still, I told my wife, they were family, they didn't have bodies to go back to, and so she let me keep kitty litter boxes in the corner of the room so they wouldn't wet our bed, and she let me teach them how to change our light bulbs, so at least they were helpful: because they could ascend and descend at will, it was easy for them to reach the ceiling.

For a while I thought I had finally tamed them, and though they occasionally chased the mailman or tore out our plumbing, unrolling a flood as proudly as a flag, they knew not to do anything truly deranged, like removing their entrails and playing lasso-the-cowboy with them, or trying to flush one another down the toilet, or plucking daddy longlegs off our walls and training them to wrestle one another. I was proud of their restraint and of how well they dressed in death, sewing their own skirts from grass clippings and stolen curtains, and at least

– – –

now they were odorless and clean, not like when they were living and smelled like gasoline and wet knives and lotto scratchers.

"We need an exterminator," my wife said, but all the ones I called were men who said they didn't deal with what was already dead. I didn't need them killed; I just needed them to go on vacation for a little while, to stalk another surname for a month or two, to reincarnate, maybe. That night in bed, with the chorus of dead cousins dog-curled at our feet, my wife said what we needed was an evacuation. She was always speaking in the vocabulary of storms, of evacuations and casualties and degrees of damage. She had the spine of a storm too: there was a stillness to her center, but her limbs were always churning the air, choreographing wreckage wherever she went. The chorus of dead cousins, though, was the one storm she couldn't predict.

My wife is a professional storm chaser. When we met, she carried a card pinned to her sleeve that said SEVERE WEATHER PHOTOGRA-PHER. I told her that was a white-woman thing to do, chasing storms on purpose. We were in the lobby of a dentist's office and she was thumbing through a copy of *National Geographic*, an issue on the Tornado Alley of the Midwest, and without asking my name she turned to me and showed me the page with her photograph printed on it.

"My photograph didn't make the cover," she said, "but they paid me eighty bucks." I looked down at the page, her wrists a silver frame. The photograph was a full page, of a tornado like a ringlet of black hair, almost too intentionally arranged. It tapered to the width of a single hair, and at the base of it, in the distance, was a thumbprint-sized town. The tornado was either leaving it or heading toward it, but it was impossible to tell which, and already it seemed implausible that anyone had ever been born there, born in a city that could be distilled into a disaster.

I looked away from the woman's hands, the fluorescence of that photograph. I don't remember seeing a sky in it, but there had to have

– – –

been a sky for there to be a storm; there had to have been an origin for ruin. I was suddenly jealous of that tornado, the way it tangoed on the page, the way her hand ran down its length like a spine. The photo was taken from the perspective of someone who loved it, and I wanted to be captured that way, to be chased from my body.

"Have you ever been near something like this?" she asked. A typhoon, I told her, when I was little in Taiwan and all my cousins were still living. My Ahma lived only with one lung and was perpetually breathless, and my Ahgong was a former soldier who slept with his gun, until one night we heard it go off in his mouth. My mother sent me to Taiwan when I was four so she could stay in California and make money. She said she would send for me in a year, but the years bred like cicadas and outnumbered my memories, and by the time I was ten I no longer remembered her face and had to look at my own in the water of the well and circle the parts of me that were hers.

The year my mother sent for me, with no more money than when she sent me away, one of my cousins jumped into the well and had to be pulled out by her hair the next morning. She was in training to be a hairdresser, and she liked to use me for practice, clamping my head between her knees until I cried. Always, when she released me, I was a new species, my hair sculpted into antlers or siphoned into a dozen braids or cut short as a boy's, which made my Ahma cry but seduced me into spending weeks looking down at myself in the well, wanting to jump just to get closer to that girl in the water.

The typhoons came in herds every summer, but there was only one I remember, the one that had my name. It was August and the bulls were being manufactured into oxen. The men did this by tying the bull's balls together and using a meat mallet to pound the balls into the texture of minced garlic so they rotted away and all that was left were the hammocks of their empty sacs. This was the only way to tame them. I knew how to plug my ears with mud so I wouldn't hear the wailing of those bulls. When the typhoon came, it rained hands, little hands and big hands, soft hands and calloused hands, and the sea's waves were hands, too, woman-hands that plucked the roof off Ahma's tin house and reached in and confiscated her, tucking her into a back pocket of the sky.

"That's not a typhoon," the woman in the waiting room said. "That's a tsunami." I told her she hadn't heard the point of the story. There was something about that tornado photograph that made me offer my losses, and I thought she might bare hers too. Maybe she would admit to having a mother like mine, a nameless island of origin. But instead she looked down at her lap—for a photographer, she had surprising difficulty looking directly at anything—and said, "I bet I've captured every kind of disaster."

"What about an earthquake?" I said, and this made her pause.

"You can't take a picture of an earthquake," she said, still not looking at me. "You can only take a picture of the aftermath." The buckled knees of buildings, the streets razored with cracks.

"Have you ever been in one?" I said, wanting her to look at me. I wished we weren't in a waiting room, side by side: I wanted to rearrange the place so every seat was facing another, so I was the horizon of the room.

She laughed and said of course she'd been in one, this is California, aren't you from here, and I said I didn't know how it felt. I'd slept through earthquakes, or I had always been in the air when they happened, flying to some funeral for some cousin somewhere, dead for reasons that were always deemed natural, though I knew which ones had husbands, which ones had medications, which ones had histories and debts and seventh-story windows.

The dental assistant called her name—even her name sounded like a storm warning, a single vowel—and I decided to stand up as if it belonged to me. She looked up at me, her head jerking up, but she didn't stop me from substituting for her. It was my first time going to a

– – –

dentist, and I thought for some reason that I'd have to undress. Before I was sent back to my mother, one of my cousins had claimed that all doctors were perverts and just wanted to strip you naked and touch everything you didn't yet have a name for. When that cousin had gone to get an abortion, the doctor had told her to insert six cloves of garlic into her vagina, and when she used chilies instead—the garlic hadn't yet grown in—we all woke up to the sound of her shouting. She ran out of the house and waded waist deep into the river and soaked like that for a full day before the pain was put out.

The dentist was a woman with forehead lines as clear and deep as if they were plowed, and she reminded me of one of my cousins who had taught me to climb trees and lick my own skinned knees. But the difference was that the dentist had perfect teeth, a bright cavalry of canines, and when her hands were in my mouth I tried not to think of biting them off. No one in my family had teeth by the age of fifty. Their molars were martyred one by one into stones, ox bones, peach pits, men's fists.

"Swallow," the dentist said, her hands clamped on either side of my neck. "This is a test," she said, while the fluorescent light flirted with me. But I couldn't swallow when I was told to, so I thought instead of the woman in the waiting room and the dust redirected by the tornado, dusking the air between us. My spit thickened into a seed and I finally swallowed, plotting to be a tree. I'd read somewhere that all photographs are self-portraits—probably a man had said that—and I wondered where she was in that photo, if she was the funnel or the sky or the town that wasn't named anywhere, not even in the caption.

After my appointment, my mouth still tasting of latex, I found the woman sitting in the waiting room. I apologized for cutting her in line, and she told me not to worry, that she had been dreading what she'd come for. "I waited for you," she said. In her palms, she held a thimble-sized plastic box. When I sat down next to her again, she lifted the box and opened it, flashing me the tooth inside, a molar still polished

with spit. Outside the context of her mouth, the tooth looked like a
tadpole, a shifting species, not yet adapted to air. "A quick extraction,"
she said. "They numbed me." The left side of her face was lagging
behind the right. Her smile was quicksand, one side sinking into the
other, teeth sucked into gums.

When the woman took me home with her, I recognized the neighborhood of teeth-bright houses and metallic sidewalks, the roads circling
themselves: a place designed to protect. Where every house was chap-
eroned by trees and the only litter was leaves. My mother used to take
me to the houses she kept clean, houses like these. While I ate worms
in the yard and sucked on doorknobs, my mother would walk through
the house with her head down, searching for strands of black hair we
had shed, collecting them before we left.

In bed, the woman tugged my hair, called me by another name. I
recognized it as mine only in retrospect, answering to it too late. Her
hand traced my spine as if trying to find a light switch along it. A flick
to flood me. She closed the curtains, the lacy kind designed not to defy
the light but to dress it. But the sky shut itself off, and in the dark all I
could see was the slick of her chin, her tongue paddling toward light,
night dissolving the moon in its mouth.

When we were lying side by side, she asked me what I did for a
living. I said I didn't do anything for the living. I did things only for
the dead. "I'm a conductor," I said, joking. She turned onto her side,
curling inward, and said, "Of music? Heat? Electricity?" She slid her
hand between my thighs and laughed, her palm griddled in the warmth
of me. For the first time, I looked at her teeth closely, wondering if she
was still numb on one side, if she could taste what her tongue had done.

"Of a chorus," I said, though my cousins were dormant then, not
yet tailing me so closely.

The QUEER
FICTION ISSUE

THE CHORUS OF DEAD COUSINS
by K-MING CHANG

ISSUE NO.
SIXTY-TWO

— — —

"Clouds are conductors," she said, ignoring me. She told me that every storm has an anatomy, and that the root of a tornado is located in the sky, anchored to the clouds and not the ground. It's our nature, she said, to assume that things grow upward. She turned onto her back and lifted her arm straight to the ceiling, told me to imagine it was a tornado descending. "Is it true you're supposed to hide in a bathtub?" I asked.

Instead of answering, she got up in the dark and ran to the bathroom. When the tub was shimmering full, we got in together and fumbled for each other underwater, sharing one rope of breath between us. My mother used to corral me into the bathtub while she cleaned the bedrooms, and when I crawled out to escape, she plucked me up and put me back, her hand descending like something divine. Even now, underwater with my legs laced around a stranger, I expected a hand to reach down and remove me from desire.

Two months before our wedding, she took me to a restaurant called the Whale's Mouth, a seafood chain where you could select a live lobster from a light-blanched aquarium in the window. All the waiters were white and bearded. I told her this restaurant was appropriating the Chinese culture of eating only what you can kill yourself. She told me to stop complaining.

In the ladies' bathroom of the Whale's Mouth, where the door was shaped like a cartoon molar, my cousins walked out of the stalls and stood behind me while I rinsed my hands. They were dark and slick as racehorses, striding out on their hands and knees. Some of them I recognized from Yilan; others were cousins my mother had brought along on her housecleaning route, their surgical gloves swinging like milked udders. I tallied their teeth, cleaned their knees. All of them told me they disapproved of me going to the dentist, because dentists were scammers. As proof, one of them opened his mouth and showed me where his molars were crowned with gold. "Fake gold," he said. "The soft stuff. I told my mother to take my teeth when I was dead. She knocked them out with a sock full of stones, and in the end they couldn't even pay off my funeral. A scam."

I told him that his experience with the dentist was one incident, an outlier, and the rest of the cousins said I was starting to sound like her, that woman, my soon-to-be-wife, who spoke about things like charts and diagrams and latitudes. One of them turned his head and spat on the tile floor, and I remembered him, the one who laughed at me because I'd thought pineapples grew on trees before my mother sent me to Yilan. "You probably think babies grow inside men," he said, and later that summer my Ahma caught him with a soldier from Chenggong Ling. She tied him to the trunk of a tree, and all night I heard him yelling for us to cut him loose.

After I left Taiwan and came home, I got a call from Ahma saying he'd run away, which I knew meant he had died and I shouldn't ask how. I cradled the landline in my palm, remembering the baby pineapple he'd plucked for me in the fields behind Ahma's yard. It was smaller than his palm, its rind not yet spiked. "This is the heart," he'd said, coring it with one stroke. "The part you can't eat." He gave me a wedge of sweet flesh, the juice cording down my throat. When I asked for more, he gave me his half and gnawed on the heart, sawing at it with his teeth. Ahma told me that only poor people eat the heart of a pineapple, which is fibrous and as flavorless as wood. Your tongue carries the splinters for the rest of its life, unable to speak anything complete.

The chorus began that year, when I was twelve. It was the summer I came home to California and told my mother, in summary, a story about testicles. My cousin in Yilan, the oldest one, who practiced castrating bulls by swinging his hammer into peaches, liked to stand beside my futon at night and cradle his balls in his hands.

The QUEER
FICTION ISSUE

THE CHORUS OF DEAD COUSINS
by K-MING CHANG

ISSUE NO.
SIXTY-TWO

– – –

"Open your mouth," he told me.

"Gross," I said. "No."

He said, "Fine," but the next night he came with the hammer and said, "Open, open." When my mother heard this story, she told me not to talk about my cousins anymore. They were attracted to shit like flies, she said, and they died at the same rate. Every time someone called with news of another one running away, my mother folded a fast-food napkin into a lotus flower and burned it.

Lotuses, she said, float on the surface of water, free of the mud that makes them. "You should learn something from this," she said, marrying her match to the paper petals. In the bathroom of the Whale's Mouth, I redirected my dead cousins to the seafood display outside. What I knew about my cousins: they were always hungry, necklaced in tongues. While they reached inside the aquarium and snatched up the lobsters, distracting all the waiters and causing a minor flood, I tugged my fiancée outside and drove us home. She was upset about not getting to eat her lobster, but I told her that escaping the chorus of dead cousins meant all crustaceans must be left behind. It was a small sacrifice.

My wife was willing to tolerate the chorus for another month, but it was nearly tornado season and now was the time for her to *focus and prepare*. In March she plotted a path east to Oklahoma and south to Texas, packing her parents' Jeep with dehydrated-food packets and water bottles and battery-powered lanterns and binoculars and her camera with its zoom lens that looked like the barrel of a gun. I told her I would come with her, and she said, "Not with them."

If anything could deter the chorus of dead cousins, I told her, it would be a tornado. They wouldn't dare come near something that could whip them into steam. She didn't believe me, but she agreed to take me anyway, and when the June heat began to circle the city like a noose, we drove away. The dead cousins watched from the driveway, waving and weeping, begging me to take them along. One of them was flapping his shirt at me like a handkerchief, and I wondered where they had learned to perform this kind of goodbye. From an old movie, maybe, about white people forced to depart the countries they've conquered. There was something false about their farewell, and I knew they were just waiting for us to leave.

My wife thought they were fluent only in the vocabulary of destruction, but weeks before we left, before they knew we were leaving, I saw the cousins in the backyard with shovels. They were standing in a row like soldiers, and when I asked what they were doing, they said, "We're making you a moat." They told me it was the season of wildfires and they wanted to make sure the flames wouldn't find us, and then they bent their heads in unison and began to dig. Some of them dug with their hands or the dishes of their detached kneecaps. All night, I could hear the sound of them knuckling into the earth.

I recognized the face of the cousin who'd initiated the digging. It was unusual for me to differentiate them, and even I began to call them by their cause of death, the way my wife did. This was the Cousin Whose Blood Did Not Clot. When she moved in with my Ahma, husbandless and with two children, we'd had to wrap the corners of the table in newspaper, bury the knives, dull our own nails by biting them short. We were afraid of touching her, because her blood was like a ribbon that could only be reeled out in one piece, one river length, unable to knot. One day we found her faceup in the pineapple fields, a man's machete in her chest and all of her blood outside her body, a red shroud we tugged over her face.

When my wife and I drove away from the duplex, my bloodless cousin was the one who cried the loudest. She hung herself up in the doorway, swinging her body like a bell. As we left, I tugged on her

– – –

voice like a thread and it kept unraveling, following us east through Nevada. My dead cousins must have hijacked the soundtrack for our drive, because every time I turned on the radio, I heard a symphony of cicadas and clacking lobster claws. The Jeep swelled with cane field smoke and I kept opening the windows, coaxing it out. Ahead, the road curved like a rib, and I imagined my cousins standing at the sides, thumbs up to ask for a ride. But all we passed was desert, delayed rain, blond dirt. Cacti as big as trees. When it was my turn to drive, I swerved off the road every two miles, mistaking a dust devil for a child. "Relax," my wife said, placing her hand on the steering wheel to steady it, but I wasn't accustomed to this kind of wind. Wind dancing the dust, erecting it into walls.

In Oklahoma, the towns were stitched farther apart and the dust barricaded our windshield. Even the landscape was illegible. The road ahead seemed to hinge, folding over us, but my wife told me it was just a mirage. My wife held a walkie-talkie in both hands, as if it were a holy object, and through the static of my cousins I heard the other storm chasers reporting on the sky's conditions: "Cloud of debris," they said. "Hail in the absence of rain."

"It's coming," she said. The sky was a darkening green, either because it was evening or because it was full of pregnant clouds, each as round and bruised as a plum. A handful of wind-lifted pebbles rained down on me, and for a second I thought maybe my cousins were here, that this whole thing was a setup just to scare me: the sky, the motel, the stolen sun. My wife said we should drive off-road and into the dusted fields, aiming to get underneath those clouds. She stood at the hem of the field with her hands offered out, waiting to catch something. The binoculars around her neck seemed comical: the clouds were as huge as houses, all the lights shut off inside them.

My wife returned to the Jeep, sitting in the driver's seat. I stood beside it, watching her through the window. "This is your chance to

The QUEER
FICTION ISSUE

McSWEENEY'S
QUARTERLY

ISSUE NO.
SIXTY-TWO

− − −

see what I see," she said, and I remembered the first time we were in bed, when she'd explained all the preparations necessary to get close to death and to deny it. I wanted to tell her that some people don't need to get closer to death. They are born inside it and will never leave. All those years my mother brought me along to houses, I felt like we were haunting them. When the owners were home, they never looked at us directly, as if we had already left or never arrived. I watched my mother pack up the car, caped in wind. She stacked the buckets one-handed, knotted the trash bags, buckled me into the backseat. We left no wreckage.

"Can you taste it," she said, rolling down the window. The clouds behind her were retracting, leaning back on their haunches, hungry. I tasted the sky's rim of sugar, smelled a cane field on fire. She was right: storms had a smell, just like a body. "Let's go," she said. "Let's get closer." I buckled myself into the passenger seat, braced myself against the window. Out in the dust fields, there were other Jeeps sewn in a line like ants, other women waiting for the wind like kin.

She steered us into the fields, and though the land was flat, the Jeep startled me out of my seat. I wanted to ask whose land this was, if we were trespassing, but realized no one else was worrying. Ahead, a cloud extended its legs, two ropes of smoke groping for the ground, braiding back together. Beside me, my wife's hands on the wheel were shaking. It was a breech birth, the sky severed from any source of light, the cloud dragging its umbilical cord along the ground. "What is it," my wife whispered, still driving. The other Jeeps ahead of us were scattering, scurrying away, but we kept going straight.

The tornado drilled into the ground. Dust beat on our windshield and broke it, glass basking on our laps. When it bent over us, the tornado was brighter than any of my teeth. It had a face. It was made of faces, eyeholes and mouth holes perforating the funnel. My cousins singing, with the entire sky as their skin, their mask. The

The QUEER
FICTION ISSUE

THE CHORUS OF DEAD COUSINS
by K-MING CHANG

ISSUE NO.
SIXTY-TWO

– – –

dust digressed into limbs, dancing out of the debris, lashing out at the landscape. They were laughing, my dust-cousins, outgrowing their borrowed skin. I waited for their mouths to make a choir around us, sucking us into their stomach, but instead they grew upward. The Jeep was rocking with the force of their laughter, and my wife held up her camera. Hands shaking, she stood up in her seat, the canvas roof of the Jeep already shredded. When the camera's flash flooded every field with white water, I reached out and covered her lens with both hands. *Don't capture them,* I wanted to say. *Let them take the sky.*

The tornado splintered, torn into tissues of wind. Into the dark, I called my cousins' names. I called them home. The air was so clotted with dust, I couldn't see my wife's face, could only feel her fist around my wrist, tugging me back into the car. But I was already out and running, the dust scouring my eyes bright. All around me, the wind rippled the fields like flags and the dust rose again, crusting into bodies. I told them to come down. "It isn't safe," I said. "There will be storms." But they hovered, constellations of dirt. They crowded my mouth, pretending to be salt. "Fine. Be that way," I said, but every word was spat dust, another cousin leaving my body. Their names populating my tongue like a pincushion. I remembered the cousin who showed me the wood-splintered heart of a pineapple, how most people discard it but it was our duty to digest it. I opened my mouth, touching my tongue to sweet dust.

MAGDELANE: EPILOGUE
by GARRETT YOUNG

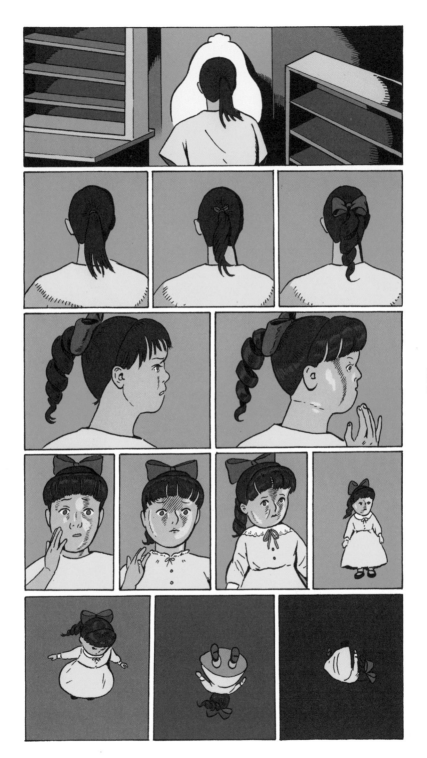

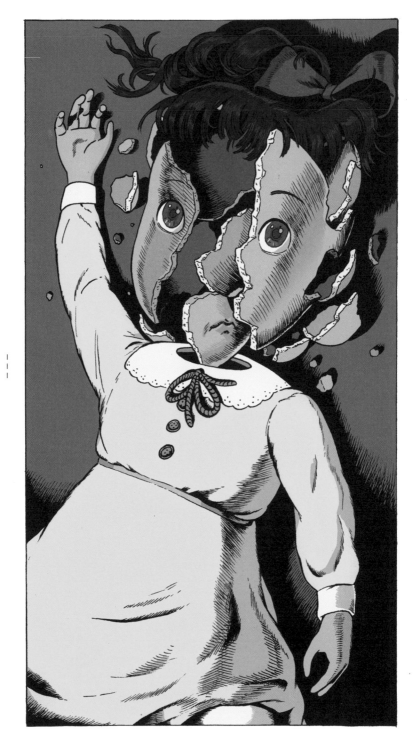

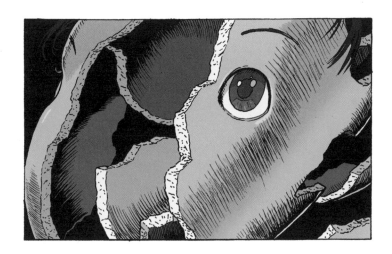

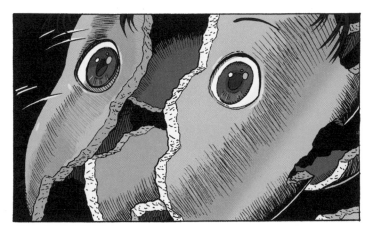

DOCTOPMARU 2020

The QUEER
FICTION ISSUE

McSWEENEY'S
QUARTERLY

ISSUE NO.
SIXTY-TWO

TRIAL
OF
GHOSTS
by
VENITA
BLACKBURN

Rowina often pretended monsters were chasing her while riding her bicycle to keep her pace effective for fat burn. She had done this as a child for fun, now for other reasons. She ran from grief. Monsters were no longer hideous, grisly ghouls. They were echoes of people she'd known, returned to her for their own purposes.

Rowina grew up watching TV shows about the dead, like everyone else. One episode was about a soccer coach that lost her whole team in a plane crash. Every single one of the players returned to her. They didn't go to their own mothers and fathers or pastors or friends. They went to her, one at a time, for a month and nine days. The audience was awed by the love they saw from those dead children, but the coach looked like she hadn't slept well since and never would again. Another

– – –

episode featured a confused man that had never been visited by anyone and didn't understand why, so eventually he developed a ghost fetish. He was not at all a mystery.

There were the best-selling books: *Are Your Dead Keeping Secret Bank Accounts?*; *How to Get the Dead to Do Their Chores*; *Sexing the Spirits*; and *I Ain't Afraid of No People: A Memoir from the Deceased*.

Rowina ran from all of them. She rode on the cement path that wound along Ocean Drive. It was hot for early afternoon—too hot. She pumped her pedals relentlessly despite the heavy warmth, tiny rivers of sweat running down her neck and arms. A man in khaki dress pants and a white tank top, with dark, hard, slender muscles and a silk tie knotted loosely around his neck, kissed the air as she passed him.

"Slow down, baby girl!" he shouted.

The man looked like someone who'd been plucked from another country and dropped here like a doll. Women with carts for stowing groceries or laundry were scattered along the sidewalks, with couples and tourists. Teens rode scooters recklessly for as long as their dollars could power them, then cast them aside like trash to clog the path. Usually, her speedy pace kept cool air rushing over her skin while she avoided the obstacles of the city, but not today. Today she raced through a veil, the air thickening as she lost energy. Rowina had pushed herself too far again, and didn't want to pass out in the street with her bicycle pinned under her like a dead horse. That would be embarrassing. The water bottle wedged in the frame of her bike turned out to be of no help—a few warm beads of liquid were all that lingered inside. Her vision darkened around the edges, little spots forming ahead of her, and she knew she had to stop for hydration.

She'd been riding for over an hour and had made it all the way to Seal Beach. Small yachts and catamarans jostled one another in the marina like friends. Fewer and fewer people appeared, and Rowina felt some relief from the absence of bodies. She knew a place to go, a small café she didn't venture to often, only when she needed a small escape from her fellow man and felt the excessive bill would be worth the price.

Though underdressed, in black bike shorts and a white, clingy T-shirt, she entered with only a little hesitation upon seeing her own reflection in the glass door. Her brown arms were firm and her shoulders square and solid from her weight lifting routine. A long, toned body paired with her soft, full features glowing with life and color from her exertions gave her nothing to be displeased with. Plus, with a bike worth as much as a used car chained out front, the staff would know she could afford to pay the check.

Once she was through the door, the air conditioning restored her faith in this world. She held up a single finger to the host without smiling and was escorted to a seat immediately. The café was just as she'd expected: nearly empty on a Saturday during peak lunch hours. An attractive waitress appeared, wearing a black apron down to her ankles and a blue button-up shirt tucked into her waistband.

"Would you like to start with some water?"

Rowina looked up and nodded with feigned desperation that earned her a small smile. The waitress returned with water and a basket of bread with a saucer of olive oil and seasoning.

"I'll give you a minute to decide, hon."

Rowina was finally alone to drink and drink and drink, after pulling the unsolicited lemon from the glass. When the water was more than half gone, she noticed she was not as alone as she'd thought.

Only two tables away, a woman sat facing Rowina and stared directly at her. Rowina couldn't be sure how long the woman had been staring and for what reason. After a brief moment of panic, Rowina looked away, as is customary when making accidental eye contact. She

– – –

looked back to make sure the woman, too, had looked away, but the woman stared on. The panic returned, hotter than ever. What did she see? Rowina couldn't help but rub a hand along the back of her head, having just cut her hair short around the sides for the first time since college. She glanced down at her shirt, which had been drying well, no sweat stains. Then she checked her own reflection quickly in the window. From what she could see, nothing seemed out of the ordinary. Another wave of panic hit her: maybe the woman was judging her as unworthy—as a fraud and a fool; maybe she could look into Rowina's wallet and accounts and see every late payment and overdue bill. But that was impossible. There was no evidence on the surface to indicate anything problematic, unless the woman was a racist or a psychopath. So Rowina decided to stare back. The other woman didn't waver under the new scrutiny. Rowina saw her strapless dress and lightly tanned skin, her dark eyes, and her hair that fell in gentle coils past her shoulders. She would've been beautiful if she weren't so invasive, Rowina thought. A motion near the kitchen distracted Rowina enough to see the staff fumbling with an order. When she looked back, the woman was gone. Or so Rowina thought, before noticing the woman walking toward Rowina's table.

Rowina prepared herself for the worst: a physical assault, perhaps, or a verbal scolding. Maybe the woman had mistaken her for her husband's mistress and planned to have it out. Rowina smiled briefly at the thought of being yanked on and cursed at by a beautiful woman in the name of a forgettable husband. She might let it go on longer than necessary. The two could laugh about it and maybe Rowina would get an apology meal out of the whole ordeal. That thought dissipated when Rowina detected subtle nerves in the woman, how she pressed her palms against her thighs to smooth wrinkles that weren't there or to wipe away anxiety sweat. What did she have to be worried about? That made Rowina worry even more. Was that what women did before they reached into a designer handbag and pulled out a gun to kill their partner's lover? Rowina thought she had women figured out but now wondered if she knew women at all, based on the curious one that was stepping closer and closer. Then it was too late because the woman was upon Rowina, and the moment had arrived for the end of her life, or something short of it.

"Excuse me, but I think I know you," the woman said.

She smelled of vanilla, and Rowina lost the edges of the room for a second. There was no anger in that voice, just low, soothing notes of uncertainty and something else, maybe hope.

Rowina shook her head, and was returning her hand to the back of her neck when the woman laughed unexpectedly and profoundly. It was an unmistakable laugh, familiar in its absurdity, like a tiny sprite gasping for dear life. Rowina knew that laugh like she knew a stone dropped in water.

"Mani?" Rowina said.

"I haven't heard that name in years. I became the whole Amani to everyone in the end."

There she stood. Perfect. She glanced at the chair across from Rowina for permission to sit. Rowina nodded and leaned forward on her elbows, astonished.

"You look... so... I didn't recognize you without the laugh. There it is."

Amani took a deep breath to quiet the giggles. The waitress returned with Amani's place setting and water glass.

"Can I get you two any appetizers?"

Rowina was already shaking her head no in response to the unnecessary, exorbitantly priced, and inadequately portioned "appetizers" the café probably had to offer when Amani replied in the affirmative.

The QUEER
FICTION ISSUE

TRIAL OF GHOSTS
by VENITA BLACKBURN

ISSUE NO.
SIXTY-TWO

— — —

"Definitely. Let's start with the salmon rolls. Right, Ro? And the mixed greens. The tuna tartare is pretty good. We can share all that."

"Sure."

Rowina stared at the menu, eyes flitting from one price to another so quickly that she didn't see the waitress disappear. When she looked up, she found Amani staring at her intently. She could feel the slump in her back, so she straightened immediately. She had a balance on one credit card to cover the sum so far, but might have to run the risk of a declined transaction if the orders progressed any further. Amani couldn't know any of that, especially if she sat upright and kept her eyes focused on the present and not the past. But what did the dead know? How far could Amani reach into her soul, her mind? Rowina shook her head. She was being silly. They don't come back for that, to know things about us and shame us with them. Amani of all people would never know any of that if Rowina held herself together. She could just say no. When the food arrived, she'd say, *No, thank you*, she thought. She could say she'd had a seafood aversion lately. That would be convincing. Rowina considered all of this with Amani's dark eyes leveled on her as if she could pull the thoughts out and lay them on the table like a deck of cards.

"It's good to see you, Ro. It's been forever."

"It has. I... I... you've been gone awhile."

"I've been gone?"

That laugh again.

"Where did I go? I never left the state before the end. You! You went everywhere."

Rowina smiled. This wouldn't be so bad, this visit. She could handle this just fine, not like the other, her mother's visit.

"I did some traveling. Lived abroad for a stint on different fellowships."

– – –

Amani nodded and sipped her water. Then she ran her fingers along the condensation.

"You were the smart one," Amani said, not looking up from the table.

Amani's voice became low again, pensive and weighty. Rowina had traveled to residencies after graduate school. Eventually, the fellowships ran out, but the wanderlust remained, fueling a wildfire of debt she had yet to extinguish.

"I know who you married, at least," Rowina said. "Everyone knows who you married."

Rowina laughed, expecting to hear that thrilling chuckle from Amani, but no sound emerged.

"Not everyone."

"Please. The waitress knows your husband, Mani. Even if they don't know you."

The last of those words moved Amani back in her chair a little. Rowina hadn't meant to be hurtful, but she had hurt Amani. The way her cheeks drew in and her bottom lip shifted from side to side, almost comically, like a baseball player about to spit. Here she was, a woman who'd once had everything, offended because she wasn't as famous as her spouse. Well, Rowina knew better than to give Amani her pity. When Amani was hurt, it was better to duck out of the way of whatever she did next. Crying was the least of anyone's worries. Rowina would know, having been the cause of some pain she hadn't thought about in years.

Amani had lived abroad until age eight, when she'd arrived at Rowina's elementary school. Her father was French and had met Amani's mother

The QUEER
FICTION ISSUE

TRIAL OF GHOSTS
by VENITA BLACKBURN

ISSUE NO.
SIXTY-TWO

– – –

in a central African country while on service duty. When her mother
died suddenly of a degenerative disease, Amani had traveled alone with
her father. She showed up in Rowina's class with the wrong accent, the
wrong hairstyle, the wrong parent. Rowina knew what it was like to have
a dead mother and how well-intentioned fathers sometimes didn't think
through an outfit carefully. Amani fit in just right with Rowina. In grade
school, they were inseparable. When two smart girls with imaginations
cling to each other, only fools try to pull them apart. Together they
pretended to be lions and hunters, taking turns at being prey and predator, gnawing at each other's limbs and judging the flavor. "Sweet. This
lion must eat a lot of cereal" or "This one is no good: too much broc-
coli." Their games evolved as they pretended to be each other's mothers.
Clumsily offering care for each other as any imaginary mother would,
spooning soda as medicine into each other's mouths and baking beautiful birthday cakes made of air and dreams. Eventually, they pretended
to be each other's sisters, then wives and husbands. Rowina would put
a hand on her hip and scold Amani for not appreciating all her hard
work, maintaining their invisible home, and taking care of their stuffed-
animal babies. Amani would take fake sips from a brown bottle stolen
from the trash, then laugh and laugh, then hug Rowina tightly in mock
apology. Then the roles would switch. Rowina would get to be the lazy
husband and Amani the overworked wife.

Not long after that, Rowina's own mother visited her.

It took her too long. Her mother waited wherever the dead wait. Rowina
had forgotten her, forgotten her eyelashes and chin hairs and smell
of astringent and lotion. Her long fingers and braided hair—none of
it seemed like part of Rowina. They were fragments that belonged in
photographs. Rowina had a mouthful of pancake when her mother
entered from the backyard, kicking her sandals off by the door. Rowina

screamed. Her father came running out of the bathroom. Once he realized his dead wife had come to see Rowina and not him, he had to leave.

"It'll be fine, Roro. I'll be back soon."

He left. He left her with a dead woman rummaging through the kitchen for a spoon to stir sugar into some coffee.

Rowina screamed at the door, more angry at being abandoned than afraid, but when the scream broke away from overuse, they were still there together.

A month later, Rowina invented the witching game for her and Amani to play at school. They sat together on the blue-and-yellow reading carpet, tearing construction paper into tiny pieces and throwing them into a circle as spells to change them into grown-ups or airplanes, anything that could fly away. A loud girl with a pink spring-loaded umbrella pulled at Amani's shoulder, then aimed the umbrella and hit Amani in the cheek just under her eye socket. The girl bent over in laughter as Amani's tears started. Rowina didn't have a chance to react before Amani leaped into the air and snatched at the girl's head, scratching her deeply and yanking that stupid umbrella away and bashing her with it until the teacher came and lifted Amani up like a melon, a wailing melon with a fistful of another child's hair, and tears and mucus running down its face. While hovering in the air, clamped under the teacher's arm, Amani saw Rowina with her little hand deep in the pile of torn paper and she stopped wailing. Their eyes met, wide and curious, believing they had made it all happen.

As they got older, the boys tugged, too, but it wasn't until the boys had something more substantial to offer than their bodies that Amani bothered to look up.

The waitress brought the appetizers, enough for five people, by Rowina's estimation. Amani wasn't as famous as her husband. Their fame didn't

The QUEER
FICTION ISSUE

TRIAL OF GHOSTS
by VENITA BLACKBURN

ISSUE NO.
SIXTY-TWO

– – –

really matter in Rowina's circles, but she knew it mattered to Amani, and that's all that counted. As a gesture of goodwill and apology, Rowina reached for a salmon roll instead of refusing the plates altogether, as she'd planned. She would pay this small price this one time.

"Did you save the world yet?" Amani asked, not eating but just watching Rowina.

To someone who didn't know Amani, those words might not mean much. But Rowina could tell she had something on her mind, and Rowina wasn't going to leave that café without making whatever it was come down on her like boulders.

"Mani, what's your problem?"

"What are you talking about? I was just curious. Your social media accounts are private, or they were, last I checked, so I was wondering what you were up to."

"You're stalking me? Ohh. You're in love with me!"

"Shut up!"

Amani choked a little on her water and laughed, as Rowina had intended.

"You're the same, you know that?" Amani continued.

"Smart, hot, super cool?"

"And kind of an asshole."

"I heard 'and,' so I won't argue with any of that."

Rowina's phone buzzed, but she silenced it without looking as Amani began to eat. So all dead can eat. Rowina was thankful for that, otherwise she might have been obligated to pay for all the appetizers. Another question surfaced, more urgent than the last. Rowina opened her mouth to speak but quickly stopped herself.

"You can ask me anything. That's sort of why I'm here," Amani said.

"Are your credit cards working?"

Amani smiled and nodded.

"Everything works. Cards. Cash. Heart. Lungs."

"So what's it like?" Rowina asked.

"What?"

"Money!"

"Oh! It's never as much as you expect, I guess."

"That sounds right."

The waitress returned, ready to take their full order, but Rowina leaned away from her as if she were being asked to participate in a medical experiment.

"We probably have plenty, and it's getting a little late," Rowina said.

Amani slid her hand across the table as if to reach for Rowina but came just short of taking her hand. "We can finish lunch, can't we?"

The words were too sincere for Rowina to bear. She would agree to anything when Amani spoke like that, as if there were no other people in the room, as if begging weren't beneath either of them when it came to each other. Rowina could only nod and eye the menu, still lurking on the edge of the table, with suspicion and scorn.

"Club sandwich for me," Amani said with such a confident shift in timbre that Rowina thought she'd been duped.

"Same."

The waitress smiled, scooped up their menus, and left them alone again. Amani looked at Rowina, not saying anything, eyelids low and with a smirk on the brink of exploding, as if she'd won something. Rowina's skin had cooled too much in the air conditioning and, as goose bumps rose on her forearms, she now felt underdressed.

"No, I haven't, by the way," Rowina said. "The world still needs saving."

"I'm sure. Who are the villains now, other than me and the whores of capitalism?"

"Ha ha ha," Rowina deadpanned.

The QUEER
FICTION ISSUE

TRIAL OF GHOSTS
by VENITA BLACKBURN

ISSUE NO.
SIXTY-TWO

– – –

"Seriously, Rowina. There's a crisis for someone every day. I worry about you, you know."

"Me? We've got widespread domestic terrorism, government complicity and abuse, income inequality like we've never seen in the history of mankind, and you know what happens to people who say something about it: death. We're in the fucking dark ages—a war—and you're worried about me?!"

"Yes, you! I didn't know about the protesters, but it is okay. It's okay, you know, to have someone worry about you."

Amani spoke to Rowina as if she were aware of her tendency toward theatrics, as if Rowina's proclamations were well rehearsed, performed, and a proper audience reaction was all she really wanted. Rowina considered all the reactions she should've gotten, the ones she was ready for—the denials, the apathy, the smug disregard for class distinctions, a safe retort about all people being spiritual beings— because it is necessary for the privileged not to worry about the safety of the disadvantaged. This makes the privileged feel safe when they rightly suspect otherwise. Rowina knew what to say to those people, the ones who want to live above the trees, where screams are buried in the wind: *Cowardly. Blind. Weak. Selfish.* Amani, however, was none of those things.

As children, they had been different but similar. Rowina was raised by a single father, but she had aunties aplenty. She went to school washed and styled and ironed. Among the poor kids, she looked pristine. Among the rich kids, she looked loved. When Amani showed up at elementary school—motherless, her hair a frizzy cloud, towing a backpack on wheels—she was teased mercilessly for half a day, no evidence of love to protect her. During the second snack time, a boy pulled her hair hard enough to draw a tear. She squeezed a packet of peanut butter crackers in her fist and, in French, told him to eat a dead man's foot. The boy stopped as if his throat had been slit. She

The QUEER
FICTION ISSUE

McSWEENEY'S
QUARTERLY

ISSUE NO.
SIXTY-TWO

– – –

said it again, a flurry of vowels and consonants, another cut. She said it again, faster, and another wound opened in his heart. The boy wailed like he'd been cursed. Rowina was in awe. The teacher came over to Amani, who stood quietly, innocently, nearly crying, too, and maybe to the teacher her wet eyes shone with empathy instead of condemnation. The teacher took the boy to the restroom to calm him down. Rowina immediately sat next to Amani without saying anything at all and could feel the heat of anger still rising from her little arms. The two of them opened their crackers and began to eat. She wasn't teased again, at least not in that class. Years later, Rowina asked what was said to that boy, and Amani confessed she'd never heard anyone say "Eat a dead man's foot" before or after that day; the words just came out of her. The two of them laughed and laughed.

"I'm surprised you're not married," Amani continued at the café. "Are you close, perhaps?"

"Are you flirting with me, Mani?"

Rowina leaned forward, and Amani's involuntary intake of breath betrayed the truth.

"You never did play fair," Amani replied, suddenly fascinated with the texture of her napkin.

"I always played to win."

In high school Rowina convinced Amani to join the track team. No one teased the athletes, but by then everyone's personal traumas had become so cumbersome that bullying had gone out of fashion, anyway. However, the two of them kept up their games of prey and predator, of mother and daughter, of lover and fool. They didn't always want to play at the same time, though. One afternoon on the track field, Rowina had bad cramps while Amani felt a joy and lightness inside that almost made her want to kill someone. They lined up in the lanes. Amani sensed Rowina's nausea and swatted at her for being vulnerable. When a predator spots a victim, there's little that can dissuade it from

– – –

attacking. Amani ran side by side with Rowina, still playfully swatting at her when Amani was sure the coach couldn't see. Rowina yelled at her to stop it. Amani bared her teeth and growled with a smile. The act of turning toward each other full-on ruined their trajectory and their feet tangled in a devastating fall. They rolled over on each other before coming to a stop, bloody elbow and forehead well earned.

"Aw, shit!" the coach yelled.

The two of them went to the locker room for a first aid kit after receiving a few more chastising swears from the coach, Rowina too angry to even speak. She went into the cage with all the equipment, opened and slammed the cabinets, looking for something remotely "first aid" in nature, then kicked a sack of soccer balls that spilled out onto her foot. Amani stood quietly by the door to the cage, holding her elbow. Only when Rowina finally found the case of alcohol and bandages did she look at Amani and see just how much damage had been done. Amani had taken the brunt of the tumble. Rowina had what might be bad bruises on her hip and shoulder but no blood on her face.

"See what you did," Rowina said. "If you'd listened to me the first time, we wouldn't be here. Kids never listen."

"I'm sorry, Mommy."

"Sit over here, you little dumbass."

Rowina gestured at the benches near the lockers. The first aid kit exploded when opened, bandages falling to the floor. After a skeptical look at the messy contents, Rowina made a selection: an alcohol wipe, some ointment, tape, and a few cotton pads. Once the blood was clean and Amani was patched up, she growled again, the urge to kill not quite satiated.

"Shut up," Rowina said, looking her in the eye.

Amani growled lower and this time Rowina growled back. Amani lunged at Rowina and put a soft bite on her cheek. Rowina screamed

The QUEER   McSWEENEY'S   ISSUE NO.
FICTION ISSUE   QUARTERLY   SIXTY-TWO

– – –

in shock and delight, falling off balance and knocking the first aid kit to the floor. Amani crawled on top of Rowina and made an exaggerated sniffing motion around Rowina's face and neck, stopping when their eyes were level. Rowina smiled and gently bit Amani on the chin, an acceptance of her bizarre apology. Amani's hands loosened their animal grip on Rowina's waist and shirt. They looked at each other, closer and for longer than they had ever before. All the clichés are true about how love strikes at the heart, how it rings like a bell in the chest and reverberates throughout the spine. Amani kissed Rowina. Her chapped lips mashed against Rowina's mouth, growing warmer and wetter and more suffocating by the second. They didn't kiss as hunter and prey or as a friendly game. They kissed like lovers recognizing each other for the first time. After a few minutes, they were calm again and sat in silence. Eventually, Rowina stood and Amani followed. They scavenged some expired ibuprofen from their coach's desk drawer and went back to the field.

The two got older, taller, stronger. Time changed their shape and altered how everyone, especially men, perceived them. The boys became their own dense units, patrolling the school and streets. Amani didn't see them until the athletic scouts came to town. Women's sports didn't come with the promise of new cars and exposure to professional opportunities. Men's sports did. Before that time, it had been enough that Amani and Rowina paid attention to each other, but a new promise emerged: money. When a senior with a new Mustang gifted by some university in Texas asked Amani on a date, she immediately sought Rowina's advice and, in a way, her permission. It was exciting for both of them, to be wanted by someone of value to the world at large. Things were fine after the first couple of dates. Amani recapped them unenthusiastically before falling asleep on the couch with her hand under Rowina's shirt. With each new encounter, Amani became more fascinated with the workings of athletic scholarships and how

The QUEER
FICTION ISSUE

TRIAL OF GHOSTS
by VENITA BLACKBURN

ISSUE NO.
SIXTY-TWO

– – –

much a contract could be worth if the trajectory toward professional status, merchandising, and endorsements continued.

One evening, they had a pot of spaghetti waiting for them for dinner, courtesy of Rowina's father.

"Are you staying tonight?" he asked Amani while halfway out the door for his graveyard shift. Amani was mid-nod when Rowina replied for her.

"Not tonight."

Amani turned as if she'd been kicked. The door closed. They looked at each other for a long time. Rowina didn't have the words for jealousy and didn't know that it was possible inside of herself until then. She could only punish them both for it. They would sleep cold and apart that night and for many more to come.

"Remember how your dad was always mad at something nobody else ever thought about?" said Amani, one hand over the other on the café table.

"Vaguely," Rowina replied, disingenuously laughing a little, giving herself away.

"C'mon! The recycling bins!"

Rowina laughed again. "I haven't thought of that in years."

"He was all, 'Why they gotta be a different color. Trash is trash. They should all just be clear, then nobody gotta be worried about a code,'" Amani mocked in a gruff man's voice.

"He got that citation from the city for putting yard waste in the recycling."

"Is that what it was?"

"That, and the horoscopes."

"Oh my god, the horoscopes! 'How they gon' know what happened on my birthday one thousand years ago when everything in the sky is

The QUEER
FICTION ISSUE

McSWEENEY'S
QUARTERLY

ISSUE NO.
SIXTY-TWO

– – –

dead anyway? Starlight is billions of years old. Those stars have long blown up. They don't even count!'"

Laughing, Rowina held up a hand to stop Amani from continuing.

"I don't know how he could be the sweetest man and harbor so much hate for recycling bins. He did have a point about the stars," Amani said.

"Did he? Sure, the body is gone, but the light is still there, the energy, maybe. All the lights in the sky are just ghosts, tugging on us this way and that. If we have to be pulled by something dead, why not by starlight?"

Amani became very still and put her hands in her lap. She didn't laugh anymore.

"How is your dad, Ro?"

Rowina smiled and shook her head. Amani sighed.

"When?" Amani was almost angry in response.

"A year ago almost."

The waitress brought their meals in the silence. Plates slid against the wood, one after the other.

"Enjoy."

"Thank you," the pair said softly in unison.

"Has he come to see you?"

"Not yet. No. No, he hasn't."

"My dad never came to see me either. I used to feel angry about it, you know. Like, who did he choose, anyway? Some hooker I never met?"

"Maybe." Rowina smiled. "So you stopped being angry about it. We weren't chosen. We weren't enough to come back for."

"But that's just it, isn't it, Ro. We were enough. We lived with those men and never had anything left to say. It was complete, a day started, a day finished. Release between the dead and the living has to be mutual. Your father loved you, Ro, and never had anything else to say about it."

The QUEER
FICTION ISSUE

TRIAL OF GHOSTS
by VENITA BLACKBURN

ISSUE NO.
SIXTY-TWO

— — —

Rowina could taste the bitter aioli and feel the muscles in her neck and shoulders seize, the ache behind her eyes.

"We're almost out of time, Ro."

Amani smiled at her. This mention of time seemed the worst event of the day to Rowina. It struck her like a cramp. She had questions. *Why did you choose me and no one else? Can it be undone? Is death temporary?* But she knew all of the answers from seeing her own mother, before she left the second and final time. They don't come back again, and you don't get more time. Amani sat quietly, smiling, her skin flushed, every freckle vivid. Her lips separated, on the verge of speaking, then abandoned the impulse. Instead she stared at Rowina, waiting. The memory of Amani continued to pulse, warm and suffocating. The dead come back to listen, Rowina remembered hearing somewhere. You can say anything to a ghost. It's supposed to be liberating, enlightening, freeing, a final judgment for things unsaid, but to be alive just then seemed laborious and unbearable and like something else, victory or avarice. She didn't hate Amani or pity her or herself or even mourn her as she should have, but if there were words for kicking a woman while she was down, Rowina wanted to say them, to gloat for having hot blood and breath and the sun on her arms, for Amani being so reckless in love and so calculating in everything else. If that could have been reversed just once in her brief life, maybe everything would have been different. Maybe they would've loved unabashedly into old age, unrecognizable to the past, doing gentle yoga classes together every other day, making love with bodies that only the young find terrifying, walking through museums with docent fierceness, reveling in that marvelous surprise of finding another person standing beside you who is yours.

Rowina's dead mother had made herself a plate of eggs and sausage before taking a seat at the table, and Rowina had continued to scream relentlessly as the eggs were eaten, one forkful at a time, the coffee drained, and the meat consumed. When only hoarse rasps remained in Rowina's throat, her mother spoke.

"Is that all you have to say to me, then? Aren't you worried about becoming a woman?"

Rowina closed her mouth and thought of herself as a thing transforming, changing like some cartoon insect in a video during science class, except in the videos the narrator never asks the bug if it's worried. She and Amani had played at being mothers, imagined them religiously, all their mannerisms and funny words. The mothers they played were perfect because they were there inside of them to call forth whenever the moment demanded. Until then, Rowina hadn't been worried about becoming a whole woman on the outside—she was unable to retreat back into the body of a child—and her mother seemed satisfied with that. As if worrying were the real lesson, the only lesson worth knowing as a girl. Her mother got up and washed and dried her plate before returning it to the cabinet. She hung the towel on the stove handle after shaking it straight, then headed toward the back door, slipping on her sandals and leaving without turning around.

At the café, Rowina felt stupid, an ordinary kind of stupid, for having wasted so much time hating someone she loved because she had been afraid of losing that love to begin with.

"You are the worst of all, Mani," Rowina finally said. "Of all my dead. This is the worst."

Amani laughed and took Rowina's hand, nails making indents in her skin, pressing deeply, unyielding, wanting, as always, to get closer than had ever been possible.

The QUEER
FICTION ISSUE

McSWEENEY'S
QUARTERLY

ISSUE NO.
SIXTY-TWO

THE
WALL
by
HURMAT
KAZMI

The wall, the wall. They are breaking the wall, they are breaking the wall. For seven years they have been breaking the wall. Today, too, they have come to break the wall. Men—seventeen men: men in shalwar-kameez; men in dhotis; men with topis; men with bedis dangling from their pan-smeared mouths; men with gold chains around their necks; pious, god-fearing, mosque-going men; retired men; old men. Our neighbors, all of them; goons, all of them. They say: The wall must go. This thorn in the side of the street: it must go. The walls of everyone else's house on our street are within the legal boundaries, but this wall, it juts out into the street like teeth protruding from a mouth. Our neighbors want to give the street a facelift; they want to break the wall. It's illegal, they say; *encroachment* is the word they use. The first time I heard this word, many, many years ago, I did not know what it meant. It sounded wrong, reminded me of cockroaches. Now I know exactly what it means. The men have come again today. They come every six months with new excuses. *Break the wall: we have to make new roads. Break the wall: we have to install new water pipeline in the street. Break the wall because our stomachs are constipated. Break the wall because we are jealous motherfuckers.*

This house—this big, beautiful house on the corner of the street—is the most envied house on our block, in our entire neighborhood. Some people call it the London house. The wall hasn't always been there. When Abba bought this house, it was cement-gray, unpainted, save for its traffic-light-red gate and a dull red boundary. Within this boundary were plants and hedges and benches and a water fountain, but no wall. Many years later, when Abba got shot in the leg during a house robbery, Amma talked him into building it: *Things are not the same anymore. We are not safe. Besides, we bought the house as it is, with the red boundary. We have the right to build a wall on it.* The wall was erected within a day; this illegal wall, a hot blister waiting to be popped. Will they finally do it today? Today they are not alone. There is a bulldozer with them: a big, fat giant with a clawlike trunk. *K——— sahab, you are a respectable man. We don't want to break this wall like this. We gave you a notice a month ago, and three notices before that. We even told you that you can build a wall on the inside first and then break this wall. We don't want to break this wall in a disgraceful way, but you have left us no choice. We must break the wall.* The men are tired; the men are angry. We have tried their patience; we have exhausted their energies. For seven years they have petitioned us, pestered us, and pressured us. The men have had it. Today they threaten us. But they don't know that Amma is a bigger giant. She will chew up the bulldozer, crumple it into a ball in

– – –

her mouth, and spit it out in their faces. Abba nods and tells them he needs to consult his family. He buys time, as he has done for the past seven years. But the men say they will come back tonight; the leeway of days, weeks, and months can no longer be given to us. The bulldozer exits the street; Abba enters the house. The wall stands, beaming. A dagger dangling above our heads, waiting to claim our lives.

Outside the house, Abba is like a puppy, his tail tucked between his legs. He just nods and says, *Jee jee, accha accha*, in front of our neighbors. Inside the house, he is a lion. He roars: S*hut up, S———! Don't give me any more tension. My brain will explode. I can only do so much. I am alone. They are seventeen. The entire street is against us, all of them. We should thank them because they haven't taken legal action yet. Elections are coming up and they are using the local provincial assembly nominee from PTI to coerce us in exchange for votes. This wall is what bothers them, right? Let's break it once and for all. I am tired of all this.* Amma, a lioness both inside the house and outside, roars back: *I just want you to speak. Open your damn mouth. Go yell at those men like you yell at me! For god's sake, do something. Even you know it's not about the wall. These people are bullying us just because we are the only Shia in this area. They want to drive us out of here. The wall is an excuse. What will they get by breaking our wall? What is our wall saying to them? Do they want to build their mothers' graves here?* Abba puts down his last card: *What should I do, then? Tell me! Shoot them all and then shoot myself?* The fight over the wall is always the same. It's seventeen men versus Abba versus Amma. I am only a spectator. But what can I do? I am fourteen. In these seven years, I have never been a part of any deliberations regarding the wall. Until today. After today's fight, Amma pulls me into a corner and says: *They will come back tonight to talk to your father, to make a settlement. I want you to go out there with your father tonight. Those men think your*

The QUEER
FICTION ISSUE

THE WALL
by HURMAT KAZMI

ISSUE NO.
SIXTY-TWO

– – –

father is alone, that he has only a bickering wife by his side. But it is time to show them that there is a son in this house too. You are a big boy now. You should stand shoulder to shoulder with your father. We won't let those bastards break the wall.

At night the men come and they are not alone. The men have brought the boys. The boys are from our neighborhood. They are the neighborhood's last weapon. Amma is stirring a pot of green ice cream soda. She is reciting something—a spell, a prayer, I think, to soften their hearts toward us, to make them leave us alone, to make them let the wall stay—and gently blowing it on the drinks. *Take the drinks out and serve them. They should know we are kind and hospitable people. They have no reason to be harassing us.* From the window in the kitchen I peep out onto the lawn, where Abba and the men and the boys are sitting. When I look at the boys, in my mind's eye the wall crashes; it crumbles as if hit by a wrecking ball, raising clouds of dust. I recognize the boys; I know all of them. They are my friends, kind of, but my family doesn't know this. I meet them secretly when I go out to run small errands. The boys are all older than me so they say I must listen—or they could cut me up and throw me into a gutter, they sometimes joke. The boys talk all funny, but I do what they say. *Sit, kneel, bend; go slow, go fast, harder; stop, please, don't stop. Don't use teeth.* In the beginning it was just one boy, a chance encounter, when I was seven. Then that boy talked to other boys, and those boys to some other boys, and the word spread like fire through a forest, consuming everything in its way. Boys approached me in the streets; boys pressed rolled pieces of paper with their phone numbers into my hand. Boys invited me to their shops and quarters, asked me if they could come over when my parents weren't home. The boys have felt me up in public toilets and storerooms. They have done what they liked to my mouth and

The QUEER
FICTION ISSUE

McSWEENEY'S
QUARTERLY

ISSUE NO.
SIXTY-TWO

– – –

hands and legs; in a mosque, outside a mosque, in the barbershop, at the tandoor, in abandoned houses, in houses under construction, in houses rumored to be haunted, in a rickshaw, in a car, in dark alleys, at night in empty streets under fused streetlights, under neem trees with bats flapping their wings overhead, under the moon, whose light makes their cum shimmer on my skin, behind bushes where thorns scrape my knees. The boys have wiped their hands on my shirt, have run their fingers through my hair and spat on my face. They have opened me up and turned me inside out. And now they are here. And I have to serve them ice cream soda. *H———, hurry up, come on, serve the drinks to all the guests.* Amma nudges me, shoving her elbow into my ribs, pushing me toward the gate to the lawn. *No, please, no,* I want to say, but I don't. Can't. As I carry the drinks outside, the large silver tray trembles in my hands. My legs shake. The boys stare at me; they smile, teeth gleaming. They curl and twist their moustaches, scratch their beards. They exchange stealthy sideways glances with one another. *Here's my son, H———,* Abba says. *Oh, K——— sahab, we have heard all about your son. Such a sweet little boy. Very innocent!* A muted ripple of laughter surfaces, and then dies. Abba looks at me, confused. A slow, warm streak leaks down my legs, wetting my pants. I drop the tray; the glasses shatter. The shards glisten in an expanding pool of green liquid. The boys smile. They smile and look at the men, congratulating them. The men know. They have known it all along. That is why they have brought along the boys. Because they know; they know the boys will not only break the wall but will bring the entire house down.

The QUEER
FICTION ISSUE

McSWEENEY'S
QUARTERLY

ISSUE NO.
SIXTY-TWO

PAPI
by
JULI
DELGADO
LOPERA

Papi and Lucía love it when Natalia is not wearing her prosthesis. They both cheer and Lucía runs to the kitchen to get more salchichitas con ketchup in a bowl and makes it back before Natalia (a.k.a. Supermodelo Amputee) sits down for another interview. She's been on every single channel for a week now, and it seems el pueblo Colombiano cannot get enough of its Supermodelo Amputee. Y, obviamente, Papi y Lucía have been obsessed from day uno. He even bought a calendar from a kid at a stoplight, who told him Natalia is the new hembrita, patrón— llévela for half the retail price. Papi lights up when he sees her: it's the one thing that gets him in the mood. On the kitchen dry-erase board, they've charted each of Natalia's TV appearances, including her live appearances at Andino, her book release ya casito, and newspaper

The QUEER
FICTION ISSUE

PAPI
by JULI DELGADO LOPERA

ISSUE NO.
SIXTY-TWO

– – –

clippings behind Citibank magnets, even though he asked her to throw
out all the Citibank stuff, but Lucía in her corazoncito knows homeboy
doesn't mean it, that this is just a temporary tantrum like all the other
ones and so she hid it all inside her closet because one day Papi will
want it back. Lucía can feel Papi going through it. Mostly because Tía
Mamadora has been hanging around more often, bringing groceries
and ironing Papi's clothes. Tía Mama with her gorgeous, harsh voice
and faint stubble that she lets Lucía rub against her cheek cuando
la saluda. She uses a fuchsia filter when she smokes and ends all her
sentences with "me entiendes mendes?"

"Lucía, is he eating?" she asks. "Call me if he stops showering for
three days straight." Pero obvi Lucía never calls, because Papi doesn't
want to bother people, but Tía Mama always shows up out of the blue
with food from Kokoriko, a maid, and books about sadness that Papi
never, ever reads. Sometimes she brings plants "para alegrar este
entierro," she says.

The TV zooms in on Natalia's butterfly jet-black lashes. You can
now buy Natalia's Lashes and of course our girl has three pairs already
and Papi has two. The tattooed lizard on Natalia's back is famous,
and even though all the niñas at school wanted it, Lucía was la prim-
erita to get one after begging Papi for days. "Only guarichas get those
tattoos," he said. But then she reminded him this had been Natalia's
idea in the first place and he conceded.

Y es que Lucía sueña con ser Natalia.

Lucía wants to be like Natalia when she grows up, presentadora
de televisión y que me pinten la cara y que mis fans me manden cartas
y cuando salga a la calle me toque taparme la cara y hacer así con la
manito como que digo adiós todo el tiempo.

Our girl has superpoderes y porte de reina, like Tía Mama says. In
her room Papi and Lucía created a little TV set. Two butacas, a glittery microphone (courtesy of Tía La Perra—more on her soon), and

The QUEER
FICTION ISSUE

McSWEENEY'S
QUARTERLY

ISSUE NO.
SIXTY-TWO

– – –

a backdrop of Bogotá that La Mama printed at her job. Here's where she works that secret magic in front of the tiny secondhand camera she saved up to buy in San Andresito.

You're still rated top two on our website as one of Colombia's hottest hembrotas. Now, isn't that amazing? Aplausos, por favor.

Now Natalia laughs and Lucía and Papi eat salchichitas on Papi's bed. The camera zooms in on the scar that made her famous, that cut half of her cheek. The music changes to a sad little melody, and we see pictures of Natalia with her other leg, before the car accident, before the-boyfriend-who-loved-her-so-much cut her cheek. There was even a campaign against boyfriends-who-love-her-so-much-they-cut-her-cheek. Activists put Natalia's face on billboards across Bogotá, but then everyone agreed she looked better as a supermodelo than as a poster child against violence. It's true. Papi and Lucía agree.

I am not ashamed of who I am, she says. *And I always wanted to be a supermodel. This is no reason to stop!* She points at her missing leg.

"Divina," Papi says. "That's the spirit."

Lucía wants more of him but he just motions for her to pass him a napkin. Lucía always wants more of Papi, more touch, more tenderness, more orear that corazón that is surely covered with layers of grime from tanto secreto. Tanto secreto tiene Papi, stacked up inside. Ay, pero let's not get started on Papi's secrets, carajo. Lucía first.

Y ahora, ahorita mismo, this is their reality: now on this queen bed with the nasty fifteen-year-old siete tigres virgin wool blanket Papi refuses to clean or throw away because, as Papi will remind you, this blanket is all he has left of Mom. "Those people took the rest of her," he says, which is not true, but you can't really fight him 'cause he will yell until your eardrums hurt and then you will have to go, *Sh, sh, Papi, it's okay.* Even Tía Mama tried throwing away the maldita asquerosa blanket. Lucía and Tía Mama teamed up on an unusual day when Papi was out of the apartment, but he came back murmuring that he'd forgotten his Colsanitas carné and caught them infragantes, stuffing the nasty gray thing into a trash bag. (Lucía doesn't understand how he wraps himself like a mummy every day in that thing. It smells, as Tía Mama would say, like a tigrillo.) They weren't even going to throw it away, just send it to the dry cleaner, Lucía tried explaining to him, but Papi's eyes swirled, palm raised, y cuando se pone así she can't deal, so she locked herself in her room and let Tía Mama handle him. She overheard Tía Mama's disappointment. "Te me estás volviendo chocho y viejo. Cuidao."

The phone rings right before the TV shows Natalia's video of herself as a little kid in ponytails, with two legs, narrated by a sad voice and a musiquita that makes you go, *Ay, ay pobrecita* for Natalia. Y, como usual, they don't answer it. Y, como usual, Papi acts like nada. Lucía try to get up but he says, "Let the answering machine get it."

Hola, Ignacio. It's Clemencia again. Por favor, return my calls. This is urgente. Ignacio, por Dios, esto no tiene cara. You can't keep evading us anymore... There are lawyers, Ignacio...

The two emcees agree with Natalia. *She's a fighter*, they say. They applaud and remind viewers that the release of Natalia's book, *Luchadora*, is only a few weeks away.

Tía Clemencia continues her rant on the answering machine.

"Pa, contesto?" Lucía asks.

He doesn't say anything and entonces she knows that's a *Do not answer the phone or else.*

We really don't have to go down this route if you'd only answer the court's orders. Ignacio? Lucía, estás ahí? Lucía, pick up the phone... Ay, Ignacio. Again, this is Clemencia. Llámeme, por favor.

Ay, Papi on repeat inside her. *Ay, Papi* without looking at him. Y se levanta to use the bathroom, y Papi, no sé qué cree but he starts mumbling and then says, "Ojo, Lucía that I don't catch you calling or talking to Clemencia, no?" And our girl flips her hair like *whatever* like

The QUEER
FICTION ISSUE

McSWEENEY'S
QUARTERLY

ISSUE NO.
SIXTY-TWO

– – –

I don't hear you, Papi, but he knows she does. "Lucía," he says in that tone she doesn't like and she turns around, looks at him with her good eyes, and they both know Lucía won't call Tía Clemencia, because what would she say to her? Plus, Lucía loves her papi, everyone knows that.

A few days later they preorder three of Natalia's books online and change the number of days left to see her on the dry-erase board to fifteen. I mean, Lucía does. Papi knows about everything—actually, he has an obsession with Catholic figurines, sequin textiles, fútbol (Millonarios, ugh, even though he's from Ibagué), the Bee Gees, the never-ending-story-with-his-hair and old salsa because Mom was an obsessive Caleña with an extensive vinyl collection that now resides—guess where?—on top of the dining table. Pero, oye, talking about the salsa collection gives Lucía una cosita in the belly that she doesn't like. Every time she passes it, she has to breathe deeply, cross herself, and count to twenty despacito, like Tía Mama taught her.

Lucía orders Natalia's book because Papi es un inepto who doesn't know how to properly use a mouse (or, better, forgets how when convenient) or how to tie a bow or shoelaces, although el mancito is surprisingly extraordinary at sewing, which he says was the only thing his mama taught him well. But, generalmente, his fingers don't know what to do, aunque trata. Try getting him to wrap a Christmas present. He claims—and Lucía calls it bullshit—that he didn't develop fine-motor skills for certain things because he grew up on a farm in Ibagué full of cows, chickens, and his BFF, Torito the Bull, so everything was about kicking, milking cows, being a real pelo-en-pecho machito, and now he has trouble being delicate. Which drives him nuts.

"Papi, ven," she asks. "Braid my hair"

"Can't you braid it yourself?"

"Papá, braid my hair, coño."

The QUEER
FICTION ISSUE

PAPI
by JULI DELGADO LOPERA

ISSUE NO.
SIXTY-TWO

– – –

He concedes after giving the loudest sigh so Lucía understands his dread.

"A ver, Lucía, siéntate. Increíble that at this age you still don't know how to properly comb that hair."

It is Friday and sunny. Although, from inside their home, you wouldn't have a clue that sunlight exists. The apartment es todo darks with thick, velvet, dusty curtains hanging in the living room that Tía Mama calls "the forever funerary of a tacky traqueto. You sure love yourself some ñero style, Papito." And how Lucía loves when Tía Mama calls him "Papito" while ashing her cigarette así, puff! Tía Mama is right. If you want some sunlight, enter Lucía's room, pero otherwise it's like it's always six in the afternoon in this casa, no matter the time. Does she care? Bueno, sometimes. And during those "sometimes" she imagines herself like Natalia and says in front of the mirror, "Ni por el chiras can you get me to live in this pocilga, corazón. Buy me a mansion en Cartagena" [ashes her cigarette].

In the mirror they always look like his Catholic figurines. The light in the bathroom is dim, with accumulated dust glowing behind Papi's head, reflecting in a semi-halo. Papi—the saint who never was. Lucía, sitting on a stool, feeling his clumsy, chunky, perfectly manicured fingers diving into her curls. Like he's fishing for something en la mata de untamed hair she inherited from him. He hasn't done this in months. The last time he combed her hair, he pulled so hard that a chunk came out and they ended up in a horrible fight that was really Papi in a long monologue of "hijueputa vida contigo, hijueputa vida la que me gané," and when Lucía whispered that he was a "campeche malnacido"—a poor little peasant—he raised his palm to hit her but then said, "Te voy a regalar, Lucía. A ver cómo te va. Let's see how much money I can get for you."

The QUEER
FICTION ISSUE

McSWEENEY'S
QUARTERLY

ISSUE NO.
SIXTY-TWO

– – –

She chuckles every time he says that.

Of course, she doesn't need him to comb her hair. A ver, te explico, she's twelve. What Lucía really wants to know is who is in charge of deleting Tía Clemencia's message from the answering machine and what's going to happen when she keeps calling or sends her maid to knock on their door like that one time. Pero Lucía doesn't say *ni pío* because you can tell Papi's thinking about it, lost in thought.

Papi will surely pull her hair again, she knows that. She knows it's gonna hurt but she's finally gotten him uncoiled from the blanket, out of the room. He even put on "More Than a Woman" and is mumbling, whistling, humming close to her so that she hears—better, she feels— Papi's vibrating chest. She wants to lock this tiny moment of the halo, of his tender hands on her hair; she wants to lock it in a little glass y save it para later. Pa' cuando Papi forgets she can show him.

"Do you ever even comb this thing?" he complains.

"It's your fault! This is exactly your hair."

He chuckles. "Respect me, culicagada."

With his precious silver comb, Papi parts her hair into four sections with the kind of concentration reserved for organizing his figurines. Hair-clips each separate section. Y lo ve que trata, he tries not to pull but inevitably the curls tangle, he yanks. It doesn't hurt pero Lucía yells all the same.

"Perdón, perdón," he whispers tenderly.

"Pa, do you think we'll get to actually see Natalia?"

Long pause. Stares at her from the mirror behind the black-rimmed oval glasses he doesn't wear in public, holding the silver comb like he's directing an orchestra. Deep in thought. Papi sometimes acts like everything is the biggest consequential thing in the world and it bores Lucía. Like, *Come on, Papi, don't take everything tan a pecho.*

"Natalia, nena—Natalia is a symbolic criatura that has been misunderstood in this país de mierda of ours. In this country you're

The QUEER
FICTION ISSUE

PAPI
by JULI DELGADO LOPERA

ISSUE NO.
SIXTY-TWO

– – –

exploited and when they have no use for you anymore pa' la calle to eat shit! Si? Me entiendes? Por eso estamos como estamos. You cannot even make a mistake. Perfection all the time, for what?"

"Papi," Lucía responds, "me perdí. You're still talking about Natalia?"

"Natalia was gonna be kicked out of her modeling career because they got no use for her without a leg. Pero, what did she do? Ah?"

"You're asking me?"

"Si."

"She wrote a book?"

"Well, yes, but what else?"

"She's still modeling?"

"Exacto, nena. She's still modeling. You know what Natalia is? A berraca."

The phone rings. When the machine picks up, it's Tía Clemencia again: *Ignacio, you will be receiving a letter...* And then Papi lifts the receiver up and slams it back down. Before he can come back to her hair, the phone rings again and Papi is just not having it. Papi yells at no one. He picks the phone up and slams it back down. Papi is like a pendulum. And you never really know which side the pendulum is swinging toward. Lucía sits still by the stool, knowing what's coming, which makes Papi's eyes swirl and he gets all big and in your face. But you can't say nothing to him or else. The phone rings again and this time he picks up the phone and throws it against the wall. It takes him a while but eventually he comes back and tells her, "I never liked that phone in the first place. Mañana, we buy a new one."

In the streets you can buy all of Natalia. Wigs of her ashy highlighted hair, eyelashes, jeans with rhinestones, pink lipstick, and a little doll that says, in a paisa accent, "Hola, supermodelo. Todo está cool," and

"Llévame de compras." Lucía kinda wanted the doll for collection purposes, pero Papi didn't understand why, at twelve years old now, all of a sudden "you want dolls, nena." "I'm collecting things!" le dice toda bothered because, *Hello, Papi, have you seen your collection-of-everything-in-the-maldito-world in the house?*

You know you've made it in Bogotá when kids sell your pirated wigs on the street for half the price. Tía Mama thinks Natalia is a bunch of bullshit like everything else in this goddamn country, where everyone only cares about supermodels and fútbol players while the putos paracos politicians are stealing all our money and people are starving. "Pero," Tía Mama continues, "if there needs to be a pretty face for all to adore"—she looks at Lucía, all smiles—"well, it should be me." Our girl agrees.

Papi did buy her the doll, after grunting, murmuring, cursing to himself, and telling the kid at the light, "Can you believe it, chino? She's twelve, with a doll," and after the kid—who is more of a jóven, pero Papi calls everybody a kid—responded, "Patrón, dolls have no age" and winked at Lucía," and after Papi told the kid, "Tranquilo, hermano. She's my kid," the kid said, "Todo bien, patrón," but Lucía caught him staring at her ass, which of course she loved because have you seen her butt? She's been working on it. She knows soon she'll be a señorita like Natalia.

Y también le encanta when Papi tells the boys she's his kid, because Papi has muscles that he shows with tight polo shirts, telling you, "Touch it, touch it. Look how strong your papi is." He has muscles and he wants you to punch him in the stomach así, like *pao*! So you can see how duro, duro like a rock his stomach is and how Papi could kick your sorry ass if he wanted to. After you punch him, he does a little silly dance that she loves, a little salsa while he whistles, "Mala mujer no tiene corazón. Mala mujer no tiene corazón." I mean, he used to do that all the time but not anymore. Which Lucía doesn't like to

The QUEER
FICTION ISSUE

PAPI
by JULI DELGADO LOPERA

ISSUE NO.
SIXTY-TWO

– – –

talk about, pero sabes? Three santísimas hours he would spend at the gym, then he would eat an entire broiled chicken with plantains and rice, todito by himself. Sucking on even the tiny chicken bones for any leftover meat, which gets on Lucía's nerves. (Her mom hated it too. She used to say, "Ignacio, por favor, and Papi would know to stop.) He would eat the chicken in one sitting, leaving the plate stacked with bones. His own little massacre. He wouldn't even share that chicken. Pero not now. Tía Mama and the family have been trying so, so hard to get him to care again and show his muscles and when they do that Lucía just runs into her room. Homegirl tells herself, Papi is not sad. Like Tía Mama said, "He's just getting adjusted." Like when her mom died and he disappeared for months. "Adjusted," Tía Mama and La Perra explained. "Déjalo, mami. It takes time."

After buying the doll, they go to the social security office to handle Papi's money-that-will-never-materialize. (See here: Papi at a ventanilla with the Brown Folder, gesturing angrily with his hands at the señorita, anxiously combing his hair, ending every sentence with a "cómo es posible.") Y cómo es posible is true. Because then there's returning all the stuff he buys off infomercials. It was Saturday, errands day. O sea, La Muerte con ele mayúscula. This meant sitting on uncomfortable magenta chairs for hours and watching Papi make conversation with every possible soul around him while Lucía scribbled notes in her shiny notebook about the next TV episode she would record later, in her room. The next one she titled "Todo Lo Que Sube Explota." More on it later.

They all know him. Everywhere they go, he knows someone. Papi is a social ho. Lucía calls him a "puta social" and he chuckles. "Me?" he says, gesturing to himself with both hands, pretending that he can't believe it. *Don Ignacio! Ignacito! Quibo Hermano! Pero look who came out of the bat cave!* Or, *Qué dice el mono!* Even though Papi's hair is dark, dark y tan, curly qué ni te imaginas. Lucía hates running errands,

The QUEER
FICTION ISSUE

McSWEENEY'S
QUARTERLY

ISSUE NO.
SIXTY-TWO

− − −

and sometimes when a friend invites her over, she can get away, not to stand on the never-ending lines at the banks to pay the water bill, the phone bill, at the supermarket to return the expired chicken, at the ferretería with that gasoline smell and the men with dark tips for fingers that always say, "La niña Lucía, how grown!" Like, duh, of course she grows. She's a teenager now and can buy cigarettes and go out into the streets alone. Sometimes.

The car is full of stuff they have to return. Papi held on to a wad of receipts with scribbles in the margins, explanations for why he's returning items he never should have bought in the first place. He buys all sorts of stuff from the TV. Especially now, with no job, wrapped in that nasty blanket all day, watching infomercials on which blond señoritas, with deep cleavage and faces that don't change, sell in a Spanish voice-over all sorts of pendejadas. Lucía knows it's a voice-over because their mouths look strange when they speak and one day La Perra told her, "That's because those are gringas. They speak Inglés." And how do they get their stuff all the way from gringolandia to Papi? A ella ni le preguntes. But the tiny appliances that fry things and manicure your nails at the same time never work. They burn Papi's fingers. Y entonces, there they are, Papi and Lucía, like a month ago, or maybe two months or maybe three weeks, but there they are in Papi's old Volkswagen that doesn't read CDs, making the rounds. Sitting in the hijuemadre malparido gonorrea bumper-to-bumper Bogotá traffic that rips your intestines in pedacitos (La Perra's words) for hours while Lucía complains and Papi listens to the news.

Caracol Radio... Three policemen were found dead after an altercation in a nearby motel en el north of Bogotá. Yasmira Guzmán has the news... Yasmira Guzmán here, reporting for Caracol Radio from Rocamar, where a woman was shot dead...

Lucía turns it off.

"Don't you turn off my news, Lucía, carajo," says Papi.

— — —

"Pa, it's so boring me quiero morir. *I* can tell you the news."

"Ay, por Dios, right now? With this traffic? I like that program. Yasmira is a good journalist. Did you know—"

"Pero I'm better."

And without asking for more permission, *Damas y caballeros, niños y niñas, jóvenes y jovencitas, acá Lucía Gonzalez Gonzalez, your favorite host, your dearest presentadora from el Altiplano Cundiboyacense, a.k.a. Santafecito, lindo y hermoso to your ears. From mi boca to your house. From this infernal tráfico via the Séptima Avenue, where a dude with no arms and a handwritten sign is pushed in a wheelchair while everybody rolls up their windows—and their eyes! And please do not clean my windows with that nasty water, hágame el favor. Carajo. Carajito. We are launching into the gray air like a comet while the entire pueblo Bogotano salutes me, waves at me. "Lucía!" they say. "Our queen! You narrate the news like nadie before! We need you, mami! Send us a kiss, por favor! We're dying for a kiss! Gritan y gritan," and I say hi with my manito. And look, what's that? A crowd holding pancartas with cutouts of my face on Natalia's body chanting my favorite Rocío Dúrcal songs and nobody says anything about my mom or my dad or my weird legs. Y aquí estamos, ladies y gentlemen. Here we go with the papi chulo pilot by my side, merenguiando that wheel, chucu-chucu to the sky. A round of applause for our very happy driver today que la mete toda and off we go above the red lights, burlando the busetas, honking at the malparidos taxis allá abajo, exploding through the fire bursting out of a kid's mouth. Like, bam! To the mountains, montañero! Oh, what's that you're saying? You love my outfit? The jeans descaderados with rhinestones and this new eyeliner (gracias, Perra!), and Papi doesn't like that I say "Perra" but that's her name and she is a bitch, a proud one, and you will meet her later. Pero right now, right now the sky is promising an afternoon of soroche followed by an aguacero so intense water will get into your feet and your butt and places you didn't even know could get water. Y yo acá with my shiny, dangling earrings and the long, luscious hair inherited by the one and only Natalia, who donated it to me because she just loves me. Look at this gorgeous, nasty city! The smog, the brick buildings, the señora selling you mazorca a mil. La Doña, who just today sold her ten-millionth mazorca! Feeding the Colombian people one corn at a time. Over here, a few stray dogs eating away at what looks like? "Another dead dog," responds our driver. Increíble, isn't it? So much food to go around. What does it feel like to eat your own? And do the dogs know? Would you, mi corazón, ever consider eating your own? Would you kill your own? We will get back to you with answers tomorrow during another round by your all-time favorite host, Lucía Gonzalez Gonzalez. Y, corte!*

Lucía es una soñadora de las tezas tezas. You don't know dream girl, you don't know TV host, until you've met Lucía. In his own way, Papi has always encouraged our girl. The story goes something like this: When our carajita was seven years old, she demanded a microphone and to be a lead part of Misi, which she begged and begged for, pero with the casita in so-so Suba, nobody could afford those theater classes. So the dusty living room turned into a stage. And Papi would sew some of her dresses with the purple sequins and the mermaid finishing that she'd cut from *Jetset* magazine. "This one"—with tiny, chubby fingers, she'd point to Paola Turbay's. "Make me look like Paola, Papi." Picture it: For four months, two braided ponytails singing a todo dar with that vozarrón in her room. Practicing for her mom. Nobody really enjoyed her singing, but you couldn't stop her. She practiced "Amor Eterno" over and over, her favorite Rocío Dúrcal song. (Papi still doesn't understand Lucía's insane pasión efervescente for romántica songs. Where did she get that from?) And you ask, "What's the big deal? Did she appear on and win some stupid TV kid show where she became Colombia's top muchachita singer and enthralled el pueblo Colombiano? Is that the story?" Wrong question, mi rey. Our girl had passion. She had tumbao. She had tres

– – –

dedos the frente and a volador por el culo that, out of all the chécheres in the attic, created a stage in the living room. Seven years old, wanting to serenade her mother. It was Alma's birthday. "Feliz cumpleanos, Mami," she'd written in cursive. For months she practiced, to the complaints and grunts of the neighbors, who called the house and demanded that somebody do something about that kid! Pero óyeme, Lucía wouldn't shut up. Papi had her rehearsing during specific hours *or else nos botan del building!* When Mom's birthday finally arrived, Lucía's belly was aswirl with nausea y una happiness que se la comía. Her big moment.

Papi was out with Alma for a birthday dinner while an older prima helped Lucía tie balloons together with thread, taping them to the entryway arch of the apartment. Now she waited. Staring at the window in full mermaid sequins, looking out into the Bogotá traffic, waiting for their car to arrive. Cual Penelope en miniatura. It was 7 p.m., 8 p.m., 9 p.m., y nada. On the stereo, "Maldita Primavera" by Yuri played, and the older prima called it that ñera shit and Lucía loved it, didn't care that nobody liked it, turned it up:

> *Fue más o menos así:*
> *vino blanco, noche, viejas canciones,*
> *y se reía de mi,*
> *dulce embustera,*
> *la maldita primavera.*

Y la niña wouldn't move. "Que no," she said when the older prima tried moving her from the window. "I *practiced.*" Oh, pero el sight: a sad, glittery cake topper staring out at the night. The older prima trying to calm things down, trying to get Lucía out of her dress pero, niña, she'd put all of that tiny corazoncito into this performance. Where was Papi with Mom?

The QUEER
FICTION ISSUE

McSWEENEY'S
QUARTERLY

ISSUE NO.
SIXTY-TWO

– – –

La maldita primavera,
pasa ligera,
me hace daño solo a mi.

Y ahí llegan. Finally. She sees the car stop at the garage, go in. "Ready!" Lucía tells the older prima to be ready with her finger on PLAY when they open the door. This is the last birthday Lucía will spend with Alma, but she doesn't know this yet. She's hidden behind the dusty velvet curtains with her hands floating just so in front of her—*like Rocío*. She anticipates her mom's smile, the clapping, the kisses she'll get. How happy Alma will be once she sees her. When they open the door, "Amor Eterno" plays, Lucía steps out from the curtains, but before she can start the first verse, before Rocío's voice can blend with hers, Papi turns the light on and tells her to go to her room. "Ya mismo, Lucía." Confused, lost, angry. "Pero *why*!" Anchored on that carpet, she catches a glimpse of her mom's puffy eyes, sobbing without breathing, how she's holding her head, negating, the way she did when she just could *not* believe it. When her heart burst with pain. All of a sudden the air reeks of alcohol and cigarettes and that repulsive energy that clings to the furniture whenever her parents fight. "Lucía," Papi repeats, "to your room ahora mismo." Lucía doesn't move. "But I practiced...," she manages to blurt. "*Now*." Papi lifts his hand. She stares at her mom's tears, how they send a horrible electric rush through her. "Ignacio," Alma finally steps in; the red of her eyes is everywhere now, "let the child stay. Tell her, a ver, show her who you really are."

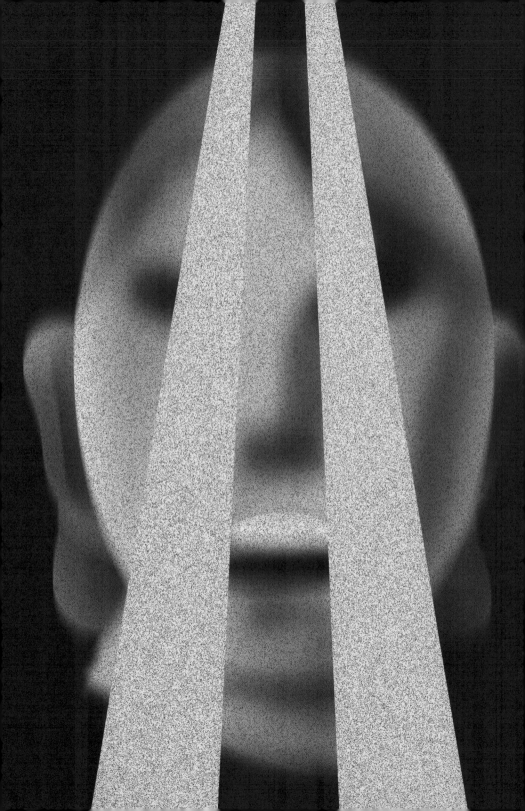

The QUEER
FICTION ISSUE

McSWEENEY'S
QUARTERLY

ISSUE NO.
SIXTY-TWO

BULLDOGS
by
KRISTEN N.
ARNETT

Spots swim in Whitney's eyes, but she can't tell if they're from the glare of oncoming headlights or if they're a side effect of the massive quantities of caffeine she's ingested over the last couple hours. Late-night driving makes her feel like things are creeping alongside the car window. It gets her worked up, so she tries out some relaxation techniques. Deep, even breaths. Singing along to the radio even if she doesn't know all the words. If she squints, the beams from approaching vehicles twinkle like Christmas lights.

Pretty, she thinks, before squinting again. Twinkle, twinkle, little star. White lights approaching.

Two cars ahead, a banged-up Ford Taurus speeds up and slows on her left, weaving across the lane. These taillights don't twinkle;

– – –

they spark a red warning in her brain. Someone's encroaching on her personal space. She breathes in through her teeth, breathes out the same way with a lingering hiss.

Exit's up ahead. Another stop means it'll take longer to get home, but she doesn't want to consider passing that weaving car. Drunk driver, sleepy driver. Probably a grandpa with a revoked license. Next exit with big lights, she thinks. Big MOBIL sign. One that sticks up far enough that I can see it from miles down the road. Twenty-four-hour McDonald's. Beautiful golden arches.

She fidgets in her seat to untwist the crunch of her spine and cranks the air conditioning until her teeth chatter and her skin gets clammy. Her hair, washed that morning in a hotel shower with yellowy, cheap shampoo, keeps whispering down her neck from where it's pulled free of her ponytail. Makes her think of bugs every time it twitches on her collarbone, as if a roach had gotten into the car. More than once she's scraped at her neck, only to realize she's trying to kill her own hair.

The Taurus weaves and slows, speeds up, slows. She pulls into the right lane. The traffic's slower there, but the aggravation she feels from tailgating a U-Haul is better than dying in a car wreck because someone was too tired to drive. Ahead, the horizon is streaked with city lights. Just a few more miles. At the thought, her bladder perks like someone's dumped a handful of pennies into it.

It's just her midsize rental sedan and the U-Haul and the Taurus on the road, bunched together, though one of them should speed up and put distance between all of them. The Taurus looks gray in the dank beams from her headlights. It has to be a man driving, she thinks. Only a man would drive like that and assume he wouldn't get pulled over. The Taurus weaves again, all the way across the middle lane, almost slamming into the side of the U-Haul.

Whitney stamps on her brakes, and her car skids wiggly until she's positive she'll jump the guardrail and slide down the embankment,

The QUEER
FICTION ISSUE

McSWEENEY'S
QUARTERLY

ISSUE NO.
SIXTY-TWO

– – –

into the trees and whatever lies beyond that. Nobody uses their horn, though it seems like an appropriate time. "What the fuck," she says. "What the fucking fuck! Shithead driver."

They're all piloting along at the same speed, rocketing down the highway at around sixty-five miles per hour as if nothing happened. Whitney decides she doesn't care what exit is coming up next; she's going to pull off and get herself a coffee. Her heart beats wildly in her throat and she can feel it pounding its way up to her temples. Sometimes Whitney gets so angry that her teeth jam together until she worries they might break to pieces in her jaw. Her anger is a thing that wants to smother her, it's so consuming.

She keeps up a litany of swears as she drives. The swearing helps. It means she won't do anything else, like pull up beside the Taurus and scream through the window, or drive so close to the back of it that she nudges the trunk with her bumper.

Up ahead, the exit ramp displays signs for a couple different chain restaurants, a motel, and two gas stations. All she's eaten on the trip has been plastic-wrapped convenience store fare. Normally she wouldn't mind, but with no sleep and nothing but coffee and the remnants of convenience store fare churning in her gut, her rage has percolated into something hot and unmanageable. She can barely see. There's only the pounding in her head, the hot pulsing in her ears.

The Taurus and the U-Haul speed past as she rounds the exit, down past the tall yellow overhead lights that outline all the potholes in the turn lane. Though she knows it's not worth it, she lays hard on the horn the entire way down the curve. "Fuck you, fuck you, fuck you," she chants, horn blaring over everything.

To the right there's a dark Burger King and a Shoney's across the street with an empty parking lot, also dark, alongside a four-pump gas station. To the left, she sees other restaurants—a McDonald's, maybe a Hardee's, as well as the green-and-white sign of a BP plaza. The lights

– – –

look more promising there, she thinks, but maybe that's because she can't clearly see what she's looking at. She puts on her blinker and waits for the light to turn, even though there's nobody coming and it doesn't look like there will be for a while.

"I should call my wife," she says as it finally flips from red to green. She turns left into the intersection. It's a thing she's told herself a lot this trip, *Call my wife*, like a reminder to herself she's set in her appointment book, but she hasn't kept up with it very well.

Sara will wake up by the second ring. Phone to her ear by the third. Her voice will be sweet and soft, because no matter what's going on, Whitney's wife is always in a good mood. *I'm just happy to talk to you*, she'll say. *Just so happy to hear your voice.* Whitney's never woken up like that. Never answered a phone dragged out of sleep, ready to smile into the receiver.

Down the block, the McDonald's is closed and so is the Hardee's, both lots as abandoned as the ones in the opposite direction. But for three in the morning, the BP is jumping. There's a white Buick LeSabre and an older-model blue minivan parked in front of a couple pumps. The lights glow halogen white beneath the wide awning, illuminating the barren stretch of dirt and brush that lines the roadway. It's an eight-pump station, a large one for such a small exit. Whitney can see an ad for wings in the window, ten for five dollars. They look surprisingly good, she thinks. Meaty and coated in a slick layer of hot sauce.

Her gas tank is three-quarters full, but since she's stopped she decides to top it off. An older man on the other side of the pump is filling up the Buick while he leans against the trunk. He's watching her get out of the car in a way that makes her want to climb back in again. Whitney's underwear is riding up from sitting so long, and her shirt has drifted above her belly button. Fishy skin shows in rolls above the lip of her pants.

— — —

"Your front tire looks flat," he says. He's pointing the windshield cleaner in the general direction of her car. Soapy gray water leaks from the end and drips down onto his sneakers. He's probably in his late fifties, peppery hair thinning at the crown. A white collared shirt is buttoned nearly all the way up to his throat and tucked into high-waisted jeans hitched in place with a braided leather belt.

Whitney hates unsolicited advice, especially when it's given by men who look like they're doing their best impression of her father. Sara does this sometimes, too, trying to be helpful but really she doesn't know what the hell she's talking about. Whitney nods in his direction, slamming the car door before remembering she left her wallet on the passenger seat. Carefully unwedging her pants from her crotch, she opens the door back up and gets her card without making any further eye contact. It's when you make eye contact that they keep talking, Whitney thinks. Everyone always thinks they know what's best for everyone else.

"They don't have any creamer." A woman in pink pleated shorts stands halfway between the Buick and the doorway to the BP. The shorts are long, almost brushing the woman's knees, and she's got on kitten-heeled sandals. "They got milk, like little bottles."

"Don't buy a thing of milk just for coffee. I won't drink the rest."

"Well, do you want cream or not. It's small. We can finish it."

Bright red lips and dark eyeliner smeared on so thick it's like Magic Marker. It's the kind of face paint that will smudge against the passenger seat as she falls asleep. Whitney gets aggravated just thinking about trying to clean the beige rub of foundation from uphol-stery. She lets the gas pump itself and turns to stare at the stretch of empty road that leads back to the highway. She's still far enough away from Florida that the outside smells weird to her every time she inhales. In the early morning hours in Georgia, it's bitter cinnamon, like sniffing off-brand cookies.

– – –

Less than seven bucks and the gauge clicks off. She completes the transaction and declines a receipt, then she closes everything: the little spin of the gas cap, the car door, and locks it all with a press of the fob. It beeps loud enough that she feels like she's trying to steal a car instead of lock one. As she crosses the lot toward the entrance, she realizes there aren't any insect sounds. Just faraway traffic, her own sneakers scuffing at occasional gravel, and the man still topping off his own car. He was filling it up when she got there and she thinks he'll probably still be doing it when she leaves.

It's not as nice inside as she'd hoped. She figured with all the pumps out front it would be one of the big places with multiple microwaves and whole pizzas, but instead it's got a Dollar General vibe and the linoleum is sticky. There's no air conditioning. The front door is propped open with a gray metal garbage can that's overflowing with paper towels and plastic bags of trash, spilling out like stuffing from a sofa. The guy behind the register doesn't even look up when Whitney walks in. He's tapping at a cheap cell phone, a pay-as-you-go kind with a shiny exterior designed to look like something more expensive.

There are other people too. A younger woman in front of a fireworks display in the middle of the store, bending over far enough that Whitney can tell what kind of underwear she's got on beneath her jeans. A man standing next to her, feeling along beneath a worn black baseball cap like he's trying to locate the rest of his hair. Then there's the older woman in the pink shorts who's messing around with the coffee maker. Her face is shiny-slick with oil and her mouth's screwed up in a knot.

Whitney really needs to pee. The feeling is like fingers jabbing into her bladder. She quick-walks the perimeter of the store until she finds two bathrooms shoved into a dank back hallway, stepping around a rolling mop bucket that holds no water. The mop itself is standing upright and the strands hang down crunchy like fried hair. She has to bang into the door to the women's room with her hip to get it to open, it's so warped from water damage.

Once inside, she almost can't get it closed again. This makes her bladder really start shouting, so she leaves it and yanks down her jeans and underwear. While she pees with her hand holding the door closed, she watches herself in the cloudy mirror directly over the sink. Her skin has that pale, sick hue she always gets when she's traveling. There's a red zit breaking out on her cheek, right below her eye, and it makes the rest of her skin look sallow. She's always got that line between her eyebrows, the thing her wife calls the permafrown, but tonight it's a canyon. If her wife were there, she'd smooth a soft finger down the groove. Try and calm Whitney down. But there's no wife, no tenderness. No gentling. Just Whitney riling herself up.

Finishing up, she declines to wash her hands and instead just scrubs them briskly against her jeans. "Who gives a shit," she says to her reflection. As she talks, the line in her forehead grooves deeper. "Who gives a fucking shit," she says again, louder, and the line draws down so hard it's like someone carved it with a knife.

When she gets out, the woman in the pink shorts is still at the coffee maker. She's fixing up two massive red-and-black tumblers that don't look like they're from the store. On the counter beside the coffee maker, which is sputtering weakly, there are pumps of flavored syrup with sugary gunk crusted around their tips. The woman smashes her hand against the hazelnut container and squirts endless pumps of it into one of the mammoth tumblers.

"Marlene, bring this to your father," she says, holding it up after the fiftieth squirt. The younger woman pokes her head up from behind the oversize fireworks display. The man in the cap is gone, possibly back to the car or into the other bathroom.

"You think Randy would like these?" the younger woman asks, holding up a plastic package of Black Cats. "Need to get birthday stuff."

– – –

"He'll blow his damn hand off."

"Yeah." The woman sets the package down and immediately picks it back up again. Her hair is frosted blond and pulled back in a pink scrunchie that matches the color of the older lady's shorts. She looks like one of Whitney's shitty ex-girlfriends, the one who bartended just so she could have a job where she drank all night.

"I'm gonna get it," the younger woman says. "I don't have nothing for him and it's tomorrow."

"Do what you want. It's not my husband."

Whitney watches the older woman pour out an endless stream of coffee into the second tumbler. Whitney isn't sure what it would cost to fill them all the way up. The woman has a smell to her like cooking grease, like something left in oil too long that's started to go south. Even thinking about fried food makes her stomach hurt.

What kind of person takes that much coffee when there's only *one pot*, Whitney wonders, making a show out of yanking a paper cup from the dispenser, leaning around the woman's body to get to one of the sleeves and a lid.

In order to calm down, she looks around the store to see if there's anything she wants to eat. It's a trick she's learned over the years: distracting herself when rage starts bubbling in her chest. There's no sign of the hot wings advertised in the front window, so that's a bust. There are helium balloons shaped like baby animals dragging against the ceiling in the far corner by the ice chest. Yellow duckling, gray kitten, black-and-white calf bump gently against one another in the small breeze from the open door. Spider web filaments connect them like cottony bedding. The cardboard fireworks display where the younger woman stands has a cartoon image of a wide-eyed panther superimposed on a patriotic starburst. It's faded along the top half where the sun comes shooting in the store window, like a black suit whose jacket gets worn more frequently.

"Give this to your father," the older woman repeats, holding out the tumbler. She dangles the bottle of milk between the first two fingers of her other hand and some sloshes onto the dirty yellow linoleum between their feet. Whitney steps back to avoid the spatter and looks up at the ceiling tiles, counting them in pairs. She gets to eight across before she realizes that the ones in the corner are dotted with dark brown mold. There's no way she wants to eat any of the food now, not after seeing that.

"Come on," Whitney hisses between her teeth. "Come on, come on."

Her rage gains speed like a freight train. Normally she'd eat something to combat it. That always seems to help, just like it helped her father. He was the kind of guy who got worked up over everything and nothing. He called himself "passionate" and said it like the word wasn't covering up an anger-management problem. "I'm passionate," he told her mother after he threw a full can of beer at the screen door when the dryer broke. Passionate meant yelling over basketball games on TV loud enough that the neighbors left well-meaning notes on their cars. It meant always driving with his hands white-knuckled on the steering wheel, ready to take out anybody who even looked at him wrong.

Her mother combated these passions with meatloaf drenched in ketchup. Big, cheesy casseroles full of starchy potatoes. Ham. Turkey. Rolls soupy with brown gravy, shoved onto an already-overflowing plate. Her father's rage would've kept him whipcord thin but for the butter and carbohydrates her mother kept handy. He slept through the anger, a hibernating bear.

The woman in front of her at the coffeemaker turns and yells, "Marlene, take this to your father! It's gonna get cold."

Whitney clenches the cup until it's smashed into the shape of her palm. The woman in pink shorts tops off her second tumbler and hands the other to her daughter, who takes it and immediately goes back to

– – –

ogling the fireworks display. She leaves the counter littered with drippy swizzle sticks and half-empty sugar packets, coffee drips splashed down in circles from the rounded bottom of her tumbler. Scooting awkwardly around Whitney, she heads to the register and asks for a pack of cigarettes and a lighter. The cashier keeps looking at his cell phone, but turns to get the cigarettes while the woman digs around in her massive black leather purse, trying to unearth her wallet.

Unclenching her hand, Whitney drops the crushed remains of the cup onto the counter and grabs a fresh one, along with a new cardboard sleeve. She opens two Splenda packets to dump inside the new cup and picks up the carafe, which feels lighter than it should. When tipped, all that splashes out is a half inch of pale liquid swirled full of grounds.

"Are you fucking kidding me?" Whitney asks. She whips around and wields the carafe overhead like a torch, shaking it. "Are you fucking serious right now. Really."

The woman's found her wallet and hands a wad of cash to the attendant. He doesn't look over and neither does she, but Whitney doesn't care. "I know you can hear me. Did you really need to take all of it? Like two fucking gallons of coffee so no one else could have any?"

Whitney isn't big, but she is stocky and there's a muscular set to her shoulders and torso that are reminiscent of a bulldog's. When she gets mad, people back up. Across the aisle, the daughter puts the fireworks down and moves quickly toward the open door. Her mother retrieves her change from the cashier and stuffs it hurriedly into her wallet, not even bothering to zip it closed before shoving it into her bag.

"That's a nasty way to talk," the woman says, hurrying out after her daughter. She doesn't make eye contact, but they never do. Not when Whitney gets riled up. "You are a nasty person."

"Fuck you! Fuck you and your giant tumblers of coffee! Hope you get a bladder infection from drinking so much, you dumb bitch."

But the woman and her daughter are already halfway across parking

The QUEER
FICTION ISSUE

McSWEENEY'S
QUARTERLY

ISSUE NO.
SIXTY-TWO

– – –

lot. Whitney sees the older woman in the pink shorts motioning toward
her, talking to her husband, and he turns around to look at her too.
This makes her want to scream. Whitney puts the carafe down and
throws both middle fingers in the air, waving them dramatically. That
gets them moving. They get into their car quick and drive away. Now
there's no one left at the gas station but her and the cashier, who hasn't
made a peep since Whitney got there. It's pissing her off, too, but now
anything would piss her off.

"There's no more coffee," Whitney says. He's back on his phone,
propped on his stool and looking bored. She brings the carafe up to
the front with her and slams it down directly in front of him. Flecks of
brown liquid pepper the register. "You're all out."

He gets up and stuffs the phone into the back pocket of his jeans.
The guy is tall, well over six feet, and he's muscular. Whitney guesses
he can't be older than twenty-two. He's got on a green-and-white polo
shirt stretched out at the neck, with a red stain over the breast that
might be ketchup or marinara sauce. His name tag reads BRYAN.
Reading his name makes her want to yell it like a swear.

Following him to the back, she stands behind him while he preps
the coffee with the speed of a tortoise under duress. "How long is this
gonna take," she asks. "It's fucking late."

He doesn't answer her, just leans over the machine to fiddle with
one of the giant fluffy filters. He's got acne on his neck and where his
dark hair curls against his skin. Fuckin' roided-out Bryan, she thinks.
Bryan with his dirty clothes who can't even fix a pot of coffee. She's so
angry it feels like her skin is on fire. It's bubbling up like paint in the
heat. She decides to go outside and cool off for a minute.

"I'm gonna go make a phone call and I'd like some coffee when I get
back, if that's not too much trouble," Whitney says, tongue twisting
into knots behind her teeth. She can hear her voice, the grating, stri-
dent tone behind it, and it makes her want to hit something.

– – –

Bryan goes back up front to his stool and sits down, slow and uncaring.

She walks through the open door and takes deep breaths of cool night air. It's very close and humid, though not as bad as at home. Every breath she takes calms her incrementally. She decides to call her wife, just because it's been two days and she knows Sara is worried. She's always worried, it feels like to Whitney, who's never worried about anything but always angry about everything. Sara loves her. Too much, Whitney thinks. Loves her more than she deserves.

It rings a few times in her ear as she stares across the gas station lot at the empty Hardee's. There's a lot of trash floating around loose in the breeze. Paper fast-food bags. Empty cola cups. The kind of garbage that could be beautiful if it were full of food.

"Good morning," Sara says. Her throat's full of mucus and Whitney wants to clear it for her.

"It's not so good."

"Where are you?" Her wife yawns into the phone and Whitney holds it away from her ear, with her teeth gritting at the annoyance. "Close to home?"

"Like five hours, maybe half an hour longer than that."

"I miss you," Sara says, and sighs. "Miss you. The dogs miss you."

"I miss not dealing with idiots," Whitney replies, and then bites her tongue to shut up, just shut up for once and not be the asshole. It's always her being the asshole. Always, always.

"What've you had today," her wife asks, like she always does. "Have you had dinner?"

"It's three in the morning. We're well past fucking dinner."

Silence on the end of the line as Sara decides how best to broach the topic. It makes Whitney feel bad, in a kind of way. Not like she used to, when they first started dating. Then, she'd been embarrassed

The QUEER
FICTION ISSUE

McSWEENEY'S
QUARTERLY

ISSUE NO.
SIXTY-TWO

– – –

and remorseful. Wanted to stop behaving like her father, who couldn't deal with the stress of the air conditioning going out, much less road travel for work. But now after her blowups at her wife, she just works to forget it. Doesn't want to remember how bad she acts. Pretends it never happened.

"Where are you? Is there something you can grab?"

Her wife's voice is like a balm to her. Like something you put on a bad sunburn that immediately soothes you, even though you're the moron who left yourself out in the heat to begin with. Whitney wonders what her voice is like to Sara. Probably like the thing that grates away at your skin until you're nothing but a bunch of fleshy, overstressed nerve endings.

"I'm at a gas station," she says, just because she can't be the horrible one any longer, and her wife sighs again into the phone and she wishes she weren't the kind of person who hates that sound.

Will I always be like this; will I always be this bad, terrible kind of person, she wonders, but then her wife is suggesting things to eat and she's yawning because it's three in the morning, so Whitney gets her off the phone and goes back inside for the coffee she's been waiting on since dumb Pink Shorts snatched all of it.

Bryan's still behind the counter with his phone smashed to his face, so she goes to the back and pours a cup of coffee. It's fine, just garbage convenience store shit, but she knows if she drinks it without food it's going to fuck up her stomach royally. She trails the aisles, looking for something to pair with it that isn't going to make her gag. There are chips and plastic-wrapped sweets, chocolatey things defiling the insides of their wrappers with grease and condensation. She chooses a pecan roll, which looks mildly bready, and then she goes up front to pay.

Bryan still doesn't look at her, even when she smacks the coffee down in front of him. She'd thought she was too exhausted to continue

– – –

feeling outraged, but it boils up instantly like a kettle waiting to spill over onto a burner.

"Could I pay for these," she asks. "Would that be too much trouble? I mean, I know it's your fucking job, but I don't want to inconvenience you."

Instead of responding, Bryan puts out his hand. It hovers in the air over her purchases, and suddenly slams down on top of the pecan roll. His palm makes a booming crack against the counter and Whitney feels her spine straighten in response. He leans forward, fingers digging into the package until she can feel his hot breath ghosting over her cheeks and her forehead.

Whitney swallows. "I'm ready to leave."

"Yeah, you're fucking ready," he replies, and keeps smashing his hand until the thing beneath it is no longer a food item. It's a mess of chemicals. It's a flattened hunk of garbage. Whitney holds out her credit card and he takes his time swiping it.

She doesn't say anything else and neither does he, because though she knows she's a bulldog a lot of the time, sometimes she forgets that other people are too. He hands back the credit card and she puts it in her purse. Then she takes the plastic bag he gives her. He's put the mashed pecan roll inside it, like it's something she'd still eat.

"Safe travels," he says, and she just nods and leaves. Nods and leaves. She doesn't even remember getting back into her car. But then she's pulling out of the gas station and she's piloted back up the exit ramp, heading south again, heading home.

"Here's the thing," her father said after one of his bouts. Her mother hovering in the background with a coffee cake, a sandwich, some chips. "Here's the thing. There's always somebody who's gonna be angrier than you."

The night is muggy and thick with stars. Up ahead, there aren't any cars. No moonlight, barely anything illuminating the way. She thinks about the Taurus, gently weaving from the passing lane to the middle, and wonders if she'll pass it on her way home. Thinks about her wife, safe and in bed. Sleepy sweet. She looks down at the odometer and sets the cruise control to a comfortable seventy miles an hour so she won't get pulled over. Her heartbeat slows, slows, evens out to a normal rhythm. She sips her coffee. She stays in her lane and turns on the radio.

The QUEER
FICTION ISSUE

QUESTIONABLE CONTENT
by LEE LAI

ISSUE NO.
SIXTY-TWO

— — —

The QUEER
FICTION ISSUE

McSWEENEY'S
QUARTERLY

ISSUE NO.
SIXTY-TWO

— — —

The QUEER
FICTION ISSUE

QUESTIONABLE CONTENT
by LEE LAI

ISSUE NO.
SIXTY-TWO

– – –

The QUEER
FICTION ISSUE

McSWEENEY'S
QUARTERLY

ISSUE NO.
SIXTY-TWO

– – –

The QUEER
FICTION ISSUE

QUESTIONABLE CONTENT
by LEE LAI

ISSUE NO.
SIXTY-TWO

– – –

The QUEER
FICTION ISSUE

McSWEENEY'S
QUARTERLY

ISSUE NO.
SIXTY-TWO

— — —

The QUEER
FICTION ISSUE

McSWEENEY'S
QUARTERLY

ISSUE NO.
SIXTY-TWO

THE CRUEL AND ASTONISHING TALE OF IMOGEN CABRAL DA GAMA
by
GABRIELLE BELLOT

"Captive people have a need for song."
—MICHELLE CLIFF

The night the gales of his misfortune blew, Derek was winding all the clocks of the house he lived in with his grandmother and dusting the noses of the cracked busts of Nero and Henry the Navigator in the living room. He was clad in the blue furisode kimono his grandmother made him wear on Tuesdays—or, at least, whenever she thought a Tuesday might be—so she could imagine him as a girl. The hot winds that had turned the world around them into a sad desert were howling like dogs against the windows of their vast wood-and-stone house, a lonely structure that seemed lost in the dust and the wilted trees that looked like castaway coral, and Derek had had to close all the windows to keep the terrible noise from filling the house.

The QUEER
FICTION ISSUE

THE CRUEL AND ASTONISHING TALE
by GABRIELLE BELLOT

ISSUE NO.
SIXTY-TWO

– – –

As he set the final clock, the one that cock-a-doodle-dooed like the withered roosters in their yard, he thought he caught the scent of guavas, but the smell faded as he heard the thud of a leviathan's footsteps on the spiral staircase behind him.

"Don't forget to water the graves," his grandmother called from the stairs.

"Yes, Granny," he replied, turning to her. She stood on the stairs with one hand on the ivory banister and the other on the fat abbess's crozier, which she used to get around. In the yellow of the kerosene lamps and the little flames of the silver candelabra by the stairs, her skin glowed like that of a great white whale.

"And don't forget to dust the silverware, and to heat up the water for my bath."

"Yes, Granny. I won't."

"And if the da Gamas ring the bell, don't keep them waiting, and have the tea ready to serve."

Derek did not answer this last request, but turned back to his work with a faint smile. It had been so many years since he had heard the doorbell ring that he could barely remember what it sounded like. Moreover, the thirteen da Gamas whose whereabouts were known, excepting Derek's mother, were buried in the yard beneath the clumps of purple bougainvillea that Derek trimmed every few months; the many other members of that sprawling family had either died in other parts of the Caribbean or had simply disappeared. The da Gamas had come originally as indentured laborers from Portugal, then had swiftly risen to wealth as landowners, drug smugglers, and robber politicians—that is, as whites well known on the island.

Derek's mother, Isabella, had produced him in an affair with a Black man, whom Derek himself had never seen, but who, he was told by his grandmother, had gotten himself killed in a drunken knife fight

The QUEER
FICTION ISSUE

McSWEENEY'S
QUARTERLY

ISSUE NO.
SIXTY-TWO

— — —

in a bar one Tuesday night. The fight, allegedly, was over one of the many other women with whom he had fathered children. Isabella, the story went, had run away the next morning and leaped out of shock and shame off the cliff of L'Abyme to her death beneath the waves of the Atlantic. With all of Derek's other family lost or dead, his grandmother, who had married the late Pedro Cabral da Gama, had taken Derek at the age of five to the da Gama family manor, sequestered herself within the walls of that mad tower of culture, and had remained there ever since, enjoying her framed prints of artwork by William-Adolphe Bouguereau and John Melhuish Strudwick, her daguerreotype of Queen Victoria, and her phonograph recording of Ravel's *Pavane pour une infante défunte*, which she thought was by Mozart.

Despite the fact that he kept the decadent house from slipping into a shipwrecked disaster, and despite how clearly the red teeth of the seasons were bared against them—for ages now, the secluded bit of the island of St. Francis that they lived on had seemed to be stuck in an interminable dry season—his grandmother was convinced that everything that went wrong in the house could be blamed on Derek's irremediable deficiencies, not the least of which was the darkness of his skin and the tight curls of his black hair. "I blame your father, not you," she had said to him many times, "but the curse is there all the same."

"But you don't have white skin," Derek had once made the mistake of pointing out. His grandmother, indeed, had faintly curly dark hair, and her skin was naturally a lighter brown than his, like milky coffee, though the whitening soaps she used each week had given it the tint of curdled milk.

She'd slapped him so hard for this comment that he had levitated for a moment, his body stretched like a Chagall figure, and then she'd pulled him back to the ground. "Your eyes are bad," she said, "which is also your father's fault."

– – –

For the most part, Derek knew only what his grandmother told him. He doubted her sometimes—he thought his skin was a pretty shade of brown, actually, and moreover he didn't even like the name Derek, which sounded so, well, masculine, compared to something like, say, Imogen—oh, how nice a feminine name would be. But each time he doubted her, he told himself he must be wrong, since he didn't *really* know anything about anything. With the exception of the two women from the capital whom she had briefly hired to teach him geometry, the piano, and French, she had been Derek's home instructor for over a decade. She had taught him all he knew of the world in general, from the way he spoke—he was not to use "de broken English of dem other people in de island, not *a'tall* at all," but rather to have his words gush forth from the clear chalice of what his grandmother called "the Queen's English," to the way he dressed—be it as a boy or a girl—to how far he dared to go if he stepped outside. He knew of the world beyond the mansion and the dusty waste surrounding it peripherally at best.

"You must never leave your granny," she had told him often. "If you do, God will *strike* you down like a bolt of lightning."

When she spoke about God, her eyes would glow and flicker like flames, and her already imposing bulk seemed somehow to take on even grander proportions, though Derek had never once seen her pray or even say grace before the meals he prepared for her. "You must think of yourself always as a spider held over a flame," she would continue. "If you stray too far, he will drop you straight in." She would grin after repeating this image. "And those with such dark skin, of course, have already been lowered nearer to the flame, so that he may test them more strongly. So you must always remain here, where I can tell you what's right."

If it occurred to her to deliver this sermon while she was in the living room, she would take down the cat-o'-nine-tails she kept hanging on the wall and snap it in the air as she spoke—"Damn it, child. Are you listening to me"—and if indeed she caught him not paying attention she would snap the whip at his feet or arms or even toward his eyes— "When I say to pay attention you must pay attention you see your father also had bad ears bad everything and see where it got him no I will not have my child brought up like that scoundrel"—and if she beat him badly enough that he bore the marks of her fury, she would later caress the bruises and rub alcohol and creams upon them, stroking his scalp and long, curly tresses and whispering, "I am sorry I hit you, but you must understand, yes, you understand, that's my lovely little da Gama," or "that's my lovely little girl," or "my dear Izzie," the latter two when he was wearing the fluttering kimono. If Derek was in pain, being called something like Izzie—short for the name of Derek's mother, whom his grandmother thought Derek resembled—helped a little, allowing Derek to imagine being called a girl's name in the long term.

Though he sometimes went for short walks in the dust after completing his tasks outside the house, he never went beyond sight of the mansion. "Go too far," she had said, "and you will see where civilization ends."

If he did stray far on a secret walk, he began to feel a prickly sense of dread. When he turned around, he was met with the vast, unseeing eyes of the tower's porthole windows. At times, it almost seemed like the house might just stand up on legs, like the homes of Baba Yaga or Howl, and follow him, and Derek was afraid. And so he lived most of his days in and around the great house.

As they had no helpers, Derek did everything around the mansion. Many years ago, the grandmother had tried hiring a pretty girl from Martinique, Yvette, to help with the chores, but the grandmother was so obsessed with the notion that the girl was trying to steal things from the house that she abused the Martinican at every turn, making her turn out her pockets before she left and excoriating her for not

– – –

adding spices to soups that she had never told the girl to add. The girl said little in the grandmother's presence, but when she was alone with Derek, she would tell him stories about Martinique while she played with his hair. Derek loved those moments. They made him feel warm, made him smile. He thought Yvette was beautiful. At times when he sat next to her, their shoulders touching, he almost felt as if he were in love with her, unsure if he wanted to kiss her or *be* her. Whatever it was, he felt at ease around her. One day, though, Yvette simply stopped showing up. "You see," the grandmother said on the third day Yvette failed to appear. "Proof that damn bitch was stealing from us." Derek had been surprised to hear this—he couldn't imagine Yvette doing anything like that—but he also believed in the inerrancy of his grandmother's teachings, and so he convinced himself that she knew something he didn't. Still, he cried in his room when it became clear Yvette was never coming back.

From then, it was all on Derek. He would bathe his grandmother each night in her Pantagruel's tub, scrubbing her cetacean enormity with a thick sponge and going over her body with her whitening soaps. Afterward, he would help her into her room, seat her in front of her grand cracked mirror, make up her face like a doll's, slip her artificial bejeweled rings onto each of her fingers, place around her great neck the pearl necklace that shone white but for a single black Tahitian pearl toward the clasp, comb straight her Pre-Raphaelite curtain of curls, help her into her faded wedding dress, place her favorite furry, wide-brimmed hat on her head, push her scarlet papal chair onto the veranda, and let her drift away on the gondolas of her dreams and muddled memories as she gazed out at the expanse of dust and dead grasses, lost under the eternal moonlight of a spotted mind. Some nights, when she began to wail into the wind or cried, with her eyeliner dripping down her face and her merlot-red lipstick speckling her teeth, she would call him into her bed to sleep beside her—"and you better damn well come, too, or I will whip you like a slave"—and he would lie there with her vast arm draped over his side, his face turned as far as he could from hers to avoid the rotten-shellfish scent of her breath. As she drifted off to sleep, she would begin reciting instructions for the house or quoting doggerel verses about unrequited love or weeping about how hideous she had become, her hands flailing and landing with the thud of tyrannosaur footsteps. And if she was not doing those things, she was snoring like the horn of an ocean liner, mouth opening as wide as Totoro's. On those nights he had many times thought of pushing her off the bed, and if she crashed to the ground she would in all likelihood never be able to get back up. But he never did, and he knew he felt better in her bed than in his own by himself, safer among the sounds than among the silence when the winds stopped.

Many nights, he would peer into the dark and wonder about who he was. Like the world outside did, the world inside the da Gama teen felt mysterious. When Derek imagined Derek, the person Derek saw was a girl. A person who looked like Derek but who was, unquestionably, a "she." Then she, Derek-by-another-name, would feel a sense of disconnect between mind and body, a sense that something was not quite right. Even in Derek's earliest memories, it was the same—a girl in the mirror of her mind—yet the grandmother had always called Derek "he," "him," "boy," and for most of her life, Derek believed these thoughts were just mistakes, maybe fragments of old dreams, maybe something of the curse passed along from the terrible bloodline of Derek's father, whom the grandmother so often chastised. But the girl never left that mental mirror. Derek imagined herself going off on adventures as a woman, doing all her chores for her grandmother as a woman, even something as simple as going to sleep as a woman and waking up with everyone knowing she was one, as well, her girlhood as bright and constant as the path of a lighthouse beam.

– – –

Sometimes Derek hid in her room, locking its door and listening until her grandmother was asleep, then slowly putting on the clothing the grandmother had saved from Derek's mother: musty dresses, tights, the furisode kimono with its swinging sleeves that nearly touched the floor and that Isabella had, according to the grandmother, brought back with her from a trip to Japan and which Isabella had always considered her most beautiful possession. Derek would sit there for hours, feeling the clothes, imagining going out like that, imagining holding a boy's hand—and, sometimes, another girl's. She imagined being some fierce, fearless superheroine, saving villagers from hell-fiery monsters. In some visions, she was alone; in others, she fought alongside some other girl or boy, who accepted her as another girl, and when they had saved the day, Derek could clasp their hands in hers, looking into their eyes, and even kissing them. In real life, she had never been kissed, but she imagined it often, loving it most when it was with someone who treated her as if she were female. She imagined how wonderful it would be to do something mundane, like walking down the road of the nearest village as herself, or buying something in a shop and being called "miss." As she thought these things, she would walk back and forth in front of the mirror, looking at her body from different angles and smiling. She would stuff bundled socks where she thought her breasts should be.

Then she would remember her grandmother, and Derek would scramble to remove the clothes. She would feel shame, afterward, at what she had done, shame at herself for having these desires, shame for having even touched or smelled the clothes. The one time she had asked her grandmother what these feelings, this mind-body problem, might mean, her grandmother had stared at Derek with wide eyes and then slapped her.

"You are a man," she said in a low voice. "God, have I raised you to be a damn fool? Is an idiot taking care of me? Don't come to me with

The QUEER
FICTION ISSUE

McSWEENEY'S
QUARTERLY

ISSUE NO.
SIXTY-TWO

– – –

this nonsense again, eh. *I* am a woman, not you. What—you think you can have a child like me? Come now. Set the table for me."

And so, after crying again in her room, she would decide that she must be wrong and that her grandmother must be right, and Derek would return to being Derek, even as the girl that Derek saw in her—sigh, his; it had to be his—imagination did not stop appearing, even as he tried to forget her. Derek's grandmother knew so much more than he did, and who was he to question her? So he tried to bury the girl in that mirror of the mind, pushing her deep into the glass until it began to crack, until it hurt. He even prayed to God to make the inner girl vanish, since it had to be some sadistic temptation from the devil. In the back of his mind, though, he still imagined himself holding a boy's hand as a girl, holding a girl's hand as a girl, and having the grandmother declare, out of the blue, that Derek *was*, in fact, a girl, and she was so sorry for ever having said otherwise.

Few things are simpler and less simple, lovelier and uglier, than being yourself in a world that does not want you to be that.

So Derek returned to the routine of setting tables, attending to his grandmother, and trying as hard as he could to be a man, telling his grandmother he would grow to be as fearsome and strong as Grandpa Pedro. But he secretly loved the days his grandmother called him Izzie, since the grandmother's mix of missing her daughter and unadulterated madness gave Derek a brief chance to freely try to raise her voice and wear her hair down and be all she wished, before she would have to disappear again, for a bit.

And so things went without variation each day, until the night of the disaster.

Derek paused as he passed by the front door. There was another gust of wind, and the smell of guavas invaded the house again. Derek frowned, though it was the most beautiful thing he had smelled in ages. There were no guava trees for miles. He opened the door

– – –

a crack. The dry roar of the wind filled the house, along with the overpowering aroma of the guavas, and for the first time he thought he heard something on the wind: a soft voice, a song as sad as the saudades of a Portuguese woman singing fado. He squinted and looked into the moonlit night. There seemed to be nothing around but the cracked yellow dirt, the trees so withered from the heat that they looked like the bones of a washed-up coral reef, the distant spires of Lovecraftian mountains, the cold strew of stars above, the fierce winds swirling around the house like the whirlwinds around Francesca and Paolo in hell.

He opened the door more, and suddenly the wind stopped altogether. He hung the heavy kerosene lamp on a nail by the door. It was a bit small for the weight of the lamp, but he figured he would be back soon. He took a smaller lamp—a beer bottle filled with kerosene and with a cloth for a wick—lit it, and stepped outside after the scent.

"I will be back soon," he said aloud; he had acquired the habit of speaking to himself when he was not with his grandmother. He felt possessed as he followed the smell's trail past the graves of the da Gamas and the ancient dog kennels and the giant gilded circus cage on wheels. He drifted in a haze for a few minutes to a dusty hill littered with boulders and the skeletons of mongooses. The scent filled the air. He glanced back at the house—he hadn't closed the front door properly, he realized. But they were alone, after all, and the wind had died down for the moment, he thought. And something about being out in the kimono and a touch of lipstick seemed wonderful. Derek had never gone that far dressed explicitly as a girl; it felt so freeing, so lovely. He—no, she—took a deep breath, let the old fears of walking too far fade. She continued to follow the scent.

A part of her wanted someone from the village across the scrubland to see her and think she was a girl in an ornate blue gown. There

The QUEER
FICTION ISSUE

McSWEENEY'S
QUARTERLY

ISSUE NO.
SIXTY-TWO

– – –

were never strangers in the scrubland, but how beautiful would it be, she thought, to find one tonight and hear them—perhaps the singer herself—call her "miss" or "ma'am." She pushed forward, far past where her grandmother permitted her to go.

As Derek descended the hill, the wind suddenly picked up again and snapped like some baleful finger straight through the front door of the house, knocking the kerosene lamp to the floor, its crash muffled under the wheezy cackle of the gale.

Derek knew none of this. It was only when she started back up the hill, after having found nothing, guava ghosts still drifting through the halls of her heart, that she smelled the smoke. She blinked. Derek suddenly realized she could hear a distant crackle. She ran up the hill, churning up dust. The smell of smoke had so thoroughly mixed with the smell of the guavas that, for a few moments, she could not tell one from the other.

Derek saw the flames before she saw the house. She froze. They were vast and terrible, yellow as the skin of some ripe fruit.

A rusting teal pickup truck stopped in the grass by a little line of woebegone buildings. There was a crumbling white-walled bread shop called Manicou's Bread, a brown rum shop, and a deserted gas station. Evening had slipped on her starry earrings, and a faint smell of smoke hung in the air.

A tall man got out of the car, and the girl in the passenger seat nudged open her door, swinging her legs over the side and throwing a piece of yellow skin from the guava she was eating into the grass.

"Don't go anywhere," the man said to her in Continental Portuguese; he had never become accustomed to the você form in Brazil. "Stay on guard."

– – –

Beija-flor, who was the man's daughter, chuckled. "Pra você tambem," she answered, picking out another guava from the brown paper bag by her side. She had gotten the bag of guavas shortly after they arrived in St. Francis earlier that afternoon, and there were only a few left.

Her father looked at her, swore under his breath, and then headed for the village.

They were in St. Francis because her grandmother, who had lived on the island, had recently passed away, and her father had begrudgingly decided to come and pay their respects. "I hated her," he had told Beija-flor when he informed her of their abrupt voyage to a new world, "but I'll end up in hell with her if I don't show up to my mother's funeral."

Neither Beija-flor nor her father had been to the island before—she had never, in fact, left Brazil—and she'd felt a mixture of excitement and trepidation as they crossed the sea, wondering if the waters would still be full of the German submarines from the war a few years earlier. She felt even more anxious but intrigued as they landed in the harbor, the island's towering, verdant mountains reminding her curiously of where she had come from. She sang under her breath when she was nervous, and she'd found herself crooning into the air as their rented truck rattled up the rough roads.

They were supposed to stay only a few days, but what her father didn't know was that she was planning never to return to Brazil. The exact details of this escape were fuzzy—all she knew was that she didn't want to go back to São Paulo. She wanted a new world, a new life, a new everything.

She took another bite of fruit. After a moment, she felt a soft wind tugging at her curls and skirt, and she began to sing, louder this time, into the wind, the breeze blowing her words through the grass, down the village's potholed road, past the men slapping dominoes with a *pax*

The QUEER
FICTION ISSUE

McSWEENEY'S
QUARTERLY

ISSUE NO.
SIXTY-TWO

– – –

onto a table outside the rum shop, over the forested mountain peaks that were burning into embers in the sunset, down toward a house lost in the scrubland she did not yet know existed.

"How'd it go?" she asked her father when he returned. He was holding a bag, in which she could see cans of evaporated milk and tins of sardines.

"Well," he said, "there was some old man ranting in the shop about tonight being an omen, or some nonsense."

"Ooh," she said with the twinkle of an imp in her eyes. "I quite enjoy a good omen."

Her father started to say something, then shook his head. "Let's just get to the inn. I need to lie down. My back feels like a bad omen itself."

She realized he was exhausted and shifted gears. "Sure, Papa. I can rub your back a little, if you like, when we get there."

"That's okay, querida." He managed a smile. "I'm glad you're here with me. I don't know what I'd do if you weren't."

She smiled back, feeling a twinge of guilt. Then they were off, driving under the evening's blanket, which had dimmed to the color of soot.

The house of the da Gamas looked like a great burning shipwreck in a desert, the dried trees alternately lit and shaded by a violent yellow-black chiaroscuro. Derek was rooted to the ground, staring, mouth hanging open. The kerosene lamp flashed through her mind. The mansion's windows had shattered, flames grasping and surging through the holes. Her bedroom was flickering orange-black, the line of flames creeping like some vast creature along the roof's gutters. Pieces of the grandmother's balcony blackened, crumbled, and fell to the sand. Smoke fumed from the windows and from the abandoned mastiff kennels along the right side of the mansion.

The QUEER
FICTION ISSUE

THE CRUEL AND ASTONISHING TALE
by GABRIELLE BELLOT

ISSUE NO.
SIXTY-TWO

− − −

"No," Derek murmured.

She ran toward the house, calling for her grandmother. Her legs felt heavy, like she was running through sludge. Was this me? Did I....

The grandmother was standing outside, hands clasped over her cane. When Derek saw her, the inner girl seemed to drop away like a dream; shame took the girl's place again. Derek wiped his forehead with his kimono sleeve. "Granny," he said.

She turned to him. He froze. Her eyes so fully reflected the yellow flames and her hands were so calmly wrapped around the top of her cane that she seemed for a moment to be some brooding judge of the underworld.

"It's the end of this world for you," she said slowly. Her voice was low, yet he could hear every word over the crackle of the flames. "You cannot even begin to imagine how much this will cost you to pay me back." A small smile crept over her face, lit by the fire, and a pattern of veins in her forehead, long and branched like some vine had taken root beneath her skin, slowly began to lengthen and swell. "Yes, my dear girl," she said, grinning now and chuckling at the ground. "Yes. You cannot imagine."

"It was an accident," he whispered. "I didn't— I don't—"

But the grandmother was still speaking to the ground. "Unforgivable. Unpardonable. Pedro. Pedro."

"Granny."

There was a *spark-pop*, and then a burning clump flew out of the conflagration, stopping just short of the kimono's sleeves. Derek fell back and pulled the kimono tighter around him. Not this too, Derek thought. I won't let this burn too.

The grandmother began to wail, and, after a moment of hesitation, Derek moved to hold her hand. They stood, staring at the grand blaze, Derek feeling helpless and awkward and wondering how, in a moment,

The QUEER
FICTION ISSUE

McSWEENEY'S
QUARTERLY

ISSUE NO.
SIXTY-TWO

– – –

the world he had known had gone up in such vast flames, and why, why he had allowed himself to defy his grandmother's orders and search for the source of that inexplicable scent and song.

"It was an accident," Derek said again slowly.

She turned to him. "You damned little fool," she said. "There are no accidents in this world."

The QUEER
FICTION ISSUE

McSWEENEY'S
QUARTERLY

ISSUE NO.
SIXTY-TWO

SHORT
STACK
by
PAUL
DALLA
ROSA

Sam was sitting in his living room, wearing his beige Pancake Saloon uniform, staring at the wall. He was waiting for the time he could leave his apartment, go down the elevator four floors, cross six lanes of traffic, and walk through the Saloon's employee entrance when his phone rang. Sam didn't recognize the number but understood that someone, somewhere, wanted to speak with him. This was unusual and exciting.

"Hi there. Is that Sam? I'm Rosa." Rosa explained that she was calling from a collection agency without using the words *collection agency*. Rosa asked Sam if he remembered a specific date. He didn't. Rosa said, "This is about your CT scan."

On that day, Sam had had an accident. He'd been at his place of

– – –

employment. He was taking out the trash, but sometimes the bin wasn't big enough for all the trash, so Sam had to climb into the bin and jump up and down to be able to fit in the new trash. Sam was jumping up and down but then he slipped and his vision went dark, shapes formed and unformed in front of him, and when he climbed out of the bin and came back into the kitchen, an hour had passed and someone said, "Hey, Sam, you're bleeding."

Rosa explained that the insurance claim he'd filled out at the hospital was incorrect. The insurer had denied payment, so he could either send in his correct insurance details or he could pay the fee for the CT scan. The fee for the CT scan was large and frightening and obscene.

Sam said, "I must have filled out the form wrong."

And Rosa said, "That's what I thought. That's what I told everyone: he must have filled out the form wrong."

Sam said he'd gone to the hospital because he'd hit his head, so his head must have been a little funny, and Rosa said, in a soft voice, almost a whisper, "Oh no," and then, louder, "Great, well, we'll need you to fill in a new form and we can clear this up." And Sam said, "Great," then quickly, "clear this up," then got off the phone, like in a movie, without saying goodbye.

Later, washing dishes at the Pancake Saloon, Sam remembered that he did not have the insurance form. Then he remembered that even if he had the insurance form, he wouldn't know where to send it. This was okay, Sam thought—ideal, really, because Sam did not have insurance.

Sam was nineteen and still had baby fat and maybe some real fat and couldn't enter bars without pulling out his wallet and repeating his birth date and star sign. The Pancake Saloon was a suburban restaurant in a franchise chain that sold pancakes drenched in concentrated high-fructose corn syrup, twenty-four hours a day, seven days a week. The restaurant had a western theme, saloon-style doors, tables with chipped laminate designed to look like dark, polished wood, and fixtures imitating nineteenth-century gas lamps that saturated the dining floor in dim, syrupy light. It was staffed exclusively by under-twenty-five-year-olds, its kitchen manned by Nepali migrants on temporary work visas.

Sam worked nights, eleven-hour shifts in the kitchen and not the restaurant. He didn't cook or make coffee or speak Nepali but washed dishes and, at times, was good at it: stacking glasses in the commercial-grade machine, blasting syrup off plates with a high-pressure nozzle, scrubbing the rubber mats that lined the floor. He was early to work, kept his uniform ironed, and was overly enthusiastic in a way most people mistook as a sign of mild developmental problems.

At times, Sam fucked up. Sam fucked up, especially on weekends, in the early hours of the morning, 1 a.m., 3 a.m., when the night bus ferrying drunk people from clubs and bars in the city back to their suburban homes would unload, its stop directly in front of the Pancake Saloon. All of a sudden, the restaurant would be full, and the customers, often people Sam had gone to school with but who were now in college, were loud and aggressive. They'd empty packets of sugar and cartons of creamer onto tables, vomit in toilet stalls, even perform partially clothed sex acts in open booths. The ambient pressure, almost barometric, moved into the kitchen, and Sam would begin to work in a kind of slow motion. Sam put clean dishes in the dishwasher and moved behind people without saying "behind," causing people to trip, vats of thick pancake batter to spill, and the cooks to loudly repeat the Nepali word for "idiot."

But then, after four, there would be calm, and by five, when the night manager left to do the night's cash drop, the floor staff would sit on milk crates behind the restaurant, next to the skip, and smoke

– – –

weed, and though no one offered Sam weed, Sam would sit with them or stand in their vicinity. Servers would say things like "I think the Pancake Saloon should blow up," or, "There should be a flood and the flood should wash away the Pancake Saloon." And as people got higher, they would become more inventive. "There should be a flood and the flood washes away the Pancake Saloon but there's a gas explosion and as the Pancake Saloon washes away it's also on fire." And Sam would say, "The Pancake Saloon sucks." Not because he thought it sucked but because he wanted to contribute. He liked the Pancake Saloon. He liked it a lot.

If someone asked Sam when he was happiest—no one did, but he held the answer close to him in case the question ever came up in some online survey or chain Facebook post or interview for an unspecified higher position—he would say he was happiest eating a stack of pancakes drenched in high-fructose corn syrup. He was happiest eating them at the Pancake Saloon with his friends who were not his friends but his coworkers.

Sam came home from work, entering his small economy apartment close to dawn. He showered, then moved around the living room in the near dark.

Sam's apartment was on the fourth floor of a poorly constructed apartment tower that sat at the intersection of two main roads, one with six lanes, the other eight. The former connected the suburbs to the city, and the latter was a freeway linking the greater metropolitan northeast to the greater metropolitan east. His apartment consisted of a small bedroom, an en suite bathroom, and a living room. From his living room, Sam could look out across the lanes of traffic and see the Westfield mall and, farther down, the Pancake Saloon, its neon sign forty feet high, a stack of pancakes blinking on and off in the night.

– – –

Sam played PlayStation and felt slightly sad. Before the shift change, as people sat on crates outside, Sam had asked if people wanted to chill at his house. Sam had asked Simon, and Sam had asked Becca, and Sam had asked Ryan if they wanted to come back to his place, and no one said yes but instead, "Maybe next time," though he had been told "Maybe next time" many times before.

Playing PlayStation, Sam imagined everyone kicking on to his apartment, where people would comment on his things and say, *That's a cool TV*, or, *Wow, is that the espresso machine George Clooney uses?* and in Sam's imagination, Sam saw himself—toggled to third-person view—making espressos for everyone, except as he spoke and used the espresso machine, he didn't look quite like Sam but like Sam if Sam were also George Clooney, or like George Clooney if George Clooney were actually Sam.

And Sam had other nice things in his apartment, some more visible and some less so. He had a Platinum Visa card and an Amex Ultimate card, as well as a defaulted payment plan for a personal loan Sam had optimistically taken out, a year earlier, for an ill-conceived trip to Japan, where he had felt largely alienated, the language barrier difficult, and had eaten a variety of foods, mainly pancakes shaped and colored to look like different foods. The defaulted payment plan wasn't physically visible in the apartment except for the fact that when he was in Japan, he had used part of the loan to purchase and take home through customs, for reasons now opaque to him, a full-size katana. He'd then hung the katana in its fluorescent green sheath on his living room wall. When Sam looked up from playing PlayStation and saw the sword, he didn't think, That's my defaulted payment plan, but rather, That is a sweet sword. Then he went back to feeling alone.

*   *   *

– – –

Sam woke at noon. Sam worked six days out of seven, and if he was asked to work on the seventh, he said yes. It was Sam's day off and on Sam's days off he didn't exactly know what he should do.

He got up, looked at the Pancake Saloon from his window, wondered what people were doing inside, then left his apartment for the mall, where he bought a large juice that was not predominantly juice but sugar and frozen yogurt, and walked from one side of the mall to the other. He walked quickly, with purpose, his arms pressed against his sides, like he was rushing to meet someone, a group of friends, a date. When he got to the end of the mall, a large, cavernous food court, he turned around and circled back.

The mall was filled with teenagers who still went to school. When Sam still went to school, he'd been excited to leave it. Though he wasn't bullied, Sam had not had many friends in high school and imagined the time after it to be one in which he'd interact with many people and all these people would like him and want to do things with him. He would smile and these people would smile and it would be like in an advertisement in which small products, an opened bottle of soda or unwrapped candy bar, led to spontaneous parties and beaches and fun. Sam thought the Pancake Saloon was a little bit like this but actually not like this at all.

Back at his apartment, Sam entered his windowless bedroom and lay on the bed. He was bored. He put some music on. Then he opened his laptop and watched an eighteen-year-old boy sit on a swivel chair and masturbate in real time. This was on a site that had previously saved Sam's credit card details.

Sam's credit card was charged to buy tokens and Sam could then give away these tokens and, for differing amounts, the boys on the screen would dance, angle their webcams lower, pull down their underwear, and put things in and out of their bodies while touching themselves. Sam tipped but was careful not to tip too much, because

The QUEER
FICTION ISSUE

McSWEENEY'S
QUARTERLY

ISSUE NO.
SIXTY-TWO

– – –

if he tipped too much the performer might climax and then quickly log off.

Sam was watching a cam boy he often watched, ShyGuy18, because ShyGuy18 was friendly, had supposedly once been shy like Sam, and often interacted with viewers. He was thin, had hair the color of aqua-blue bubble gum, and cammed from a small, carpeted bedroom somewhere in Virginia, a light projector making faint disco patterns across the walls.

Sam could interact with him by typing messages. Sam thought that if ShyGuy18 and Sam lived in the same city, they would be friends. Sam often typed messages into the chat window and ShyGuy18 would talk to him, or not to him specifically, but to the chat room as a whole. He would talk about his day and then send links. It was kind of like hanging out at the mall because the links would take Sam to the world's largest mall, Amazon, to ShyGuy18's wish list, a large, white screen where you could scroll across product icons and buy the things he wanted. The list was similar to other cam boy wish lists: better recording equipment, a swivel chair made to look like the seat of a race car, sex toys, the latest *Grand Theft Auto*, but also more-original requests—a Mixmaster, tropical fish, an officially licensed *SpongeBob SquarePants* Pineapple House aquarium ornament.

Sam bought ShyGuy18 the *SpongeBob SquarePants* Pineapple House and then typed, "I bought you the Pineapple House" into the chat window, and ShyGuy18 said, "Yay," and then he spoke to Sam by name, not Sam's real name but Sam's username. He said, "Thank you shortstack2013." Sam blushed. Every now and then, Sam tipped him and his browser made a sound of coins falling and Sam felt happy. Then it was over, and Sam was alone again in his apartment.

He left his bedroom. It was dark outside. It was ten.

Sam could tell whether or not the Pancake Saloon was busy by counting the number of cars in the lot. He could count them, standing there, looking out from his living room window. The lot was full. Sam called his manager and asked if they needed anyone to come in tonight. Sam's manager said no.

Hours passed. When Sam spent too much time alone, he thought of himself in a series of adjectives, rapidly cycling between *helpful*, *friendly*, and *slightly obese*.

Rosa called again. She asked how Sam was. She asked about Sam's financial situation, and Sam misinterpreted this as her taking an interest in his life. Sam described the Pancake Saloon in great detail. Rosa absently said, "Okay, okay," then asked Sam if he had insurance.

Sam didn't like to lie to people who were kind to him. He said he didn't have insurance.

Rosa said she was glad he had told her. Rosa explained, again, that Sam would need to pay for the CT scan. The CT scan was three thousand dollars. Rosa asked if Sam understood her. Sam nodded. The line was quiet. Then Sam said, "Oh, I nodded," and Rosa said, "Great."

At the Pancake Saloon, Sam stood in front of the manager's office door and waited. Sam didn't want to knock on the door but to seem to be there coincidentally when his manager came out. Sam's manager, Kelly, was twenty-four and would sometimes sit on a milk crate smoking with everyone and say, "The Pancake Saloon should blow up," and other times would yell at them to work. It was variable and, like Kelly's frequently changing hair color, had to do with things happening, unseen, in Kelly's personal life.

When Kelly came out of the office, Sam asked if he could have shifts during the day. Kelly said they already had a dishwasher during the day, and Sam said, "Okay," and then Kelly said they needed a server. Sam said he could be a server.

Kelly paused, then said, "Yeah, whatever." And then, "You'd be working double shifts, though." Sam said this was fine.

Sam went back to the kitchen and imagined all the money he would make as a server. Sam imagined his rapport with customers. Sam smiled and imagined having regulars. Sam imagined serving his regulars and his regulars going on to have lovely days because Sam had served them.

He was so excited that when he got home, he felt like he couldn't sleep, so he didn't. He waited for the mall to open and then, to celebrate, walked to EB Games, where he bought himself the latest *Grand Theft Auto*. He thought he shouldn't spend money but then he thought, It's important to celebrate when things are worth celebrating. When you get a promotion, you should celebrate. That isn't a bad thing to do.

At the register, Sam's credit card was declined. Sam took out another card.

During his first shift in the dining room, Sam's customers were not particularly friendly. They were like the non-player characters in *Grand Theft Auto*. They were impatient and said rude things when Sam accidentally bumped into them.

It was a weekday shift and that meant it was slow, though it didn't feel slow to Sam. Moving through the dining room, Sam felt his inner voice take on the tone of a reality-television chef that visits people's restaurants to yell at them about how shitty they run their restaurants. The voice swore at him to be better, to be faster, and because the voice swore at him, he made stupid mistakes. He took orders to the wrong tables. He got confused with substitutions. He poured non-decaf coffee into a mug filled with decaf. When people complained, he said, "I don't know," "Beats me," "That's weird." When a family said they wanted to talk to a manager, he said, "That's okay," and then, "Your meals are free."

– – –

Then Sam's manager, the daytime manager, the franchise owner's son, told Sam to come into his office. The manager was in his twenties, was tanned, and sometimes took money for cigarettes directly from the register. The office was a small, windowless room crowded with a desktop computer, the Saloon's safe, and four large filing cabinets the color of pancake batter. Inside, the manager told Sam that he could not comp people's meals. "That's bad business."

Sam said, "Okay." Then Sam stood on the dining room floor and his reality-television-chef inner voice gave him orders using sporting metaphors that Sam didn't fully understand. The voice said, *Step up to the fucking plate, Knock it out of the park, Fucking call the shots.*

At Sam's apartment building, in Sam's mailbox, was a letter. It was from Amex. His card's credit limit had been increased.

Between Sam's day shift and night shift, he watched ShyGuy18's cam show, used his Amex to buy gifts off ShyGuy18's Amazon wish list—a Sunbeam Mixmaster, an LED ring light—then played *Grand Theft Auto.*

Sam played through the opening scene, a bank robbery, a car chase, and then found himself with a fresh start in a vast computer-generated city, an open world. Sam didn't like doing missions or following the story, because the missions were boring and often difficult, and Sam didn't like killing people, because it didn't seem very nice.

What Sam did do was run out onto the street and steal a car—it didn't have to be a good car; it could be a Toyota Camry that for licensing reasons in-game was not a Toyota Camry—then drive on the freeway toward the horizon. He toggled the radio until he hit the all-pop, all-hits channel, then cruised.

When Sam felt particularly pumped up or aspirational, he would try to steal a private jet. But it was hard to steal a private jet, because

– – –

driving onto the airport's airfield brought a lot of heat, and to deal with that heat required a level of coordination with the PlayStation controller that Sam lacked, so he would get arrested or killed. Sometimes Sam paused the game to watch a YouTube tutorial on how to hijack a private jet, and in the YouTube tutorial, it seemed easy: the player should approach the jet just as the uploader, a teenage boy, said, "Yeah, yeah. This is what everyone wants. Grey Goose, baby. Private planes."

But that wasn't really what Sam wanted. As Sam played, he would think of a minigame in one of the old *Grand Theft Auto*s in which you could drive a scooter and deliver pizzas or takeout noodles. In some games, you could even enter fast-food restaurants and order a burger and fries. Sam thought it would be funny if, in this *Grand Theft Auto*, he could work at a Pancake Saloon. He would come home from work, open his save file, then have his character do a shift at the Pancake Saloon, entering through a 3-D-rendered employee entrance, wearing a uniform identical to Sam's, and then come back to his crib, which would be filled with all the cool shit Sam would buy.

That was what Sam wanted.

Sam answered calls and the calls were Rosa. Rosa was very understanding and said things like "I understand." Rosa said she would email paperwork for a payment plan but that it was very important that Sam send the signed paperwork back. Sam said he would send the paperwork back, and then when it arrived, he thought, I don't have a printer. Sam thought maybe he could use the printer in the Pancake Saloon's office. Sam visualized doing this, walking in and booting up the manager's computer, printing and signing the paperwork, the things he would say if the manager came into the office. He would say something like *Oh, hey.* Because Sam imagined each of these actions

– – –

so vividly, he then didn't do any of them. When Sam remembered he hadn't, he'd think, Well, I don't have a printer.

Other collectors called Sam. These were for his personal loan, his Visa card, but not yet his Amex. Sam was in his apartment. He added the figures together. Sam spent almost half of his paycheck on rent and bought groceries on credit, because when he used credit he also got points. The savings on the points were significantly less than the losses to interest. Sam didn't fully understand this. He worked day and night. What Sam understood was that he needed more money. He needed more income.

Between work and playing PlayStation, Sam thought, he could monetize his other activities, like touching himself while watching other people touch themselves online. Sam could cam. Clicking through the cam site's rooms, less out of Sam's own sexual interest but to fill time, Sam knew there wasn't one thing people wanted but a multitude, and in that multitude, somewhere, someone might want him. They would want him and want to be his friend. They would say, *You are amazing*, *You're so cute*, *Take my money*. Sam imagined stacks of crisp bills.

The thought made him giggle.

Sam sat on his couch and set up his laptop on the coffee table. He used his Amex card to upgrade his membership from viewer to performer. For a moment it looked like the payment wouldn't clear, but then it did. Sam angled the screen up and opened his room.

The room's name was the same as his username, shortstack2013. Sam saw himself and his apartment on the screen. On the webcam, Sam's economy apartment looked like an economy apartment. He looked at the resolution and thought his apartment would look better in high-definition and that he should invest in a better webcam—that is, if he wanted to do this professionally.

The QUEER
FICTION ISSUE

McSWEENEY'S
QUARTERLY

ISSUE NO.
SIXTY-TWO

— — —

Sam put on a black ski mask he had bought and then never worn on his trip to Japan. He put the ski mask on because he was shy and thought the ski mask might be liberating and, to viewers, erotic. His lips and eyes were visible. He took his Pancake Saloon shirt off but felt self-conscious, then put it back on. He placed his arms across his chest. He thought that ShyGuy18 must also be shy, but ShyGuy18 had worked past it and seemed to have a good time. He thought he shouldn't think about what he was doing too much but be spontaneous.

Sam put his feet up on the coffee table in a way that was suggestive. He took his socks off. Then he put his socks back on, thinking he'd take them off when there were viewers. There were feeds on the site where boys were tipped to sit on a couch while another man massaged their big feet, sucked on their toes. That seemed okay to Sam. That seemed easy. But Sam did not have big feet. Or someone to suck on them.

He put on some music and kind of nodded his head. It was exciting. He was exciting. He thought about all the products he would put on his own Amazon wish list once he'd settled his debt. He saw each product in front of him, floating, suspended in empty white space.

Sam's browser made a noise. A viewer had entered the room. Sam tried to make a sexy face by thinking, *Sexy face,* and pouted his lips through the mask. Then Sam stood up, inhaled, and began to lift his shirt. Slowly, he exhaled. His belly filled the screen and resembled, more than anything, a smooth milk bun. His viewer was watching. Sam stepped from side to side. Then Sam lowered his underwear. Sam was still. His laptop made another noise, a different noise, a kind of sad noise. Sam said, "Hello," then realized his one viewer had left the room.

Weeks passed. When Sam answered the phone, it was Rosa but it wasn't Rosa. It was Bad Cop Rosa. Bad Cop Rosa said mean things.

– – –

She said, "Pay the money." She said, "I don't care. Pay up!" She said, "You're in a bad situation. You're going to go to court." She yelled, "Compound interest!"

Sam owed $6,000 on his Visa card, $4,500 on his Amex, $5,600 remained on his personal loan, and then there was the cost of the CT scan. Plus interest. This was all unconsolidated.

At work, Sam told the daytime manager that he thought the Pancake Saloon should cover or help cover the cost of his CT scan.

The daytime manager said, "What?" and Sam said, "From the time I fell at work." The manager asked if Sam had filed an incident report.

"I don't know," Sam said.

"So how can the Pancake Saloon know you actually hurt yourself working," Sam's manager said. "To allege that you injured yourself here, so the Pancake Saloon pays for your personal medical fees, well, that's a serious allegation. That's not the kind of Pancake Saloon employee this Pancake Saloon employs."

Sam said, "It was at work."

Sam's manager said, "Go back to your tables." And that's what Sam did.

Later, at home, Sam sat in his living room, lit by the television's glow. Sam didn't have a shift that night and felt a kind of restlessness he associated with drinking too many energy drinks or espressos from his espresso machine. He played *Grand Theft Auto*. He drove across one freeway, then merged onto another, weaving between traffic.

It was late. It was past three. Sam gripped the controller and stood up, looked at the Pancake Saloon through the window, then sat back down. Occasionally, thoughts raced through Sam's mind, and the thoughts raced so quickly they left ghost trails. The thoughts were: MONEY, Money, money, and CASH, Cash, cash.

Fuck the Pancake Saloon, Sam thought. If the Pancake Saloon were in *Grand Theft Auto*, he would use a rocket launcher and blow

– – –

it up. He would plow an SUV through the Pancake Saloon's front windows. If the Pancake Saloon were in *Grand Theft Auto*, the rocket would explode on the Pancake Saloon's exterior and the SUV would hit it and then bounce off. The buildings in *Grand Theft Auto* were indestructible.

Sam turned the PlayStation off. From his living room window, Sam realized he could watch the night manager, Kelly, walk from the Saloon to the bank to deposit the night's takings. It would be close to five. His eyes could follow Kelly leaving the restaurant from the employee entrance, waiting for the traffic light, crossing the six lanes to get to the mall, then walking alongside the mall's parking lot, shadows lengthening under the streetlights, until she stopped at the bank's deposit chute.

The restaurant had strict procedures that were written up in the Pancake Saloon's employee manuals. When the night shift made the cash drop, two people were meant to make it: the night manager and someone else. But the Pancake Saloon that Sam worked at was a franchise, where the procedure, especially at night, when the owner's son wasn't there, had, over time, been replaced with a new one, which was to follow the corporate procedure as little as possible. Kelly took the money alone.

Sam thought he could take that money. Sam imagined this as a mission in *Grand Theft Auto*. Sam would cover his face with his ski mask, then, at 4 a.m., go downstairs and wait in the mall's parking lot. He would wait for Kelly to cross the road, and then, before she reached the bank chute, leap out from the dark.

Sam would speak in a low voice. Maybe even use one of those machines that you press against your throat, a voice changer or vocoder. Sam would say, *Give me the money*. Sam would speak like a gangster from *Grand Theft Auto* if the gangster were also using a vocoder. He'd say, *Give me the money, bitch*, and raise a fake gun. Sam realized he didn't

– – –

have a fake gun, so in Sam's imagination he was holding his katana, still in its sheath. He would wave the katana and say *Bitch* a few times. Then Sam would grab the money. Then Sam would run.

This scene was followed by a quick montage: Sam in his apartment, counting money, counting so much money, more money than the Pancake Saloon would make in one night. Sam at work, unsuspected, later that day. Sam's debts being settled. Sam buying himself nice things. Sam living his life.

But Sam wouldn't do this, any of this, because Sam was bad at missions and knew that if he tried, he would fuck it up, or he might scare Kelly, and he didn't want to scare Kelly, or Kelly might scare him and pull out a canister of mace.

Sam accepted this. Sam's heart beat rapidly in the dark.

At work, there was an incident. During the morning rush, a woman had come in with two children. If the woman were in *Grand Theft Auto*, she would be a character walking on the street in the business district. She wore a suit.

Sam brought the woman her order: three plates of pancakes smothered in high-fructose corn syrup, and a coffee.

The woman said, "I made a request, and it was a simple request, and you haven't done it. My daughter wanted ice cream."

Sam picked up one of the plates and said he would add a scoop of ice cream.

"Make them fresh. The pancakes should be fresh."

Sam said, "Yes." Sam said he would go to the kitchen and be right back.

In the kitchen, Sam put the plate of pancakes under the heat lamp. Sam waited a few minutes, then asked if someone else could take the pancakes to his table. No one replied. Sam put a scoop of ice cream onto the pancakes and returned to the dining room with the order. He set it down.

The woman sipped her coffee. Then she let the coffee fall out of her mouth and back into the cup. She wiped her lips with a paper napkin. She said, "This coffee is tepid."

Sam said he would replace the coffee.

"It isn't about the coffee," she said. "It's about the level of service. I was having a good day and now I'm having a bad one. My children are having a bad time." The children seemed happy. They were doing what Sam wished he were doing. They were eating pancakes.

"Do you understand?" the woman said. The woman spoke to Sam like she thought Sam had made poor life choices and she was personally offended by those choices. She communicated that she was training her children to be members of society, members who would not serve people pancakes, or have debt, or if they did have debt, they would have the good kind of debt, the kind that could be leveraged.

Sam said, "That's okay," and the woman said, "No, it's not okay," and Sam said, "Your meals are free."

When they finished eating, they walked past the register and into the parking lot. Sam watched them getting into their car, an expensive car, through the Saloon's plate glass, the woman buckling the smaller child into a safety seat. They drove away.

The daytime manager was standing behind Sam. The daytime manager said, "Did you just comp their meal?"

Sam was asked to leave. At home, Sam lay in bed. Sam watched ShyGuy18's cam show but didn't have any tokens. So Sam sat and looked at ShyGuy18, and ShyGuy18, shirtless, seemed to look through his webcam and through Sam's screen, making eye contact, and ShyGuy18's eyes were communicating and what they were saying was *Tip me* but Sam couldn't. His cards had maxed out. Sam typed "Hello" into the chat window, then ShyGuy18 stood up and half pulled his underwear down and then pulled the underwear back up. Sam typed, "How are you?" ShyGuy18 sat on his swivel chair for a while, then got up and left the room. In the corner of the room, Sam saw a small aquarium. Inside the aquarium was an officially licensed *SpongeBob SquarePants* Pineapple House ornament. ShyGuy18 came back with a Coke Zero. Sam wrote, "I had a bad day." ShyGuy18 concentrated on the can of Coke Zero, then on the screen, and then on something off-screen. ShyGuy18 typed, "I'll cam later." The feed cut to black.

Sam received calls from unlisted numbers. They called in the morning, the afternoon, the dead of night. Sam's debt was sold to one collection agency, then to another. His debt was swapped and traded alongside other people's debt like Yu-Gi-Oh! cards. Sometimes Sam answered the calls. Sometimes he didn't. When he answered, he would say, "I cannot take your call right now. I am at my place of employment," and they would say, "Pay us the fucking money!" and Sam would say, "Goodbye," disconnecting the call with a kind of giddiness, his heart beating fast, then slow, then fast again, until the feeling faded away.

Sam was no longer a server. This made sense to Sam. He was a terrible server. Sam still worked at the Pancake Saloon. He washed dishes. Sometimes, as Sam sprayed dishes, his inner voice would yell, *Bankrupt!* like he was on a game show or playing and winning a variant of Yahtzee. At certain shift intervals, he mopped the kitchen floor.

When Sam got home from his shifts, he placed his phone in his fridge's vegetable crisper. Then Sam played *Grand Theft Auto*. Sam had gotten better at *Grand Theft Auto*. Sam stole a car and drove to the airport. Sam wanted a private jet. There was a chase. Explosions. Multicar pileups.

Almost every time, Sam died, but then one time he didn't. He drove through the mass of concrete that was the airport and reached

– – –

the private jet. He jumped in. He floored the jet's engines, police officers running across the tarmac, SWAT team members in helicopters,
bullets raining down. And then the jet was on the runway and the jet
was moving faster and faster. It began to lift.

Sam was in the air. Then the city was below him, all its freeways
and fast-food restaurants and shitty apartment towers like Sam's
shitty apartment tower, and a calm came over him. He angled the
plane up, flying higher and higher, until the altitude maxed and the
game's draw distance glitched, and each direction, above and below,
collapsed into sky.

The QUEER
FICTION ISSUE

McSWEENEY'S
QUARTERLY

ISSUE NO.
SIXTY-TWO

PEPPERSOUP
by
TIMI
ODUESO

I am making a savory stew.

On the blue plastic tray that Auntie gifted to me when I was to begin schooling at Kongo, I have chopped purple onions in fine ring slices; I will fry them in hot palm oil before adding some locust beans.

In my makeshift oven, a chocolate cake bakes. I have mixed some cinnamon into the batter; I have beaten the egg whites till they formed peaks that stood erect as I plucked the whisks from the mixing bowl. I have poured the stickiness into a heart-shaped tin and covered it with groundnuts. There is a profusion of smells in my kitchen now: the smell of batter slowly rising and releasing the nutty aroma of nutmeg, and onions caramelizing in hot palm oil, begging to be laced with iru and thyme, waiting to be ladled with thick melon paste.

The QUEER
FICTION ISSUE

PEPPERSOUP
by TIMI ODUESO

ISSUE NO.
SIXTY-TWO

– – –

There is something about Fulani boys that reminds me of good egusi soup: the pink of their lips, peppers that have escaped the wicked blades of my handheld blender; the dark hairs that caress their heads, pods of delicious iru that refuse to melt in oil; and their very skins, miracles like well-boiled cow skin that beg to be savored by hungry tongues.

If you are asking yourself if I'm having a feast, lay your questions to rest: I am not. I am not cooking for myself or a platoon of soldiers. I am cooking for one only. Nuruddeen is coming over.

This is why I am stirring powdered crayfish into my melon paste; this is why I am making a savory stew—in hopes that I will be eating something else later. I mix very carefully; you must never stir too hard or the lumps will not form. When I am done, I spoon my paste into the oil and watch the bubbles erupt as the ground melon seeds begin to fry. Do you know what they say about good egusi soup? They say you can tell how it will taste long before you add the paste to the oil.

I do not know what this proverb means; all I know is that Nuruddeen will eat well. All I know is that there is no staple that goes hand-in-hand with egusi soup like pounded yam, so I take a sharp knife to a tuber and carefully skin the bark off the creamy whiteness hidden inside. When the slices are swimming in a pot of clean water on the cooker, I walk through the back door to drag in my pestle and mortar from the veranda.

Let me tell you, it is not every day that I cook for a man. Do not think I am one of those people who often trap the hearts of men in their pressure cookers, boiling away their humanity with spices till all that's left is a skin that yields at the bequest of milk teeth. In my four years here, in Kongo, I have cooked for four men only, and if all goes well, I will not be cooking for another for a while. The first man I cooked for, when I moved here, had skin the color of cocoyam, with a papery texture I was sure would shine if enough oori was rubbed into

The QUEER
FICTION ISSUE

McSWEENEY'S
QUARTERLY

ISSUE NO.
SIXTY-TWO

– – –

it. He reminded me of elubo, of cassava flour, and when he came over that night, I filled his stomach with a vegetable soup I had spiced with black pepper and turmeric; and after he had eaten his fill, when his tongue had licked the oil that ran from his fingers down to his elbow, when he had fiddled with the blue plastic tube of toothpicks and rid his teeth of the strands of goat meat that hid there, I led him into my bedroom and let him fill me up in return.

I stick a fork into the yams and find they are soft enough. I pick them out, one after the other, and drop them into my mortar. The end of the pestle makes the first contact and turns a slice into pulp. I begin pounding the yam, forceful dropping motions that blur the shape of the slices into mush. Do you know what the true spice of pounded yam is? They have lied to you, it is not the clean water you boiled the yams in. It is not even the soil the yam seedlings were planted in. It is not the sprigs of wood that splice off the mortar and pestle and melt into the staple, the splinters that make you pick your teeth and think you have a fish bone stuck between your roots. It is the sweat of the pounder. The little drops of nectar, of energy and hard work that travel from the crown of the pounder as they make the meal and drop into the staple, are the true spice of pounded yam. It is why your fingers find solace in each mold you make; it is why your throat finds it easy to push the mash down—because the pounder has lubricated your meal with their love.

The second man I cooked for here came one year after the first, during my second year in Kongo. He was the butcher at the stall where I bought my meat, and he told me he liked the way my fingers pointed at the meat whenever I ordered him to cut it into smaller pieces. I told him I liked the way the muscles in his arms flexed when he raised the wuka to cleave meat from bone. For him, I left Kongo to slave under the hot sun of Sabo in search of fresh banana leaves. For him, I steamed the banana leaves filled with ground beans, hot peppers, and

The QUEER
FICTION ISSUE

PEPPERSOUP
by TIMI ODUESO

ISSUE NO.
SIXTY-TWO

– – –

boiled eggs; for him, I made a spicy moimoi that melted in his mouth and made him say, "Walahi, may Allah punish me if I don't take care of you." For him, I laid out a mat in the sitting room and pushed him down onto it before burying my face in his groin; and as he groaned, as he tried to push my head away after his pleasure erupted in my mouth, as he screamed, "Stop, stop, no more," I felt his juices melt in my mouth and took back from him every morsel of me he had swallowed from my table.

I wrap the fluffy white staple in a transparent nylon and stuff it into a cooler. I move to the cooker and open the pot to find that my paste has mixed with the oil to turn from a pale yellow to a bright orange. I grab my spice basket and add, first, half a teaspoon of curry. As I measure out black pepper and crushed seasoning cubes, I think of the third man that ate at my table in Kongo. I think of Peace, whom I cooked for in my third year in Kongo.

He was not like the others, Peace. For him, I didn't cook a meal I had learned to make from Auntie's hand. I didn't take a keke to Sabo to search for fresh snails or smoked grass cutter, I didn't use iru or ogbono, and I didn't make a savory peppersoup with uziza seeds. Instead, I made one of the meals I'd seen in a handbook: I walked to the Shagalinku superstore on my street, bought a vial of dark soy sauce, and made chicken fried rice. I chopped spring onions and sautéed chicken breasts in honey and white pepper. I bought a new rolling pin and lined brown sugar, cinnamon, and nutmeg into dough. I laid cinnamon rolls out to rest and the smells wafted upward till the maigida, who owned the house I rented and was almost never around, walked down the stairs on his way out, knocked, and asked, while pulling on his beard mischievously, "Adun, you don't cook often. What is happening? This one you're cooking for us today, are we safe?"

If you ask anyone else why Peace's meal was different, why someone as traditional as me would deviate from custom and make something

The QUEER
FICTION ISSUE

McSWEENEY'S
QUARTERLY

ISSUE NO.
SIXTY-TWO

– – –

unknown for another man, they will tell you it is because I liked him. They will say it is because his smile made my heart race; they will say it is because when his hands touched mine, the skin on them burned and yearned for cleansing; they will even tell you that my soul longed for his love. They will tell you nothing but lies. The reason Peace's plate was garnished with sprigs of fresh thyme, the reason I bought scented serviettes for him to wipe his mouth with, the reason I brought a bib out and tucked it into his collar before he began eating, was that he was serious about the beads he wore around his neck. It was that he had waited five months before he began speaking to me. It was that, unlike every man I had tasted, Peace spent half his time with me fiddling with the rosary that hung around his neck.

I had heard of his type before. Amid her lessons, as she taught me never to cook beans to watery mush, as she told me how to spot which omorogun would be best for turning eba and which for amala, as I learned from her hands the quickest way to men's hearts, Auntie told me about people like Peace: people who took their beliefs as seriously as we did ours, people whose words would actually break my bones. "Whether it's a tasbih or a rosary they carry," she said, "most people are the same. They don't really believe. The very few that do, though, can smell the other spices we have boiled into the stock fish. They can taste the truth in your efo riro, and if you even try to taste them, just a single lick will burn your existence away."

"But we're immortal," I'd said. "We will always exist."

"That doesn't mean our bodies can't die. It is like a pot of fresh peppersoup: as long as you don't open the lid or dip a spoon into it, there will always be something left in the pot, fresh or stale. That doesn't mean the pot can't be destroyed. That's how our lives are: we are vats of peppersoup ever resting in cauldrons. Tip the cauldron and you will have to start afresh, gathering every single ingredient for a fresh pot. We will always exist; it doesn't mean we cannot die. You must be careful

The QUEER
FICTION ISSUE

PEPPERSOUP
by TIMI ODUESO

ISSUE NO.
SIXTY-TWO

– – –

with men like that. Their hunger, much like their search for salvation, can only be filled by things that come from other continents."

Let me tell you, it was difficult, finding the kind of people Auntie had spoken about. It was like frying fish on a hot skillet, salivating at the thought of crunching on crisp bones while tensing up as the pan sputters hot liquid in your direction. When I first came to Kongo, in my early days as a student at the university, my eyes roamed across the men that walked the streets, the ones who wore white caftans on Fridays and fingered their tasbihs consistently, the ones who seemed to spend every living moment in church, at a rehearsal for a special program or an all-night prayer session. The watching drove my insides to a thirst that made me remember the abundance in Auntie's house, with its terrazzo floors stained only by the footprints of the many men who strolled the halls. The thirst made me remember Auntie's words: "Once a year is enough. Don't get greedy or people will start to notice." The thirst drove me to the corner of Sabo market where men in tank tops sold beer and peppersoup to people who drove to the spot only when the sky had sent the sun on its way. It was there that I met that first man, the one who told me my efo riro was better than anything his wife had ever cooked, the one who wore a heavily embroidered caftan and asked me in a silky voice, as he rinsed his hands of the eba I had made, if I was ready for him down there; the one whose voice rose to a brittle pitch that whispered of the many children he had left in a house in Kano; the one whose eyes darkened with despair as my mouth latched onto his neck and he realized I wouldn't let go until he was like the diaphanous plastic bottle on my table: empty, wrinkled, and devoid of everything that made him alive.

I would have left Peace alone; I had been in Kongo three years and I knew where to find men whose eyes wandered too far, but he smiled once at me, on a day I sat next to him as we wrote an exam. I felt his gaze on the sheets in front of me and I slid them farther to the left, to

– – –

a position I was sure his vision could reach. I turned slowly and found behind his thankful smile a longing I had seen too many times.

Peace had hidden it well, that longing. He hid it in the collar of the pressed shirts he always wore, burning away the creases of his desires with an iron fueled by his beliefs. It was there in the way his fingers lingered on the rosary around his neck, waiting for the plastic beads to suck the yearning from his skin so he could drown it in holy water. He hid it in the careful bites he took of the chicken I served, mindful not to eat too fast, afraid of appearing hungry for too many things.

He hid it so well, my fingers hesitated before they broke down the walls that boy had spent all his life building. When his hazel irises looked into my dark ones, my throat closed up, and the hunger I had been building for a year began to evaporate. At least until he told me how scared he was, till his confessed fear brought the appetite rushing back.

"I've never done this before," he said. "Not even with a girl."

"Me neither," I responded. As I brought my lips to his, I almost forgot to savor how pure he tasted, like olive oil untainted by the acridity of onions; like boiling water waiting to be sprinkled with curry and turmeric powder; like fresh peppersoup waiting to be spooned into wet, hungry mouths.

When I hear three knocks on my door, the food is already laid out on the table. I have broken the cake into cubes and lined them up in clear Tupperware containers; I have spooned a generous portion of egusi soup into a gold ceramic tureen and topped it with smoked catfish; I have used my omorogun to smash ice into pieces that will fit in my water jug. For later, I scrub myself clean of the putridity of locust bean with a black soap Auntie makes for special nights like these, then I lace my wrists with drops of oud. I wear nothing but a black djellaba that hugs my chest too tightly. Underneath, the silky spandex underwear I reserve for these moments cups my testicles nicely. I have made several meals just for Nuruddeen.

The QUEER
FICTION ISSUE

PEPPERSOUP
by TIMI ODUESO

ISSUE NO.
SIXTY-TWO

– – –

I meet him at the door. He is wearing a deep gray caftan. Beneath his left eye, a tiny mole shifts as his spreads his lips to reveal white teeth.

"Welcome," I say, ushering him into the room with my eyes. His shoulders relax and he lifts his head into the air.

"You really cooked, fa? I swear, Adun, I thought you were joking," he exclaims.

"I don't play with food," I reply. "And besides, you're a special guest." I lead him to the table and he sits, his lips parted as I spoon the soup into a bowl. "But all this for me?"

My hands find themselves on his as I say, "For us, Nuruddeen, for us. For tonight, at least."

Nuruddeen's hunger appears instantly, a ferocious one that burns a look onto his face. The look stays there when his fingers slip the first ball of pounded yam between his lips; it stays there as he bites into the catfish, slurping at the soup that has hidden itself between the silky skin; it is there when he swallows the cake and asks if he can have one more piece.

When I stand before him an hour later, in nothing but the silky spandex underwear I have kept for these special nights, the look is still in his eyes and it makes his fingers wobble as they loosen the knots on his trousers. It stays there, hidden behind his eyelids, when I move in for our first kiss, my tongue pushing his lips apart to taste his insides, my hands roaming below to find a turgidity that pokes hard at mine. It stays as my tongue slips out of his lips and traces its way down his neck, savoring the saltiness hidden in the lines that run around it; it stays and doesn't begin to disappear until I bite down and he whispers, "Too hard, Adun."

I bite deeper and let the sharpness sink into his flesh. I look up to find his eyes darkened and his lips spread apart in preparation for a scream.

The QUEER
FICTION ISSUE

McSWEENEY'S
QUARTERLY

ISSUE NO.
SIXTY-TWO

– – –

Did they not tell you about us? I think, as the blood flows onto my tongue and begins to douse the thirst that has been pent up in my throat for a year. Did your fathers not warn you to refuse food from the hands of a person whose house you have never seen before? Did your mothers not hold your ears and pull tightly as they told you tales of children and men whose bodies had changed form after they ate from the hands of a stranger? Did you not grow up hearing of me, listening to tales of people who can poison your judgments with isiewu and suya?

My hunger grows and my stomach rumbles as I think of nipping into the toughness of muscle, of sucking marrow from the hollow crevices of bones, of the stringiness of skin that sticks between my teeth. I bite down harder as Nuruddeen's screams rebound off the four walls. My throat guffaws at his screams for help, knowing that the maigida is not within the gates of the compound. His legs flail in the air as he grabs at my hair and tries to pull me off him. It will not work: I have the strength of four men now.

I suck harder, and as his screams turn to low moans, as his hands begin to lose the vigor he undressed with, as my eyes whisper to him that I will devour him in the same manner with which he emptied my pot, his juices leak from the open wound in his neck, from the spaces my lips cannot reach, and spread out onto my mattress, a bright red stain I wish I could bottle and make a sweet tomato soup from.

The QUEER
FICTION ISSUE

McSWEENEY'S
QUARTERLY

ISSUE NO.
SIXTY-TWO

THE
PLANT
GAME
by
KAYLA
KUMARI
UPADHYAYA

The spider plant was the first to die. It happened gradually, browned tips the first sign of suffering. It was an easy enough fix, Cass thought. There was probably salt in the tap water, so she switched to distilled and thought little of the spindly spider plant. It was, after all, one of the most resilient plants in their home.

Her girlfriend, Lana, had given it to her the week they moved in together. "To add to your collection," Lana had said, holding out the spider plant, whose draping arms in turn reached out to Cass.

We will be happy here, the plant told Cass, and she agreed.

I think I'm in love, she said to the plant.

"*Chlorophytum comosum*," Cass said, holding the *m*'s on her tongue and letting them melt there until Lana leaned in and tasted.

– – –

Cass and Lana often played the Plant Game, something they'd invented when they started dating. Lana would point to a plant, a tree, a flower, a leaf, sometimes just a piece of stray bark, and Cass would produce its scientific name. She had a degree in plant biology, but even within her field, Cass was a bit of a freak.

The spider plant took three weeks to die. It agonized, rotted from the outside in, the sickly brown spreading from tip to root before deepening to doom-black. Cass found it gnarled and crispy in its pot, beyond repair even for her. She tried everything in the days leading up to its death: collecting rainwater to give it, moving it around the apartment, asking the spider plant where it hurt. But it didn't answer, and that's when Cass knew it was serious.

"It doesn't make any sense," Cass told Lana as they sat on the couch eating boiled eggs speckled with salt and pepper.

"Don't plants just die sometimes?" Lana bit the top off her egg, exposing its soft golden core.

Cass shook her head. She explained that spider plants are particularly easy to take care of, adaptable, able to withstand abuse. Lana nodded along, nibbling at her egg, and Cass knew she was rambling, that Lana was just barely tolerating her plant talk. Lana liked playing the Plant Game and she liked taking photos of all the plants in their apartment, the one that used to be just hers, but Cass could always sense her drifting when she went on too long about the life cycle of a geranium or the ideal climate for a sycamore tree.

Lana didn't have much of a green thumb. Before Cass, she'd owned only a few air plants that she'd bought for too much money at a bodega. They sat in glass cages with little pebbles, and she kept them alive, but she didn't care for them.

The first time Lana brought her home, Cass had been struck by the vast blankness of the apartment. Nothing lived on the white walls.

The QUEER
FICTION ISSUE

McSWEENEY'S
QUARTERLY

ISSUE NO.
SIXTY-TWO

– – –

All of Lana's furniture was some shade of black or gray. She felt suffo-cated by the straight lines and flatness. So, leading up to the move, she gifted Lana houseplants every chance she got. She talked to her girlfriend about these gifts as if they were people, new friends to share space with. She introduced her to black dahlias (the goths of the flower world), daylilies (drama queens), and philodendrons (secret roman-tics). Lana's previously barren, minimalist apartment filled with life, and Cass apologized profusely to the neglected plants Lana had owned before, injecting them with new life. *I'm sorry*, she said. *We're glad you're here*, they answered.

By the time she moved in, the sterile apartment had transformed into a private forest, right in the middle of Prospect Heights. It teemed with green and colors that only nature can produce. It smelled like outside, that good, heavy smell that made Cass feel safe and alive in her own skin. She breathed much easier, and Lana marveled at the beauty of it all. Sometimes Cass wouldn't leave the apartment for days on end. It was easy to get lost between the walls of this place. And Cass preferred talking to plants over talking to people, anyway.

"Anyone can care for a spider plant," Cass continued. "Even—" she stopped herself.

"Even me," Lana said. She huffed into the kitchen, and Cass imme-diately followed, pulling Lana back toward her and insisting that's not what she'd meant. Cass kissed her, and she still tasted like egg and coffee, but she moved her tongue around the wet cave of Lana's mouth.

"I care for the plants, and you care for me," Cass said. *Nice save*, the mischievous ponytail palm on the counter said, and Cass ignored it.

Lana left for the restaurant where she bartended and made so much money that it seemed she would never go back to art school.

The QUEER
FICTION ISSUE

THE PLANT GAME
by KAYLA KUMARI UPADHYAYA

ISSUE NO.
SIXTY-TWO

– – –

Cass tried to get rid of the dead spider plant. If she had been back home, she would have buried it in the yard as if it were a pet, returning it to the earth. But there was no yard at Lana's Brooklyn walkup, and Cass didn't have time to walk to the park. Apologizing even though she knew it couldn't hear her anymore, Cass dumped the plant's remains into the trash can and rinsed out its pot in the sink.

She couldn't have a dead plant in the house; it was bad luck, but it was also bad for business. She ran a plant care clinic out of the apartment. People paid—too much, Cass thought, but Lana regularly encouraged her to hike up the prices—for one-on-one appointments with her about their ailing plants. She sold plants, too, ones she sowed and raised herself, and affixed handwritten care cards to them. It had all started as a side gig to keep her sane while she was working in a research lab with a bunch of men who snickered when they caught her whispering to seeds.

The side gig took over, and she left the lifeless lab. It was Cass's work, but Lana handled the business side, marketing the speakeasy shop on Instagram and handling the money and sourcing ceramic pots from artists who came into the restaurant. Cass's natural gifts became profitable. By the time she quit the lab, she was already known around town as the Plant Whisperer.

Cass made her rounds, checking all the plants in the apartment a little more carefully than usual, spooked by the spider plant's peculiar demise. She stroked the loping leaf of a fiddle-leaf fig tree that didn't look quite as a bouncy as usual and felt a prick. When she pulled back her hand, there was blood on her pointer finger, and she instinctively brought it to her mouth, sucked, and spit the blood back into the tree's soil base. Maybe that's what the spider plant had needed. A blood sacrifice. Cass didn't give her menstrual blood to plants anymore, after Lana had asked her not to.

I'm scared, the tree confessed, and Cass massaged its leaves.

I won't let the same thing happen to you.

By afternoon, the apartment filled with people. Two butches debated whether they had space for another ficus tree. A tall blond man with a messenger bag kept picking up plants and setting them down as if their weight were significant to their worth. A woman with long braids was most interested in the hanging plants and walked between a collection of them, letting their tendrils touch her face. Cass sat on the floor, repotting a cactus. Anxious, she was careful not to prick herself again.

Some of her clients got the basic stuff. A watering schedule, soil, explanations of the plant's significance in various cultures. Often people wanted more. They came for the Plant Whisperer, and they wanted Cass to play the role of a deity. They were in search of some exciting mysticism they could reap for themselves. These particular clients—the Takers, Cass called them—were almost always white. Sometimes she'd give them what they came for: a show. She'd hold her ear close to their plant and dramatically tell a Taker they needed to stop keeping so many secrets, because their plant thrived on emotional transparency... in addition to water and direct sunlight.

The truth, Cass knew, is that not all plants need to be talked to. Some require more care than others. And plants don't listen to just anyone. They're more discerning than humans. They can tell when someone doesn't believe, and they can sense lies. Only some people can talk to plants and be heard.

The fiddle-leaf fig tree started to die. Like those of the spider plant, the warning signs were subtle at the start before rapidly spiraling. Leaves shriveled and sloughed off. Cass tried the only solution she

The QUEER
FICTION ISSUE

THE PLANT GAME
by KAYLA KUMARI UPADHYAYA

ISSUE NO.
SIXTY-TWO

– – –

could think of: a beheading. Lopping off the top of a fiddle-leaf fig tree's trunk could usually stimulate new life. She used her sharpest pruning scissors to snip the struggling tree, but nothing changed. It was dead in a matter of days, and not once did Cass hear another word from it. She looked at its neighbor, an old and wise maidenhair fern. *Something is wrong*, it warned.

Most of the plants weren't talking to Cass anymore, as if it were her they were scared of. She wanted to tell someone, but whom was there to tell? Lana believed in it all only insofar as it was something other people believed in and therefore paid for. The only other person Cass had known who heard plants talk was her grandmother, and she was dead. How lucky she had been that her grandmother had been visiting their little white house when she, still a child, ran through a field of black-eyed Susans, pressing her palms against her ears as the clamor of thousands of gossipy flowers filled her head.

Her grandmother had known immediately. Small and scared, Cass clung to the fabric of her grandmother's sari and listened to her calmly explain. She promised never to tell anyone about the secret language of plants, and she had broken that promise only once in her life. Two months into their rapidly progressing relationship, she'd told Lana she could communicate with plants.

Lana came home to Cass snipping the decayed fiddle-leaf fig tree furiously into debris. If the plants hadn't been scared of her before, they certainly were now, the sudden violence of Cass's destruction surprising even herself. These shears were meant to stimulate new life, not take it, and here she was committing plant murder in her own home. She was at a loss, confused by her inability to make things better. Lana ran to her and gently eased the scissors out of her hand.

"Dearest," Lana cooed, "it's two in the morning."

Cass hadn't even noticed the time. She slumped against a wall, defeated, and Lana sank to the ground next to her. "You smell like *Lavandula angustifolia*," Cass said, inhaling a spot behind Lana's ear when she leaned in to hug her.

"Like what?"

Cass sniffed her again. "Lavender," she said. The soft scent tickled her nose.

"Say it again," Lana whispered.

"*Lavandula angustifolia*." Cass breathed against her neck before kissing it. She felt the weight of the fig tree's death lifting off of her before Lana giggled and pushed her away, their lips unsticking with a smack.

Cass saw it then, something barely perceptible in her eyes. It wasn't like when Lana got too drunk and they lolled around, although Cass could smell on her breath that she'd definitely been drinking at work tonight, as she did most nights. But Cass saw a burst in her eyes this time. Or maybe, she realized, a bloom, a subtle pulsating of Lana's irises that was gone almost as quickly as she noticed it. She thought maybe Lana wasn't getting enough sleep.

Lana pulled herself up and left Cass sitting among the bones of the fig tree massacre. "Can you clean up some of that shit?" Lana called from down the hall. "It's even dirtier in here than usual."

Cass looked around. Except for the mess she had just made, the apartment looked pristine. She was always careful to clean up spilled soil and dropped leaves, because she knew disorder bothered Lana. She threw what was left of the fig tree into a garbage bag. *I'm sorry.*

Lana worked later and later, and Cass slept less and less, always worried about her plants in a way she never had before. She was used

The QUEER
FICTION ISSUE

THE PLANT GAME
by KAYLA KUMARI UPADHYAYA

ISSUE NO.
SIXTY-TWO

– – –

to worrying. Anxiety blossomed in her constantly. But never about this, about her ability to maintain lush, precious life. That had been the one thing she could count on.

A flower on the amaryllis turned an impossible black. The rest of the flowers gleamed red, and Cass stroked each of them, hoping they wouldn't meet the same fate. She moved the plant to a different window and snipped the cursed flower. It rolled in her hand like the bent-neck head of a snap-trapped mouse. When she fingered it, it turned to dust. She felt something lodge in her. An invisible thorn.

She didn't have time to address the amaryllis before the apartment filled with people. It was a Sunday, her busiest day, the one that brought in a post-brunch crowd still buzzing from booze and eager to buy plants that they might or might not take care of. She tried not to think too much about the fate of the creatures she sold away, especially now that she couldn't even keep the ones that lived with her safe.

The customers were needy today. All Takers. One asked if there were any spells she could cast to make her plumeria bloom more boldly, and Cass calmly explained that she didn't know any spells at all. This did not satisfy the woman with the thin ponytail, who wanted more from her plumeria and from Cass. She produced a crystal from her bra as proof that she believed in an otherworld, one where plants could talk and be talked to. Cass sighed. Lana was always suggesting that they add crystals to the shop's wares. Maybe she was right.

That night, Cass woke to the sound of Lana slamming the front door. This was a disturbance she was used to; Lana didn't possess awareness of the sounds she made in the middle of the night. Startled the first dozen times it happened, Cass had eventually become accustomed to the clamor of Lana returning home from a late-night shift. But the less she slept these days, the louder the noises became.

"I was wondering if you could maybe close the door a little more softly when you come home from work," she said when Lana finally appeared in the bedroom.

"I didn't know it bothered you."

"It doesn't. But it might be, I don't know, bothering the..." She hesitated.

"The plants?"

"Forget it."

"Always so concerned about the fucking plants."

"Forget it."

She didn't think it would be wise to try to explain the real needs of plants to Lana, who was always exhausted after work.

The small office in their apartment became a graveyard. Usually a nursery where Cass brought her customers' sick plants to prune and repot and mend them, as well as a studio where Lana drew, it was now a place of death and decay. Orchids and sword ferns and begonias were the latest victims of whatever curse had overtaken their home. They sat withered and worn in the office, where even Lana's wood desk was a grim reminder of plants that were no more. Cass still couldn't sleep, and she ordered in most meals, even though it wasn't in their budget. All her time was spent trying to solve the problem.

One night, Cass heard a stir. She turned, but Lana wasn't in bed with her. The devil's ivy hanging in front of their bedroom window caught her eye. It had grown improbably long, but the leaves weren't their usual green. They were black-blue bleeding into sour yellow, like bruises.

More rustling. Recently convinced that rats were breaking in to eat and spread some sort of medieval plague to her plant children, she got

– – –

up to investigate. The sound came from the office, and Cass slipped through the open door. A figure perched over Lana's desk, and it took Cass a second to realize it was just Lana, drawing.

"Lana," Cass said. "Jesus, you scared me. I didn't think you were home. Why didn't you come to bed?"

Lana didn't answer or even turn around. She kept drawing, furiously, as if she were scribbling out a mistake. She looked wild. Cass stepped closer.

"Lana. Why are you drawing in the middle of the night?"

Still no sound from Lana other than the scratches of her pencil, like fingernails on flesh. Whatever trance she was in, Cass couldn't break it. She got close enough to peer over Lana's shoulder. She saw a wild tree, its branches gnarled and threatening. The picture shifted. It wasn't a tree. It was a woman with branches for hair.

She got close enough to touch, and she placed her hand on Lana's shoulder, gently, but Lana spun around as if attacked. It was there in her eyes again: the bloom. She ripped out her earbuds.

"What the fuck, Cass?"

I'm sorry, Cass said. Or did she say it? She wasn't sure. She blinked, suddenly in a trance of her own. Thorns scratched at her insides, and she felt like she might puke.

"Are you going to say something?"

"I'm sorry," Cass said. "I'm just surprised to see you home. I thought you would have come to bed after work."

"Can you just let me have this one thing?"

Lana explained that she never had time to draw. She explained that she had had a burst of inspiration. She explained that now that she had been interrupted, the inspiration was over. "My apartment used to be so clean," she said, swiping a smattering of dirt off the top of her desk and onto Cass's bare feet. "I let you come in here and change

The QUEER
FICTION ISSUE

McSWEENEY'S
QUARTERLY

ISSUE NO.
SIXTY-TWO

— — —

everything. How am I ever supposed to draw when this doesn't feel like my space anymore?"

"I'm sorry," Cass said. Something about seeing the bloom in Lana's eyes, now lingering unlike earlier, when it had vanished so quickly, made her think she shouldn't bring up the fact that it had been Lana's idea to turn the spare bedroom into a shared office. But it was also true that Lana had stopped drawing around the time Cass moved in, and she worried it really was her fault. The shop took up space and time, and the apartment looked nothing like before. Maybe Cass had been spending so much time caring for her green things that she had forgotten to nurture this thing between them. This thing that was also a life. This thing that could die.

"I'm sorry," Cass repeated.

"Why are you sorry? Stop saying you're sorry," Lana said, and Cass felt nipped in the bud. She tried to mend the moment by admiring the drawing.

"Who is she?"

Lana shrugged. "It's you."

She handed her the drawing, and Cass stared at the woman with branches for hair.

"But it doesn't look anything like me?"

"Of course it fucking does."

All night Cass dreamed of marigolds, growing first in the apartment, replacing all the death, then beyond, then inside of her, and she pulled fistfuls of invasive blossoms from her chest cavity, and they came out with bloodied ends. When she woke, she clutched at her chest, and all she found was the steady beat of her too-human heart.

Lana said she thought Cass had been sleepwalking. But I remember

The QUEER
FICTION ISSUE

THE PLANT GAME
by KAYLA KUMARI UPADHYAYA

ISSUE NO.
SIXTY-TWO

— — —

everything, Cass thought. She remembered the arch of Lana's back over the desk and the claw scratches of her pencil. She remembered the bloom. She remembered apologizing on a loop, and she remembered trying to kiss her in bed afterward, only to accidentally tongue a salty bit of her ear as Lana rolled away from her. She had never sleepwalked before, but then again, she had never gotten so little sleep. Maybe Lana was right.

She closed the shop for a week and then another. She was too tired to form a coherent sentence, and she was too depressed about her dying plants to even move around the apartment without feeling like someone had stuffed her full of soil. The space that had once felt so alive to her became suffocating again. So many things were dead or dying.

Scientific curiosity no longer gnawed at her. There was no rational explanation for the rapid death, and the more Cass worked to stop it, the more feral it grew. If science couldn't explain the problem, then maybe she was to blame. Maybe she had upset the delicate balance of life.

There were more dead things than not in the apartment, and Cass turned her attention to Lana. She started cooking again, making soups and stews and things of sustenance to warm the chill between them. She watered her with masala chai and broths yellowed by turmeric, tended to her with hand massages, fed her love notes and praise. On Lana's days off, Cass asked if she wanted to go out into the world and do something, but Lana only ever wanted to watch television, said she was tired from all the work. Cass couldn't complain; she wasn't sleeping either. So she cozied up to Lana on the couch, and they re-watched movies they'd already seen, until Cass inevitably fell asleep and Lana left her there, in the forest that was their living room.

The closer Cass pulled Lana in, the further away Lana got. She clipped every kiss short. She picked up extra shifts despite complaining

– – –

about how tired she was. She often interrupted their couch time to get up and clean the fallen debris around the apartment.

"I'll do that. You sit," Cass insisted, but Lana sighed and continued. She seemed, Cass thought, both too close to ever come into focus and too far away to even hear her.

A hand shook Cass awake. She opened her eyes, and Lana hovered over her. It felt like the middle of the night, but she quickly noted that Lana was dressed for work, that sunlight was just peeking in. "What time is it?" she asked, and Lana replied that it was four in the afternoon. Cass rubbed at her sleep-puffed eyes, confused. Even though her sleeping schedule had changed dramatically when she'd started dating Lana, she never slept through the day like Lana sometimes did. The sun would be setting soon. It was as if a whole day had been taken from her. All things have circadian rhythms. Even plants. And even they can be ruptured.

"I need you to clean the office," Lana said.

"Okay."

"Before I get home from work."

"Okay."

"And reopen the shop. What's the point of all these plants sitting here if we can't sell them?"

"We can't sell them if they're dying."

"Figure it out."

I'm trying. Can't you see how hard I'm trying?

A noise awoke Cass. Another disturbance. She could barely remember a time when she had woken up of her own accord. This time it really

- - -

was the middle of the night. She wondered if Lana was drawing again, and she checked the office first this time, but it was empty.

She tiptoed back into the hallway, and the sound became more like a whisper. Was it the plants? Were they finally talking to her again? She strained to listen. It was low and rhythmic, like the thrum of a drum. *Die, die, die.* She froze. That couldn't be it. *Die, die, die.*

She stared down the length of the hall and saw a dark shadow looming over a crest of green. "Hello," Cass asked out loud, though she was unsure if she was speaking with a plant or a person. The shadow turned and something fell off of it like a shed petal. She sucked in her breath and immediately felt woozy, palmed the wall, too tired to even know what she should be afraid of. The shadow moved toward her. It was Lana. It was just Lana.

"You have to stop sleepwalking," Lana said in a low, strange voice. "You're going to hurt yourself."

In the morning, Cass made a promise to herself to leave the apartment. It was only then that she couldn't remember the last time she had. By the time she woke up, Lana had already left for work, and the shy winter sun was already setting. So she wouldn't get much natural light, but at least she would get fresh air, Cass resolved. She dressed and heated up old soup to eat before booting up and leaving her death-stricken house.

She walked around the neighborhood, looking at the dormant trees readying themselves for a long winter before regrowth in the spring. Eventually, she got on the train and realized that the only place she knew how to get to without consulting her phone, which she'd left at home in her daze, was the bar where Lana worked, where she used to go most nights at the beginning of their relationship. She headed there. She could pick up flowers on the way to give to Lana. She tried not to think about what might happen to those flowers if they brought them home, but at least cut flowers had an intentional expiration date. They were temporary joys.

Cass didn't account for it being a Saturday night, and the restaurant was buzzing. She found a seat at the front bar, shed her layers, and looked around. At least the plants here were thriving. She clocked a sturdy snake plant behind the bar and wondered how much longer until the one back home would slither to its end.

A woman behind the bar slunk over. "Can I get you anything?" she asked. Cass looked up and felt, yet again, short of breath. Choked. Wilted. Standing before her was someone so familiar, so captivating, that she thought for a moment it might be one of the many nameless women she had kissed in dark bars before she came out.

"I'm sorry; you look so familiar."

The woman smiled and tucked her hair behind her ear, and that's when Cass figured it out. Her hair. It looked exactly like tree branches: wild strands in every direction. Her skin was pale, nearly translucent, like the unshaded body of a figure drawing. There was no mistaking it. She was the woman with branches for hair, the woman Lana had insisted was Cass despite zero resemblance.

Before Cass could say anything, she felt a jab on her shoulder and turned to see Lana, eyes full-bloom, no smile of surprise. "Babe, what are you doing here?"

Cass turned to look back at the woman with branches for hair, but she was already at the other end of the bar, talking to someone else. Cass asked Lana who she was. "Oh, that's Jade. She's new," Lana said, her eyes shifting to the flowers in Cass's hands.

"For you," Cass said, handing her the flowers. She felt the thorns again, the urge to puke up her soiled insides. She also thought she might be smelling lavender, but this time it burned her nose.

Lana explained that she was busy. She explained that Saturday

The QUEER
FICTION ISSUE

THE PLANT GAME
by KAYLA KUMARI UPADHYAYA

ISSUE NO.
SIXTY-TWO

– – –

nights are always horrible, didn't Cass remember? She explained that
she would put the flowers in some water but that she needed to work
and that Cass should order some food, eat, go home, wait for her.

Cass did as she was told.

Lana didn't come home. Cass waited until three in the morning, then
four, then it was past five and she couldn't bear the waiting. Lana
didn't answer her phone, and Cass felt the same as she had for weeks
when she tried to reach out to the plants and heard nothing in return.
She was alone. She couldn't reach anyone.

Cass imagined Lana dead, and then she imagined her with the girl with
branches for hair, and then she imagined herself covered in ingrown
marigolds again. She couldn't decide which vision was worse, and they
began to blur together in a mix of yellow plumes, crooked branches,
and glassy eyes. She filled a glass at the sink and downed it and then
another, trying to clear her head, trying to fix herself with water the
same way she'd thought she could save the spider plant.

She drifted into the spare bedroom, not quite sure what she was
looking for. Clues. Anything. She looked at the plants left in the room
and willed them to answer her, but they were silent, disconnected,
like Lana's phone. The looped ringing still played in her head from
the thirty-two outgoing calls she'd made since she got back from the
restaurant. She shuffled the papers on Lana's desk, but the girl with
branches for hair wasn't there, just unfinished sketches.

Cass knew this was an intrusion, that glimpsing these drawings was
like sneaking a look at Lana's brain. But she wanted to understand. Plants
were easy; people were harder to crack. Lana was one of the first people

The QUEER
FICTION ISSUE

McSWEENEY'S
QUARTERLY

ISSUE NO.
SIXTY-TWO

– – –

who hadn't completely confused Cass, but something had shifted. People are supposed to know each other better the longer they're together, but the opposite had happened with them. An estrangement. Cass traced her finger along one of the unfinished drawings and thought about how the first trees on this planet had had to rip themselves apart to grow.

What if she never comes back? Cass asked a wilted succulent. *What if none of this was real?* She didn't expect to hear anything in return, but the silence still stung.

She opened the cabinet next to Lana's desk. Lana kept her art supplies there, always organized neatly in some sort of system that Cass never got right, so Lana had long ago asked her not to clean up after her. It had been a while since Cass had looked in the cabinet, but right away she knew something was off. There were several bottles and cans inside. Had Lana picked up painting without telling her? She lifted a jug to inspect it.

It wasn't paint. It was a massive bottle of diquat. Herbicide. She pulled the other contents out of the cabinet. Bleach, weed killer, bug spray, drain cleaner, endless aerosol cans emblazoned with toxic warnings. She felt her own throat close as if she had taken the poisons herself.

The death wasn't an accident. The death wasn't a curse. The death was a distraction.

"Cass?"

At the sound of her name, she dropped a bottle of poison, caught catching. Cass slunk backward until her back touched the wall. Lana stood in the doorway, light behind her. Her long-limbed silhouette reminded Cass of a knotted milky mangrove, the tree whose skin can blister and blind. Most plants have a defense mechanism, but some are more cautious than others.

– – –

"Babe?" Lana stepped forward, and Cass felt the limb of an ivy plant snake down her back and gently clasp her wrist. She couldn't tell if it was holding her steady or trapping her.

She couldn't move, her mind working overtime to connect the dots, still fuzzed from sleepless nights. The loss of sleep, the fixation on fixing, the distance—none of it was as inexplicable as she had thought. It was designed, like sketched branches on a page. The death was a distraction, a game, maybe. But Cass couldn't even begin to comprehend who would play such a game. She looked at Lana and hoped to see something she might have missed before, but her girlfriend looked exactly as she always did.

This amount of effort was something Cass had never seen from Lana, not even in her art, which was perpetually unfinished. Lana gave Cass a hard time about her obsession, but Cass couldn't understand how someone could move through life without one. But here Lana was, plotting. She'd sown something magnificent and frightening.

Lana came closer, and the ivy tightened its grip around Cass's wrist until something wet dripped down her hand. She still couldn't move, still couldn't tell if the ivy was protecting her or pulling her closer to the hurt. Either way, she felt trapped.

Lana splayed her warm hand on Cass's cheek and looked genuinely concerned—frightened, even. Cass willed herself not to trust what she was seeing, to remember that the blindness caused by milky mangrove was only temporary. The ivy choked her wrist. She thought of the spider plant and its unceremonious demise, snuffed out by a slow poisoning. The edges of her vision blurred, and she became even more aware of the ivy's grip, certain it had broken the skin. Lana was a shadow in front of her, close enough that Cass could smell the lavender on her again. It choked her too. Lana's hand was still on Cass's cheek, and it felt firm, like the ivy's grip.

— — —

"Were you sleepwalking again?" Lana asked.

Despite everything Cass had unearthed, despite knowing in her gut that sleepwalking wasn't something she did, wasn't something she ever had done, she wondered if she was.

The QUEER
FICTION ISSUE

McSWEENEY'S
QUARTERLY

ISSUE NO.
SIXTY-TWO

LONELY
NOT LIKE
A CLOUD
by
VI KHI NAO

She recently returned to Vegas from a conference in Texas, where Joel Osteen recently denied humans affected by the flood shelter at his luxurious megachurch. Joel Osteen lectures and speaks sweetly, but his arms are the size of half-broken twigs. What would Jesus do?

Upon her return, another fellow Christian asks her if she will walk from Lake Mead to Hoover Dam with him and she says she would love to.

Since she is carless, he comes to collect her to take her to Lake Mead. They walk the long walk. She wears a long gray coat the color of postindustrial revolution, and blue jeans and a blue sweater and blue shirt to match the expansiveness of the sky. They walk the railroad passageway. Many other tourists, mostly fit, are walking along with them that day. They walk through the tunnels, tall and wide enough

– – –

to fit the train's waistband. The tunnels have been carved or bombed or dug from mountainous rocks and there are short passages of open air with no mountains between them.

"How many days do you think it took them to carve through that large mountain?" she asks him.

"I think they blew through it with dynamite."

"Look here. They must have gotten excited by sanding the edges, but boredom and lack of time may have prevented them from finishing their sanding, because the rest seems very rugged."

"How many bombs do you think they went through to dig all of that tunnel?"

They walk somewhere. The wind passes through their coats and sweaters. She zips up her sweater and gathers the edges of her coat and hugs her own shoulders. It is only sixty degrees. When they are not under the vigilant gaze of the sun, it feels to her like forty degrees. No one else is wearing a coat. She looks like an Eskimoed bluebell among a sea of daffodils. But she doesn't seem to care and neither does he.

Eventually, they sit down on a sand-colored bench and look at the expansiveness of the blue lake before them. She takes out a grapefruit and a plastic container of precut mangos. She offers them to him and he takes the mango. Acidity does not get along with his stomach, but he takes one or two bites to show her that he is not a true asshole but a team player. He also eats the energy bar she offers him. He actually enjoys eating it and this diminishes her temporary guilt about his stomach's aversion to acidity. She wants to take the mango from him. She wants to take everything from him except his manhood.

A healthy woman with short hair, in shorts and in her late forties, runs past them.

"She is too healthy," she observes.

"Not your type?"

"She seems like a woman who is hard to be intimate with. I wouldn't want to date her."

"What do you mean?"

"If you were in the mood to have pancakes at 2 a.m., she wouldn't eat with you. She is too healthy. Intimacies are built around shared experiences. It's hard to get close to people who are rigid about their meals."

"Watching you eat those pancakes could be intimate too."

"Being as healthy as she is, she would prevent me from even preparing the batter, let alone placing the butter on the grill."

"Extremely healthy people are a danger to society."

They get up and they start walking again.

"Have I told you the story about what it is like to date a vegan?" he asks.

"No."

"She was obsessed about me not eating meat in front of her. She said, 'Are you going to eat meat in front of me? If you are, don't.' She wanted to control everything I did. That's not love. I don't think she loved me. We would do everything together. Have sex, watch movies, and do other things, but when it came to food, I couldn't eat what I wanted. And she was one of those poor vegans, too, so she couldn't afford to have expensive, healthy vegan meals. She would eat really bad vegan things, not beans and rice, but things without any moisture in them."

"Why does she need to eat food with moisture in it?"

"It keeps the food fresh."

"It does? I thought it was the opposite."

"She only ate vegan chips. She ate chips all the time."

"That's a lot of sugar and oil and starch."

"I know."

"I would try to leave her, but she would stalk me. She would find me

The QUEER
FICTION ISSUE

LONELY NOT LIKE A CLOUD
by VI KHI NAO

ISSUE NO.
SIXTY-TWO

– – –

and throw a smoothie at my windshield and try to get me to come back to her. I tried to come back but she returned to her old ways and wanted me to be vegan like her. Why couldn't she be normal? Being a vegan doesn't seem that political or humane. Why can't she protect dogs—"

"That's a long way down. Do you think the trains derailed and tumbled down these high edges?"

"I don't think they derail. But maybe."

"So you were saying about being humane."

"There are ways to fight for causes without hurting another being. She hurt me."

"I am sorry she hurt you."

When the man pulls into the apartment complex's main-office driveway, she exits his car and stands outside the gate. She and her father could not open the gate to their apartment complex because they had lost the gate beeper. When her father went into the office to ask the landlord for a replacement, the landlord informed him that it would cost fifty dollars. So her father told her they would just live without it, and hopefully in a few months they could move out. They waited until the gates were opened by their neighbors, who came in and out of the complex on a regular basis. Sometimes the wait time was only one minute and at other times, ten to fifteen minutes.

After the man drops her off, she roams the vacant streets of Vegas, moving from one establishment to the next. She doesn't leave of her own volition, but due to the insensitivity of the establishments' workers. Smith's closes at 1 a.m. but its franchised Starbucks is open only till 7 p.m. Hiding herself in the obscure corner of the Smith's Starbucks during post-closing hours, in a dark recess where light from the bright fresh fruits and vegetables and bakery can't reach her, she sits, watching YouTube videos of Lady Gaga, alone with her MacBook Pro, not disturbing a soul. But Smith's cashiers and staff have been noticing her ubiquitous nocturnal presence. And although she does not harass

The QUEER
FICTION ISSUE

McSWEENEY'S
QUARTERLY

ISSUE NO.
SIXTY-TWO

– – –

or hurt or even bother them, her esoteric, nonconforming, antihuman behavior is a sore on their eyes, and that evening a staff member, not a manager, approaches her in the darkness of Starbucks's one-person leather sofa to let her know she can't be here after 7 p.m. The staff members like to make fugacious rules, rules they invent overnight, designed just for her, when her abnormal behavior appears to threaten no one. It's as if those dark maple, wooden Starbucks chairs blocking the entrance to the café had been erected as a barricade to prevent her from entering, so that she couldn't sit down in the dark to watch Lady Gaga or the alcoholic flights of antiheroine Jessica Jones, her face, which gives off the glow of a neon sign, randomly haunting the staff members' waking hours, especially those insomniac hours when they can't shut off the master-bedroom light of their minds, when their minds won't shut down and they feel totally dead on the inside, not like zombies but like those stale, leftover French baguettes they are forced to discard every day into large gray garbage bins.

After being kicked out of Smith's, she roams the streets of Vegas again. It's 1 a.m. She has a home, but her shoulders walk like a homeless person, droopy and a little hunched. Her eyes search the streets for 24-7 grocery stores or gas stations or casinos. Turning her body to the left, she notices the empty parking lot of the night. To the right, blinking neon lights of gas stations and restaurants compete with the loneliness of the obscure, unblinking bright signs of other businesses. She desperately does not want to return home, despite feeling utterly exhausted. Her eyes are falling asleep and her mind isn't awake. But she is afraid to return home, to her father's place. She isn't afraid to confront him or even to be around him. She is afraid she might forgive him. All he would need to do is smile or ask her if she has eaten. She has begun to see that forgiveness is reigniting the cycle of abuse. She does not want to forgive her father. A smile from him would be a killer.

The QUEER
FICTION ISSUE

LONELY NOT LIKE A CLOUD
by VI KHI NAO

ISSUE NO.
SIXTY-TWO

– – –

A quarter of a mile from her father's place, she spots a pub, not hidden from public view, but hidden from her until now. In fact, the pub is a massive orange building and it has always been there, so close to her own home. The pub is open 24-7. She stands in front of its entrance and, when she finally decides to try to enter, finds it locked. A sign catches her eye. It says to use the buzzer if the gate is locked. She hesitates. Should she go home and share a bed with her father? And face the inevitable? Or should she roam the vacant streets some more, or should she push the buzzer that would let her in, where she would be physically safe but maybe not psychologically?

A buzzer clicks the gate open. To test-drive her intuition, the door is unlatched. And, true to her calm but not cautious sensibilities, she walks in. The dining area is as bright as day, but no one—not a single soul, no waitstaff—is around. The pub is divided into three sections. The first section has been converted into a restaurant, the second into a bar room, and the third into a party room. Everything has the appearance and energy of a David Lynch film—polychromatic and dark and sultry and sad and fatuous. She unlatches the door to her right and walks in. She doesn't want to order anything. At Smith's she'd eaten a carton of Cheerios and isn't hungry. She just wants to watch the rest of the Kristen Stewart interview on YouTube. But the waiter's persistence activates her guilt and she caves in. She orders the apple crumble with ice cream and asks if it is okay to use her laptop.

She watches Kristen Stewart's jittery legs in nine interviews. One with Ellen; one with Jimmy Fallon, in which they take turns wearing earphones while trying to guess each other's spoken words; one with Kelly Reichardt and the actresses from *Certain Women*; one with *Camp X-Ray* director Peter Sattler (that one is boring); one with *Vanity Fair* editor Krista Smith; one with Peter Travers; one with Juliette Binoche. And so on and so forth. When she watches these interviews, she studies Kristen Stewart's body language and discovers that Kristen's energy

The QUEER
FICTION ISSUE

McSWEENEY'S
QUARTERLY

ISSUE NO.
SIXTY-TWO

– – –

vibrates at a different frequency than that of anyone she has ever known.

Later that evening, when she climbs into bed, she masturbates while thinking of Kristen. Kristen Stewart isn't her type, but she could be her type, given time and understanding. She masturbates thinking about her because she wants to sow telepathic energy between them, the sexual thread as a portal or a gate in which she could use the unfathomable, cosmic vim between them to encourage their two souls to vibrate at the same frequency. She masturbates to force herself to fall asleep fast, but also to open the cosmic window of Kristen in her soul. Only time will tell if their souls will align. Only time will tell if her orgasm has been effective in achieving her future endeavors.

She knows that it's time to head home when she begins to watch the ten most attractive men in the world. When she sees Prince William on the list, she tosses her hands in the air and leaves the pub immediately. Omar Borkan Al Gala is sexy, but William? She also wants to see Godfrey Gao's name. She considers his name to be the most sexy name in the world.

Before she falls asleep, she wonders why Kristen Stewart isn't her type.

Before she leaves the pub, the waiter introduces himself and calls himself Brandon. He says that the next time she wants to enter, she can press the buzzer.

She wakes up early but forces herself to fall back asleep so the daylight hours of her existence extinguish fast—like a chronic smoker who wishes not to experience the luxurious nicotine aftertaste but just wants to greedily and rapidly suck in all the smoke in one long, castrated inhale. But her lungs do not have the capacity of a swimmer's, and after taking one or two small, intermittent breaths she is awake. Fearing that her father will return home from his night with his girlfriend and thus force the inevitable encounter, she takes the

The QUEER
FICTION ISSUE

LONELY NOT LIKE A CLOUD
by VI KHI NAO

ISSUE NO.
SIXTY-TWO

– – –

quickest shower in the world. When foam from the soap collects in large batches of frothy clouds around her ankles and ambuscades the existence of her feet, she knows that the stress of homelessness and the stress of being in her father's home have exponentially grown; hair falling out in elephantine amounts is a symbol of female impotence and has the potential to block the flow of water, the flow of life from the top of her head down to her feet. With the dexterity of her toes, she lifts the lightweight metal strainer from the bathtub manhole and moves it a few inches to the left so that foam, soap, and water can pass through without her hair adding another layer of sieve. Out of the shower, she pumps the bottle of lotion, but nothing comes out. She presses all of her weight onto it, but not one drip. She nearly loses her balance putting all of her effort into it, but catches herself by clinging to the towel bar near the mirror at the last second. She notices a pair of red scissors leaning in a jar, and she uses them to cut the lotion bottle in half so she can apply its insignificant dribble of lotion onto her skin, already desiccated from the brutal dryness of the Vegas air. Despite the pump's inability to reach the remote regions of the bottle's corners, there is still a significant amount of lotion left, enough to cover her entire body. Cautiously, she opens the bathroom door, fearing that her father may have returned already, but the silence and darkness of the kitchen confirm otherwise. Naked, she opens the kitchen drawer near the refrigerator, and in one short, swift motion, she polyvinyl-chlorides the cut lotion bottle to prevent air from solidifying it. This extra step will allow her to use the remaining lotion for another day. She tosses the cut container into the large drawer of the bathroom cabinet and gets dressed.

In the evening, she walks out of her apartment complex and comes face to face with a fluffy terrier. It does not have a leash or a collar and appears to be lost and ownerless. She stares at it for at least a minute. The dog does not move and reciprocates her stare. It continues to

The QUEER
FICTION ISSUE

McSWEENEY'S
QUARTERLY

ISSUE NO.
SIXTY-TWO

– – –

stare at her until she begins to cross the street. It leaps in the air in an attempt at fake excitement for its existence and then, mimicking her, it crosses the street without looking to the left or right. It crosses the busy intersection mindlessly and a truck plunges forward. To her, it appears as if the dog has been squashed or flattened under the truck's wheels. The truck comes to a halt. There is massive confusion and the traffic stops. A surprise to her, the furry animal emerges from beneath the truck. It appears uninjured, or it appears injured but hyper and so gives off the appearance of having no injury. It runs all about while cars stop in the midst of the traffic. The hyper dog runs toward the traffic light and a woman gets out of her truck to chase after it as it runs quickly away from her. While all traffic halts on behalf of the dog and on behalf of her running after it, she catches up to the dog, curls it into her arms, and walks back to her truck. The driver, her husband, drives off once she enters with the dog in her arms.

The QUEER
FICTION ISSUE

McSWEENEY'S
QUARTERLY

ISSUE NO.
SIXTY-TWO

I KNOW
HOW THIS
DREAM ENDS
by
DENNIS
NORRIS II

I.

Mama's worried about me. She looks at me, eyes wide and round. She pulls me close, hugging me so tight I can't breathe. I complain. She says what Old Teacher used to say: "Sometimes a boy needs to take a deep breath and let it happen." Then she smiles, her lips stretched tight across her face, her eyes like fat water balloons ready to burst. She brushes her hand across my chest and down my sleeve, smoothing every wrinkle. "You ready?"

I nod. Good boys are supposed to be easy.

I am ten years old, and Mama says it's time to get baptized. I don't want to—I hate going to church—but Mama says it's past time I got this over with. She stands up and puts her coffee mug in the sink. "Let's hit the road."

The QUEER
FICTION ISSUE

I KNOW HOW THIS DREAM ENDS
by DENNIS NORRIS II

ISSUE NO.
SIXTY-TWO

— — —

I don't mind listening when the choir sings, but then Pastor starts preaching. He gets real big and loud. He says he's like the Big Bad Wolf: he huffs and he puffs and he blows the devil down. I don't mean to roll my eyes when he says that; it just happens.

Mama and I have been going to church every Sunday since school started—ever since she became friends with Old Teacher. He doesn't go to church anymore; he doesn't even live in town anymore, and when he got run out, I thought that was the end of church for us. But nope, not for Mama, and not for me either. Last week, at the end of service, she grabbed my hand and we marched down the aisle to officially join the church family. That means we dedicate our lives to Jesus, and that means we get baptized. Mama bought me a brand-new shirt and bowtie. She's been looking forward to this day all week.

I usually fall asleep in church. I have this recurring dream where I'm lost in the woods in winter. I'm surrounded by tree trunks and snow as far as the eye can see. Night has fallen, there's a sliver of moonlight to guide me, no squirrels, no birds, no life. Nothing but dead branches, moss, and rotting brown leaves poking through the snow. I take small steps, careful not to break any twigs. I hold my arms out, palms open, intercepting tree trunks, bark scratching my hands, moss soothing the skin around my scrapes. I'll never know if I am saved, because Mama pinches my arm when she catches me dozing. She hisses in my ear, telling me to wake up. I hate the way she sounds when she does that, like a snake slithering under my feet.

I am cold when I wake up from that dream, and sometimes I think maybe baptism is Mama's way of saving me. She says she's doing the best she can with me, and that this is one way I can help her out.

This is how it works:

At some point during the service, Pastor will bring all the people who're getting baptized to the wading pool in front of the sanctuary. It's all the way past the pulpit, where Pastor and the other ministers

The QUEER
FICTION ISSUE

McSWEENEY'S
QUARTERLY

ISSUE NO.
SIXTY-TWO

– – –

sit during the service, and past the piano and the organ and the drums, and even past the section where the choir sings. To get there, you walk to the front of the church, go through a door on the left, turn right, and take the stairs. The stairwell is wooden and very narrow. It's dark, and there are no windows. Any light that makes it into that stairwell comes from the top, where it opens onto the wading pool that sits behind the pulpit, against the wall, elevated as though resting at the top of a hill. Above it hang fluorescent lights and a giant wooden cross that extends almost to the ceiling. Pastor will stand inside and guide us, one by one, into the pool.

Most of the time, I don't want to be baptized, and I never want to go to church. But Mama says I need to be covered in the blood of the lamb—the lamb being Jesus. She says it's the only way to know you're truly safe, because it means God is protecting you. I don't know if I believe all that, but I do know that I'm not going to convince Mama to let it go. This morning she woke me up extra-early because our car broke down and we had to walk. Mama says she hasn't had time to get it fixed, but I know the truth, even though she won't admit it: She doesn't have enough money to get the car fixed. She never has enough money.

We walk down the driveway past the car, and turn right onto the sidewalk. A few doors down, we see Jeremy and his nana locking their front door. I watch them as they turn around and start walking to their car. When Jeremy sees me, he stares hard and stops, his mouth bending down into an ugly frown. His nana looks at Mama, puts her arm around Jeremy, and opens the car door. He climbs inside. They are going to church, too, but it's no use asking: they won't give us a ride, and, anyway, they go to the white church, on the other side of town.

"Come on," Mama says. "Forget about that boy." She points my head forward, and together we walk, her arm still tight around my shoulders.

– – –

We walk several blocks in silence. I'm looking at the sidewalk, trying not to step on any cracks. Mama warns me that we'd better walk faster or we're going to be late. Then she asks me why Jeremy seems so mad at me.

I shrug, even though I know the answer. I just don't know how to tell Mama. She's been through enough. I start to grab her hand but then I realize we're passing Mimi Kennedy's house. Her family walks to church every Sunday because they live in the nice part of town, only two blocks from the building. In the grass of their front yard, I can see the shadow of the cross that hangs off the side of the church. It reminds me of the wooden balance beam on the playground that I use every day during recess. I do jumps, turns, cartwheels. I land perfectly every time, and I throw my arms over my head, like the girls on TV.

I stop walking on the sidewalk and start tracing the edge of the cross-shadow in the grass with my toe, which I'm pointing inside my shoe. I'm about to do a leap when Mama grabs my arm and yanks me back onto the sidewalk. "Enough of that," she says. "We don't want you messing up the Kennedys' lawn. You've pissed them off enough. Let's go."

A few days ago there was an incident. Mimi Kennedy, who thinks she owns everything, was hogging the swings on the playground. The swings are really popular, so Principal created a rule: You have until one hundred *Mississippi*s to swing, and then you have to jump off and let the next person in line have a go. But you can get back in line as many times as you want to until recess is over. Mimi Kennedy wanted to swing real bad so she pretended like she had forgotten how to count to one hundred. I was next in line. I tried to wait patiently, but after another minute or two I told her that her time was up. She ignored me, so I pushed her off the swings, real hard, and she fell, landed in the

The QUEER
FICTION ISSUE

McSWEENEY'S
QUARTERLY

ISSUE NO.
SIXTY-TWO

– – –

wood chips, and skinned her knee. Jeremy was the first one by her side, but all the other boys followed right after, along with New Teacher.

Everyone likes Mimi Kennedy because she's light-skinned and she has good hair. Mama says I'm pretty too—too pretty for a boy. She says the other boys are scared of how pretty I am, and how soft. She says sometimes she is too.

Mimi Kennedy doesn't realize how good she has it. A few years back, her daddy built a swing set in their backyard. We have a backyard, too, but it's empty, nothing but prickly brown grass. Mama doesn't water it enough. When I play in the backyard, I can hear it crunching under my feet. Jeremy used to say the crunching sound was actually the grass screaming, but I'm not so sure. Old Teacher was at our house once, and he said brown grass is dead grass, and I said, "How can dead grass scream?"

Mimi Kennedy's backyard is full of soft green grass, just like her front yard. Her own daddy, her own swing set, her own green grass. She has everything! That's why I got so angry when she kept swinging. It was my turn! I watched as she pumped her legs, kicking and tucking, going higher and higher, and it felt like a volcano erupted inside me, the molten lava like energy coursing through me. Mimi Kennedy is always taking something away from me, and for once, I stopped it. I figured out how to be my own hero. Mama says that's how you know you're becoming a man.

I used to think Old Teacher might be my way out of the woods. He had a way about him, as Mama used to say. He could calm anyone with the slightest touch. Right before Thanksgiving, there was a fire in the school. It wasn't huge, but it was close to our classroom. He lined us up and walked us to our fire exit and out of the building. He chose me to lead the line. At one point, I felt him staring at me, and I knew he could see how scared I was. He walked next to me for a few minutes, his big hand on my back between my shoulder blades. Once everyone

– – –

in the class was outside, he kneeled next to me and put his arm around my shoulders. He was so close that his beard tickled my ear. He pointed near the wooden ship at the far edge of the playground. That was our fire safety spot. I had to lead the class to that spot while he stayed behind. He was so warm I felt like I was cocooned in a thick blanket that had just come out of the dryer. I had been trembling, but I stopped. I led the entire class that day, walking carefully and in a straight line. I was prepared to quiet everyone but there was no need. When we reached the ship, I stood hugging the main mast. I thought the other kids could hear my heart thumping hard against the wood. We watched as the fire truck arrived and the firefighters jumped down and started unraveling their hose. Jeremy stood next to me, the hair on his arm brushing against mine. I looked for Old Teacher, and when I saw him, I saluted him. I pretended I was a sailor at sea, with a hat made special for collecting my broken pieces. There was nobody but me and Jeremy on that boat, not even Old Teacher, and not even Mama—who keeps saying she can be my best friend now that Jeremy doesn't like me anymore.

When we arrive at church, we shuffle into the building. We used to slip in easy, but ever since Old Teacher left, people look at us and whisper.

"Good morning, saints," Mama always says. That gets her a few "How are you?"s, and sympathetic handshakes. But all the old women love me. They give me hugs and offer me candy, though Mama makes me wait until after service to eat it. She doesn't want me crinkling wrappers during communion. Today we hurry to our usual seats, near the back of the sanctuary.

Pastor is preaching a three-part series called "The Three L's of Life: Love, Lies, and Loss." I don't usually pay much attention to his sermons but this sounded like a miniseries I'd watch with Mama on a Saturday night. Two weeks ago was Love, and last week was Lies.

– – –

During Love, Pastor told us we have a responsibility to tell people we love them, even when it's obvious, and especially when it's not. He admitted it can be confusing to know if you really love someone, but he said he knows how to make it simple. He said you know you love someone when seeing them makes you the happiest you ever are—even if you don't get to talk or touch. Even if they're angry with you. This made a lot of sense to me because sometimes I'm angry with Mama, but I still love her so much it hurts.

I kept thinking about love two Sundays ago, and all through school that Monday. I thought about Jeremy, and how he was my best friend. I thought about how we watched *Are You Afraid of the Dark?* at his house, and the way he put his arm around me during scary parts. Or how his leg would press against mine in the backseat when his nana drove us to McDonald's. I thought about how I was always happy to see him at school, even though he pretended we didn't know each other. I realized I loved him.

Jeremy is the person I love.

That night, he came over. We went to my room and started watching TV. He wanted to watch something called the Stanley Cup. It was boring, but he leaned back and put his arm out, wanting me to cuddle next to him and to lay my head on his chest—just like we saw couples do on TV when we used to play at his house and his nana was watching her soap operas. Jeremy had a can of Pepsi in his other hand, and he kept pointing it at the TV and explaining the rules of hockey to me.

I pretended to care about what he was saying. I kept nodding and asking questions, but all I could think about was my responsibility. It began to feel like something heavy, like a thing I shouldn't share. After a while, I got quiet. I played with a loose thread on my T-shirt, and then I started crying. I'm not ashamed to cry in front of him, not like I am with the other boys. Even though it felt hard to breathe— and even though I sat up and then Jeremy sat up and interlaced his

The QUEER
FICTION ISSUE

I KNOW HOW THIS DREAM ENDS
by DENNIS NORRIS II

ISSUE NO.
SIXTY-TWO

– – –

fingers with mine, like he sometimes used to do when we walked to school and no one was looking—I knew I couldn't tell him what I'd realized in church the day before. I knew I'd figured out something that is the worst kind of secret. So I stayed there, curled up in my bed, crying into my knees.

For a few minutes, Jeremy held me. He rubbed my back, leaned in close, and said, "It's over. He can't hurt you anymore. He's gone." And even though I wasn't crying because of Old Teacher, I nodded. I cried harder and louder until Jeremy pressed his forehead against mine. He lifted my chin in his hand, cradling my jaw in his fingers. And then he kissed me. His lips were soft and still, and I felt small and safe.

This is why I love Jeremy.

When I calmed down, he stood up. He put his shoes on and left. I didn't know what his leaving meant until the next day, after school, when he had a bunch of boys over to his house to play basketball. Now he spends all his time with them, and with his girlfriend—Mimi Kennedy.

And that's the problem with girls like her: they steal everything from boys like me.

II.

I hold Mama's hand and listen as the choir sings. The church fills quickly. After the holidays, attendance seemed to dwindle. But when Pastor announced his three-part series, people started coming back. I watch as the saints file into the sanctuary. An old woman who sits near us gives me a piece of gum; her husband pats me on the back. My smile passes quickly, my eyes unable to keep from roaming the room. The last few minutes before the service begins always feel like a fashion show. Everyone's on display in their Sunday best.

It's only a few minutes later, when we are fully into the service, and a deaconess is giving the church announcements, that I find Mimi Kennedy's parents. They sit next to each other, and a few feet over sits Jeremy's nana. And tucked in the space between them is Jeremy! Suddenly I want to disappear. I do not want to get baptized, not today, in front of all these people, and not in front of Jeremy. His head tilts to the side, toward Mimi Kennedy, staring straight ahead at the pulpit.

I try to count the number of times I've invited Jeremy and his nana to come to church with us.

I bite my lip until I taste blood. My heart sinks to the soles of my feet.

Not long after that, it's time for those of us who're getting baptized to make our way down the aisle and past the front of the church. There's a room on the other side of the stairwell where a collection of white paper gowns are kept for the baptism ceremonies. They're nothing more than hospital gowns, but they beat being dipped in the pool in our church clothes.

I stand and grab Mama's hand, but she stays seated. She crumples her brow, confused.

"Come on," I say. "We don't want to be late."

She gestures for me to go without her, and when I don't, she frowns. "Oh," she says, "I'm not getting baptized. Sweetheart, I was baptized years ago." She looks off into the distance, out a window. "When I was about your age, actually." She smiles at me and shoos me off. I turn and look at the others. Most of them are walking down the center aisle, but Mama and I are sitting closer to the aisle on the far left. I take off, moving quickly. I am swift, light on my feet. I don't want to be seen. I try to make myself small. I know it doesn't matter—everyone will

– – –

see me once it happens. But I feel suddenly, painfully exposed—like everyone in town knows everything about me. I keep my eyes trained on the door I need to go through, and when I pass the row where Jeremy sits with Mimi Kennedy, all the way on the other side of the sanctuary, I make no movement to look in his direction. I remind myself that I am my own hero, and that after today, I will have God on my side.

Mama says I should be thinking about something holy as I'm getting baptized so I start wondering what Pastor will have to say about loss.

I unbuckle my suspenders and slide my pants down my legs. In my head, memories play like scenes from a film. I know the other people can't see or hear them, but I feel as though they can. I see Old Teacher, sitting in the pew next to Mama, looking over at me. I see him watching me on the playground during recess. I hear him saying, "I see you," as I dance and leap across the balance beam. My body tingles, hearing the smile in his voice. It feels so good to be seen.

I slip my bare feet into a pair of flimsy sandals with thick plastic thongs that go between my big toes and the rest of them. It's uncomfortable, and when I take steps, the sandals flop loudly against the soles of my feet. They are light blue—ugly and inelegant—and I hate them. By now I am in nothing but my underwear and the sandals. In this room, everyone looks at the ground as they undress and robe themselves. I pull a gown from a hanger and wrap it around myself. The gowns are one-size-fits-all, and I am the only child being baptized today. On top of that, I am small for my age. I pull the belt tight around my waist. The robe is too long for me, so the hem will have to drag along the floor.

We are told to wait until the choir starts singing, then to make our way into the stairwell and wait in the dark as Pastor finishes his remarks. In the room, we gather by the door. We stand in single file, oldest to youngest. This is the order in which we will be baptized. On the other side of the stairwell, we hear the singing begin.

"God's a-gonna trouble the water."

"God's a-gonna trouble the water."

Every month, during baptisms, the choir sings a different arrangement of "Wade in the Water." This month, three of the women sing a cappella.

Near the front of the line, just as the door opens, an old woman I've never seen steps out of line and comes close, cautioning me. "Sit," she says. I find a chair, and she kneels before me. She starts rolling up the hem of my robe. "We don't want you tripping as you climb those stairs." She looks up into my eyes and smiles. Her hands work quickly, folding and creasing the extra material. In the flurry of her movement, I see Old Teacher. I feel his hands move up my legs. I watch his fingers spread over my thighs, and I think of spiders scurrying all over my skin, looking to feed. Sometimes he growled when he touched me.

I shiver. Goose pimples rise all over my skin.

"Don't worry," the woman says as she stands up. She puts her hand out for me to hold, and sings with the choir. "Just follow me down to Jordan's stream. God's a-gonna trouble the water." Her voice makes me think of soil—brown and rich, both warm and cold.

We exit the room and she leaves me in the back of the line, moving toward the front, where she belongs, seemingly disappearing among the others. I watch as Pastor turns toward us and gestures with his hand, indicating the first in line to step into the light, and into the water. Each baptism takes no more than a minute or two. In the background, the trio continues singing, their voices sometimes precise and percussive, other times melodic, and always perfectly harmonious. When the soloist sings the word *children*, her voice easily

The QUEER
FICTION ISSUE

I KNOW HOW THIS DREAM ENDS
by DENNIS NORRIS II

ISSUE NO.
SIXTY-TWO

— — —

soaring through the sanctuary, I see my school. I see the sun shining through the leaves on the trees. I hear my classmates running around outside. I see Old Teacher watching me on those days when he asked me to stay inside for recess and do my balance beam exercises on a crease in the carpeting of our classroom. I feel his knees bumping against mine when we sat cross-legged in the beanbag chair reading books, his arm slipping around my waist. It wasn't every day, but it was many days.

As each baptism happens ahead of me, I move forward. With each step, I move closer to the light of the sanctuary. I feel Old Teacher as though he were still here, his whiskers tickling my cheek, his voice quiet in my ear—"I see you"—as though his voice had a direct line to my ear under the noise of the service.

I'm on the precipice now, about to step into the water. The front of my body is bathed in light, and I can barely see. I hear Pastor call my name, and I step down into the pool. The water is warm against my skin. He holds my hand, guiding me into the center of the pool. I feel his other hand, strong against my back, keeping me steady. Pastor's voice barrels through me, filling the sanctuary. As he speaks, reciting a few Bible verses, I look out into the audience. I see Mama, near the back, sitting on the edge of the pew, her hands clasped, her eyes wide with excitement. The women sitting around her lean close and congratulate her. I see Jeremy, and Mimi Kennedy. Jeremy is expressionless. It's Mimi Kennedy who draws my eyes to hers the longest. They squint. Her face is grave—as though someone had died. The only other time I've seen that look on her face was the day she walked into our classroom during recess. She needed to use the bathroom and the one closest to the school entrance was locked.

* * *

The QUEER
FICTION ISSUE

McSWEENEY'S
QUARTERLY

ISSUE NO.
SIXTY-TWO

– – –

Pastor looks me in the eye and nods. He dips me backward, submerging me fully in the water. The rules of baptism state that I must remain under water for seven seconds while Pastor says a quick prayer.

I close my eyes. I lean into Pastor, his arm supporting me, holding me up. I hear him speaking, but his words are muffled when they reach me. Despite the fact that I have no physical control, I feel completely safe with Pastor holding me under the water. I think of the woods from my dream, only this time it's spring. I look to the sky, its blue electric, its clouds like giant cotton balls, and I become aware of the snow melting around my feet. Dewdrops scatter like pepper flakes along the branches, pink and green buds aching to bloom.

And Jeremy.

There he is, behind me, wrapping his arms around my waist, his lips against my neck like a warm, wet washcloth. We are men now. Butterflies surround us, flitting from branch to branch. Warmth from the sun beats down on our skin. I know how this dream ends.

Pastor pulls me up. I gasp for breath, water streaming down my face. My hands immediately rub my eyes as I open them, the fluorescent light seeping in.

"God's a-gonna trouble the water."

The congregation applauds. Mama stands. More saints rise to their feet, their applause expanding until it drowns out the singing. I watch as Jeremy, and even Mimi Kennedy and her parents, stand and clap. As Pastor leads me out of the pool, I see Old Teacher, leaning against the school building.

I dismount from the balance beam, throwing my arms up and my head back.

He claps, sticks two fingers into his mouth, and whistles.

* * *

The QUEER
FICTION ISSUE

I KNOW HOW THIS DREAM ENDS
by DENNIS NORRIS II

ISSUE NO.
SIXTY-TWO

– – –

One Saturday a few months ago, there came a knock on our door.
Mama was busy in the kitchen so I ran to answer it. On the other side
I found Jeremy and his nana, and behind them, Mimi and her mama.
They were there to play with me while the women talked with Mama.
That Monday, our class had a substitute teacher. I watched through
a window when, just before lunch, Mama arrived in the parking lot.
I watched as police officers escorted her into the building. Mimi
Kennedy and Jeremy were the only people who would sit at my table,
though Jeremy wouldn't speak to me. Mimi wouldn't look at me until
after lunch. We colored together. I drew a forest of dead trees and
a ground covered in snow. She drew birds, and butterflies of yellow,
brown, and red. As she colored them in, she said, "Do you think your
Mama knew? Since they were dating?"

Something in her eyes—pity or pride or disgust—made me want
to run as far as I could from that school, that classroom. This town. I
even wanted to get away from Mama.

The thing is, even though Mama says we're a team, I understand
now that I have to be my own hero. Mama gets upset about Old Teacher
from time to time. She cries and calls herself a bad mother. She says
things like how could she not have known what that man was doing to
her boy. She says he used her to get to me. Sometimes she asks me if I
think he'll come back, but I know he won't.

A year passes.

Every morning Mama makes me breakfast before I head off to
school. She has a new job, which she says is half the battle. I think
she wishes she had a boyfriend, or at least a best friend, but no one
comes near our house. She brings me to church every Sunday, but it's
the same as everything else—we arrive, we sit alone, we leave. I think I

The QUEER
FICTION ISSUE

McSWEENEY'S
QUARTERLY

ISSUE NO.
SIXTY-TWO

– – –

understand her now when she tells me she can be my best friend. She's all I have, and I'm all she has. It's just the two of us in this world, and sometimes when it's like that, you wish you could be everything—and everyone—to the other person. We both know she can't be my best friend, because she's my mama, and I can't be her boyfriend, because I'm her son. But it doesn't stop you from feeling like you're failing the other person, does it? It doesn't stop you from feeling like you're not holding up your end of the bargain.

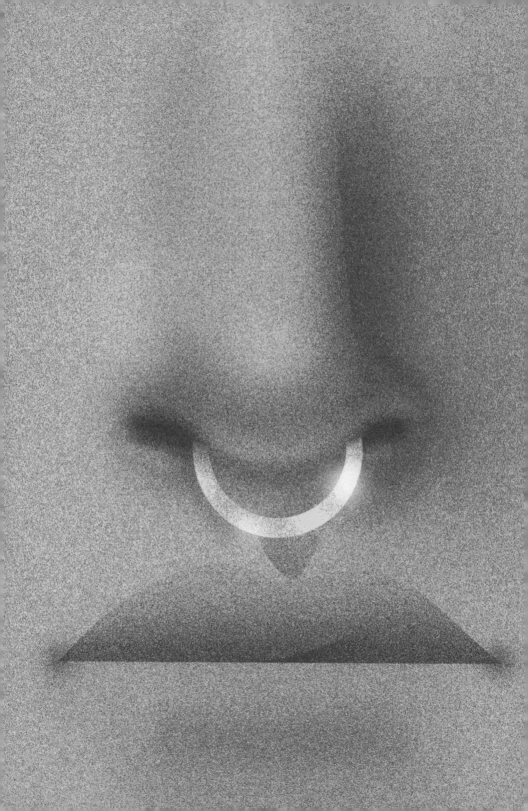

The QUEER
FICTION ISSUE

McSWEENEY'S
QUARTERLY

ISSUE NO.
SIXTY-TWO

GLASS
by
SARAH
GERARD

"Similar to other pain play, you experience a loss of control," said
Jesse. We were at an East Village monastery-themed biergarten where
the walls displayed murals of sodden monks pissing and fucking and
self-flagellating. Sitting on the patio, hidden from passersby behind
a vined lattice, I asked her what it feels like to be hit in the face. She
invited me to come fighting with her, but I confessed I was afraid she
would hurt me. She was small and I knew she could fight dirty. I'd
seen her get jumped in high school and laugh as the other girls beat
on her—I mean laugh hysterically—and they all scattered, disturbed.
"The rush comes from the flood of endorphins," she told me. "I've seen
people orgasm. I've seen them go into convulsions." She was bragging.
She liked that I was speechless. She'd always needed to be the center of

The QUEER
FICTION ISSUE

GLASS
by SARAH GERARD

ISSUE NO.
SIXTY-TWO

– – –

attention, needed to wield power by knocking a person off-balance. It had been sexy when we were teenagers, when other kids were afraid of her, but this was only because I was never the focus of her aggression until later. Rather, she'd never aimed it at me. Even when she did, in the end it only made me crave the restoration of her approval. But I was naive to think that if she scared other people, it meant she wasn't also afraid of them. Or afraid of me.

I was gauging all of this, sitting before her as an adult, framed by a tromp l'oeil of a row of reliquaries. Jesse was giggling. She thought she had shocked me.

"Pain play," I said, my expression neutral. "Is that a phrase you use often?"

"I like pain," she said. "I'm not sure if I should say more about that. I don't want to cross any boundaries."

I knew she did, though. This show of reluctance was a trick of our mirror neurons, her recognition of my introversion, a way to draw me in with a promise of safety, or danger, as I so desired. I hadn't seen her in over a decade but our familiarity in the flesh was immediate. I felt that she felt it. Her email, from out of the blue, said she'd moved to New York from Chicago with Ana, after a falling-out with their band. *I might only be saying this because I'm on ketamine, but I always had a crush on you*, she'd written, and I'll admit I was not in a good state of mind when I received this email. My husband had left me a month before, for his daughter's mother, a record producer more solvent and sober than I was, plus more attractive. A week later, my best friend since the second grade had died of a gunshot wound to the heart that the police called a suicide. I'd wanted to reach out to my ex-husband when I found out, but for legal reasons I was not allowed to, and also he'd blocked me.

In eleventh grade, Jesse had kissed me on the cheek in the student parking lot. She was a brassy blonde back then, with long roots, Sharpie eyeliner, stick-and-pokes, and self-inflicted scars, which I'd thought were impressive; I'd imitated them. Yes, I'd idolized her. I'd projected everything onto her.

"Let's save that for another time," I said now, and her eyes narrowed. A smile crept into the corner of her mouth. Over her shoulder, Ana approached from the bar. I'd lurked Ana online in advance of our hangout: she was doing erotic witchcraft on OnlyFans and maintaining a website, Sexcraft, which offered video tutorials, private divination sessions, and a sexstrology blog. Jesse had moved in with her the summer after high school, which seemed very adult to me at the time. She was four years older than we were, a significant gap on the cusp of adulthood. I remembered seeing her at punk shows, her head half-shaved, red lipstick, piercings, fighting, drinking, smoking, swearing. Now she writes about working with sigils for healing sexual trauma. She refers to her featured dildo of the week as her caduceus.

"She looks terrified, Jesse," Ana said, joining us. "Did you tell her the story about baptizing me? Jesse loves that story. She tells all her new girlfriends." She slid my beer across the table and our eyes met, hers hard and brittle as glass. She looked away, indifferent, lighting a joint from her purse.

"You tell her," said Jesse. "You're the one who broke up with me."

"We were drunk and on coke."

"You told me to kill myself."

"So Jesse grabs a knife from the kitchen, slices her wrist in front of me, and blood is spraying everywhere, like a geyser, in my mouth, all over me. I was in awe of her."

I said something incoherent, but they were laughing too loudly to hear me. My sense was that they were laughing at me directly. I flushed. Jesse held her wrist up and pulled the sleeve down for me to see, and the scar was there, ragged and translucent, a cross-section of stich marks down either side, like a caterpillar.

– – –

"I sat with her in the hospital for three days," said Ana, holding up that many fingers. The smoking joint was pinned between two of them, the cherry tilted toward me like an accusatory finger. "Then she did it again."

The second time Ana broke up with her, Jesse severed the major artery in her left thigh with a utility razor. She did this completely sober, they said, and the only reason she survived was because, at the last minute, she called Ana to say goodbye. Ana rushed home to find her in the bath, unconscious in cold water dyed red.

They finished this story and waited expectantly. Until now, I'd assumed the scar on Jesse's thigh was from an accident. I'd seen it immediately, as she'd made no attempt to hide it—was almost highlighting it with cutoff shorts and combat boots and knee-high stockings. It was over an inch wide at its middle, and the length of my hand, purple and smooth. It made my own scars look like a child's scrawls. Everything I did seemed childish compared with Jesse. Who had experienced real suffering. For love. Of Ana.

I owe much of what transpired over the following month to the fallout from that first night, after the bar. We stumbled a few blocks to St. Marks. It was after midnight but the street was thick with crust punks pickpocketing tourists, buying heroin and blow jobs from street-walkers. The kitschy bars and sidewalk cafés were still open. Jesse's parents had bought her an apartment on Avenue B. As it turned out, since being fired from the bike shop in high school, Jesse had never been expected to keep a job or pay rent. I would come to learn that she was incapable of doing these things. Her biological mother was a crack addict. This had had certain neurological consequences. Her adoptive father was an insurance actuary, a millionaire who threw money at the unsolvable problem of Jesse, indulging her every whim, then

– – –

repeatedly, at the last second, saving her from the grave. Her adoptive mother was a retired special ed. teacher who hoarded wine bottle corks in a steel washtub on top of the refrigerator. I remembered this being the case when we were kids, anyway.

By contrast, Ana paid rent to Jesse's parents for the apartment's second bedroom. She and Jesse had broken up two years before our reunion at the biergarten, yet continued living together. Yes, they had shared a bed for another year after Jesse's second suicide attempt, they told me. "Then Jesse made me move into the other room."

We stopped outside of a tattoo parlor two blocks from their apartment. Ana turned to me abruptly. "Jesse," she said. "Can you actually imagine her in a midriff?" She was easily half a foot taller than I was. She towered over me in a set of kitten heels. Jesse and I were at eye level. She looked at me and her gaze drifted to my clavicle, then to my belly button, and downward. "Would you dye your hair?" she asked me.

"I mean, I haven't since high school," I lied. Once, in my early twenties, I had bleached it, and I'd never admit I'd been thinking of Jesse when I did this. "But I'd consider it, based on the color," I said.

It had crossed my mind, in the days since Jesse's email, that she might have reached out to me specifically, recalling the longing I'd once had for her—sensing it emanating across time. I believe that's why she kissed me on the cheek in the student parking lot in eleventh grade. Even then, I imagined that she did it to stoke my desire, or to give me something to stoke it with, to keep it alive. I had touched myself so many times thinking of Jesse, even in recent years. I'd redacted color from my own body for her, marked it for her, purified it for her—in a certain sense, I'd carried her like an icon.

"She can sing too," said Jesse. "I remember."

"Let me hear it," said Ana.

People passed on either side of us. Had I not been drunk and drowning in grief for my friend and my marriage, I would not have

The QUEER
FICTION ISSUE

GLASS
by SARAH GERARD

ISSUE NO.
SIXTY-TWO

– – –

picked a Barton Carroll song, a song to drink alone to, to audition with. And it felt like that: an audition. A plea to take me in, for salvation, acceptance, and tenderness. As it happened, I sang the first two verses of a song called "Pretty Girl's Going to Ruin My Life (Again)."

Ana was stunned. We stood silent for several seconds after I finished, while she took in my performance. "She's Annie Clark," she said to Jesse.

"Listen," said Jesse, taking my wrist. "We're going to have to get more vulnerable with each other."

My arm lit up and she guided me toward the door of the tattoo parlor. "What are you doing?" I said, attempting a laugh, but her eyes were set, and the pressure of her fingers, and the feeling between my hips, shut me up. The air was antiseptic, electric with the buzz of needles outfitting guns.

"Think of this as an 'intimate-friend collaboration,'" she said. We stood before the display case. "I want to see you with a septum piercing." This statement replayed in my head several times: *I want to see you.*

"What happened with your last band?" I asked her.

"Why?"

"The album is hers," said Ana, appearing behind us, referring to their former lead singer. "Her name is the only one on it, but I think she'd agree we cocreated it."

Jesse was silent, her eyes on the jewelry. Her irises deep and translucent, a rich brown like rust, or like old blood dried on the sidewalk.

"We'll always love her," said Ana, "but she's hurt us, and she knows it. She'll need to prove that we can trust her again before we work with her."

"She wants to do another album with us," said Jesse. "I don't really want to."

It clicked all at once that they used to fuck. "You don't owe her anything," I heard myself saying. "You don't have to be her friend."

– – –

Jesse smiled and slid the consent form toward me. She handed me a pen. She paid sixty dollars, or her parents did, and she bought the jewelry. She held my hand while the piercer brought his instrument to the hard tissue between my nostrils. She tightened her grip when I closed my eyes, and he forced the spear through.

I was working at the Joe Coffee in Union Square. I'd get up at four in the morning to open by six. I had to build in time for my thirty-minute commute from Midwood, and would catch extra sleep on the train and eat croissants while counting the tills. After clocking out at two, I went around the corner to class for the second year of my MFA program, or I went to my part-time internship at a literary magazine, rejecting slush pile submissions and stuffing padded envelopes with tote bags. For some reason, I'd believed this internship would take me somewhere creatively. Jesse said it sounded like bourgeois capitalist fuckery. "You're filling the pockets of the rich," she scoffed. "All those magazines are backed by corporate money. Why don't you write some lyrics for us instead of wasting your time on unpaid labor you don't enjoy?"

I remembered that one of her favorite hobbies in high school had been debating with people about the finer points of Italian fascism-Bolshevism. She had been in favor, though she admitted it was utopian. I had kept the secret of her parents' money from our classmates, intuiting that for the sake of her self-image, she was ashamed of needing it, and ashamed of enjoying it, and I'd felt some sympathy for that. Not many people were invited to her house after school. I was one of the few.

I proceeded to her apartment from my internship for our first band practice. I was looking forward to showing her that my septum was healing nicely. I was flushing it twice a day with warm saline, as directed.

The QUEER
FICTION ISSUE

GLASS
by SARAH GERARD

ISSUE NO.
SIXTY-TWO

− − −

I arrived to discover that Ana was busy on camera and wouldn't
be joining us. "She's doing a new-moon collaboration with a friend,"
said Jesse. "They'll be in there for a few hours. You and I can lay down
vocals."

She picked up her guitar and began playing it. I paced the
living room. Her apartment was an expansive two-story loft with an
elevator. Scanning it now, I was unsurprised to find that Jesse was an
avid collector of what she termed "transgressive culture." Her DVD
collection spanned an entire wall, and was diligently alphabetized
by genre of exploitation, then by director. There were standards like
Gaspar Noé and Lars von Trier, *The Human Centipede*, and *Salò, or
the 120 Days of Sodom*, but most of the films and their makers I'd
never heard of.

The opposite wall was a tangle of cords connecting four levels of
mixing boards and pedals, an electronic drum set, a keyboard, two
amps, and a microphone.

I looked into the dining room, lined with books.

"What do you think?" she asked me about what she'd just played.
It was pink and fuzzy, rough textured, fed through distortion pedals.
My Bloody Valentine. Ride.

"I like it," I said. "Record it and I'll write you something this week."

"Write something now," she said.

"I can't."

"Why?"

"I'm too shy."

"That isn't real."

She began the song over again. I stood in the middle of the room
with my hands in my pockets, awkwardly shifting from foot to foot. I
laughed and looked at the floor, scrambling to decipher a melody amid
Jesse's chords, now midway through their first repetition, and on to
the second. She played four more bars and nodded for me to come in.

The QUEER
FICTION ISSUE

McSWEENEY'S
QUARTERLY

ISSUE NO.
SIXTY-TWO

– – –

I felt my pulse in my temples. I began to hum but my voice caught in my throat. I turned in panic to look at Ana's bedroom door. Blue light escaped from the crack beneath it.

"What's wrong?" said Jesse, stopping.

"I don't know if they can hear me."

"Who cares?"

I stood frozen.

"You sound amazing."

"No, I don't."

"Yes, you do. Again."

"No."

She was stunned. She had not expected me to disobey her. I glanced over my shoulder again at Ana's door, and heard now, faintly, music playing on the other side. Had it been playing before? Had she turned it on just now, to drown us out?

"She hears people sucking all the time," said Jesse.

"So you admit that I suck."

"Don't put words in my mouth."

I had touched a nerve. It gave me the distinct feeling of wanting to disappear. I ducked into the bathroom and locked the door. I slid to the tile and breathed into my hands and listened to her resume playing without me there. I'd failed to think of the simplest melody. My musical background did not include courses in composition. I thought I'd be learning songs that were already written. I had never written one. I'd had only a few guitar lessons from my autistic uncle, Marty.

I wanted to hang myself. A part of me had believed that Jesse resurfacing when she did was predestined. It happened just when I'd needed her. I'd needed her to fill the void of my ex-husband, my dead friend. I'd needed to channel my sadness, or avoid it, or I would drown in it. I'd needed the band to save me. And, yes, I thought I could save Jesse too. If she needed me.

The QUEER
FICTION ISSUE

GLASS
by SARAH GERARD

ISSUE NO.
SIXTY-TWO

– – –

My throat had constricted from crying. I stood and opened the shower and cranked it to its hottest setting. Her fixtures had been updated: brand-new tile, a glass brick window looking out on Tompkins Square Park. I sat on the shower bench and held my feet under the water and closed my eyes. I let my heart settle. I breathed from my diaphragm and felt my throat relax.

"Were you taking a shower?" Jesse said when I returned. She had opened a bottle of Ardbeg Scotch and was pouring herself a double.

"I was steaming my vocal cords."

"You're weird."

She poured me a glass and handed it over, but I declined. "I actually can't stay long," I apologized. "Sorry to waste your time. I have to get up at four in the morning tomorrow."

"Why?"

"To open the café."

"Isn't the café, like, right around the corner?"

I gathered the implication. She sat on the chair beside me and looked up from my breasts into my face. Her knee fell just within my sphere of sensation. The hairs on my calf stood up.

"Does that help you feel more relaxed?" she said.

"It does."

"Then relax."

I sat and she passed me my drink. She began playing a different song. This one was softer and slower, a bluer hue. "In a sense, the trick is to not pay attention to what's happening right in front of you," she said. "Fool yourself into hearing the melody without meaning to. Don't think too much about it. We can talk."

The thing is, Jesse saw my potential. She initiated me into a state of being I had never seen for myself, yet had wanted blindly. My husband had never seen it. No lover had ever seen it. No teacher or editor had ever seen it. Jesse saw it.

We talked about her plans for future body modifications. She collected them the same way she collected books and movies, and the difference as I saw it was that, whereas the pain of her cultural collectors' items was a depicted one, the pain inherent in body modification was lived. So then would it be reductive to say here, in no uncertain terms, that Jesse was a sadomasochist? What I mean is that, despite how it may seem in the end, I was only a masochist.

I slept through my alarm and awoke just before I needed to leave. I tried to wake Jesse to say goodbye, but she was sleeping so deeply that for a minute I worried she wasn't breathing. We'd finished the bottle of Ardbeg and I was still drunk when I left a note on her nightstand, thanking her for being patient with me: *Who knew our voices would sound so good together?*

The sun rose over Manhattan.

In the afternoon, she texted me twenty seconds of the song we'd written. **Come over tonight and finish it**, she said.

I rearranged everything. It was understood that there would be band practice whenever I had my internship, since Jesse lived nearby. Then she discovered that my school was around the corner, too, so I quit my internship and began reporting directly to her apartment after class. Staying with her was easier than commuting from Midwood; it saved me an hour on the train, round-trip, so I slept an hour later. I fantasized about the band progressing to such a degree that I would be asked to move in and pay rent to Jesse's parents like Ana did—I would do it for the privilege of sharing her bed, though I did not sleep better at her apartment; I slept very little when I stayed there. I would do it for the satisfaction of being seen by my ex-husband's child's mother, the music producer.

The QUEER
FICTION ISSUE

GLASS
by SARAH GERARD

ISSUE NO.
SIXTY-TWO

- - -

Between practices, we maintained a constant stream of correspon-
dence related to the band. I came to understand that, although I was
the vocalist, Jesse was the bandleader: she loaned me a Telecaster and
a practice amp, booked me an appointment at Seagull Salon, sent me
links to shirts and skirts and boots, tattoos, songs and videos, scraps
of songs she was writing, and designs for logos, and it was understood
that I would build upon these ideas prior to our practice each evening.

One day I arrived while she was at boxing. "She's not here," Ana said,
disappearing down the hallway into her room. I closed the front door
and felt small beneath the vaulted ceiling. I stood staring at Ana's door
for several minutes and considered knocking, but she might have been
broadcasting, and I might have already interrupted. And if I were to
interrupt her again, standing in the frame of her doorway, backlit by
the soft light of Jesse's hall, what would I do, then—join her? Tip her?

Ana had not participated in any practices. At a certain point, I'd
suggested to Jesse that we might want to start a band group text so
Ana could be included in our collaborations and wouldn't feel left out.
Jesse hadn't made a move to initiate this, and I hadn't asked her why,
afraid to know the truth. I chose to believe for this early period that
Ana's cam schedule conflicted with ours for the band. I wanted her
to want to be kept abreast of our new collaboration so that, when the
camming and band practice schedules aligned for her, she would be up
to speed. Perhaps her sex work was more seasonal than I knew—I had
never done it. Perhaps it was the season of Beltane, or the transit of
Venus, or the new moon in Leo, or some shit.

I'd asked Jesse what Ana's contribution would be to certain songs we
were composing, but her answers were always vague: "Later." I set my
backpack by the drum kit and opened the window to sit on the sill, as
I'd seen her do. I imagined her spotting me as she came up the street,

The QUEER
FICTION ISSUE

McSWEENEY'S
QUARTERLY

ISSUE NO.
SIXTY-TWO

– – –

my silhouette looking down on her, watching her approach. She came in sometime later, sweating and dirty, bruised and panting, looking feral. I followed her into the bathroom and watched dumbly as she turned the water on. She peeled off her clothing. Her hands were taped; she unbound them. I asked why Ana hadn't been practicing with us.

"Oh, yeah," she said. "She doesn't like you," she added, as an afterthought.

"She doesn't?"

"She never has." She sank into the tub. She leaned back on the plastic cushion she kept for soaking. I sat on the closed lid of the toilet, staring into the roar of the faucet. "She never wanted me hang out with you, you know," she said, "even after high school."

"Was she jealous?"

"No."

"Why did she suggest we start a band?"

Jesse laughed. "Because it's funny."

She closed her eyes as the room filled with steam. I recalled the experience of asking Jesse to prom. She'd said yes and I was elated, made my own dress, arranged to borrow my father's car. Then she started dating Ana. Canceled on me at the last minute. Said Ana had told her to.

"Why do you care?" Jesse said. "Ana sucks."

"I thought you were twin flames."

"I can set boundaries without telling her I'm setting boundaries."

We sat in silence. She drained the bath and suggested we order Seamless. Jesse never cooked, nor did she buy groceries. Only liquor. Now that I'm thinking about it, it was as if Jesse didn't care much about her life; she was complacent and self-destructive, had possessions but no purpose. Didn't have any attachment to her possessions; rather, she was a collector of objects and of people as objects, as tools for her enjoyment and disposal. Jesse lacked a soul so she attempted

The QUEER
FICTION ISSUE

GLASS
by SARAH GERARD

ISSUE NO.
SIXTY-TWO

— — —

to fill the lack with others'. But just as a soul is endless, so is the void where a soul is missing.

After laying down vocals for "Cracklove," we got drunk and watched *Cannibal Holocaust* on the leather sofa, and around the time that the film crew started hacking open the turtle, Jesse reached over and ran her hand up the inside of my thigh.

"Ana is right there," I said, pointing to her door, feet away, suggesting we move to the bedroom.

Despite my marriage, or perhaps because of it, I didn't know what good sex could be like. With a woman or with anyone, I had very low expectations. Jesse's sex toys were Ana's throwaways from passed-up endorsement offers. Ana's image was curated. Sustainable, all-natural, organic, nontoxic, glass or quartz, and her color palette changed astrologically, or according to that day's featured tarot card. I knew this because I'd watched all her videos.

By contrast, Jesse kept a loose-weave basket beneath her bed: vinyl ropes, party-store handcuffs, mass-produced designer dildos manufactured in China, harnesses, ski masks, ball gags, collars, a dull knife. I performed as if this was kinky. I didn't know better, thought I was supposed to. I didn't know kinky. It wasn't something I believed came from within.

Also, sex was not what I wanted from this relationship. It would have been preferable to the alternate purpose I wanted it to serve, however, which was to heal my broken childhood, though I wouldn't have been able to articulate this to myself at the time. I had to learn it. I had to learn consent. Among other things.

Jesse strapped on Ana's leather harness and a vibrating purple dildo with sparkles. I got on all fours, asking for doggy-style.

She was sloppy; it was sad.

– – –

"Want to see how Ana likes it?" she said. She pulled out and rolled me onto my back. Swung my legs over her shoulders. "She gets horny when she's on her period," she told me. "This is how I'd have to fuck her."

"Why are you saying this?"

I watched her face as she entered. She saw my horror, I'm certain. "Sometimes I'd pretend I was spitting on her," she said. She pretended to do this. I struggled beneath her. "Then I'd choke her until she'd squirt."

"Please stop."

"Don't be a baby." She stood abruptly. She walked away, naked and hung, slamming the bedroom door.

Jesse habitually slept until four in the afternoon. I was never able to wake her, and her snoring scared the neighbors. They pulled me aside in the vestibule and I'd tell them Jesse had a sleep disorder. It was not completely a lie; it was why she took Ativan, so she claimed. I asked Jesse if her psychiatrist knew she was drinking. "It's fine," she grinned, as if it was funny. Since joining the band, I had moved continuously through a cloud of increasingly potent chemical agents: Xanax, Vicodin, fentanyl.

I asked Jesse to help me come down from Adderall. I'd been using it during the last week of the semester and hadn't slept for days, hadn't eaten, felt like a tweaker. She fed me and gave me two Seroquel. I slept through the weekend, and when I awoke, Ana was looking down on me.

She and Jesse were laughing. My mouth didn't work; I couldn't feel it. When I tried to form words, it took a huge effort.

So I remained silent, nodding off in the kitchen.

Ana had been messaging with their ex-bandmate, she told us. I learned her name was Gretchen. "She's such a good girl," Ana said.

The QUEER
FICTION ISSUE

GLASS
by SARAH GERARD

ISSUE NO.
SIXTY-TWO

– – –

"An old soul." She smiled at Jesse. "We've grown close again," she said. Then she smiled at me. "We're recording."

I brought Jesse to the birthday party of my friend from high school. Jesse remembered Hannah as a mousy rule-follower, but that's because she didn't know that in high school Hannah's parents' best friend had paid for her abortion. We took the Long Island Rail Road, and to pass the time, Jesse suggested we play a game. It reminded me of a game I'd played with myself when I was a teenager: I'd pour salt on my arm and hold an ice cube over it and let the salt burn a layer of skin away. At first it would be numb, then the pain would set in slowly. I guess the fun was in getting to lick the salt. Today, there's a section of skin on my arm with no freckles.

Jesse told me the rules of our game. Each of us would bite the other as hard as we could. Whoever pulled away first was the loser.

I went first. I took a fold of her skin in my teeth. It came up from the back of her hand in a thin tent. I increased the pressure of my teeth until I was using the full force of my jaw. Long Island slid past outside the windows, ugly as hell. It felt good to bite something. I stared at the endless interlocking parking lots, making escape impossible. The expanses of no trees. Jesse's skin was supple and I imagined my teeth biting clear through it. Bone meeting bone. She pulled away.

"Stop it, you pussy." She gawked at it. A bruise was forming. "Fucking freak."

I presented my own hand. I decided I would not pull away, no matter how much she hurt me. I closed my eyes and prepared myself. She lowered her head and pain shot through my arm. I opened them and watched her coolly. "It doesn't hurt."

* * *

The party was stiff with libertarians. Hannah had married a day trader twenty years her senior who was paying for her M.Ed. at Hofstra. He had fathered the baby she was carrying. Her maternity dress was royal blue and seemed to expand around her. Their house was a replica of a Polly Pocket with a waterfall pool. Jesse expressed her boredom by drinking four Coronas in the space of thirty minutes and subtly mocking people around the patio table. She thought they were too dumb to notice but they were too polite to say anything. I wondered what she thought of me bringing her. I hadn't wanted to, but she'd insisted on coming with me to the event that was causing me to miss band practice.

I reminded myself that I was not responsible for her behavior. I met her eye but couldn't hear what she was saying to the person next to her. She smirked, seeing Hannah lean into me.

"I overheard Jesse say you're in a band now," she said.

"We're working on an album."

"Are you...?"

I waited.

"Who's the vocalist?" she managed.

"I am, but it's more Jesse's band," I said. "The hair was Jesse's idea." I turned my head to show her. "So was the septum."

She smiled sadly. Then her palm flew to her mouth. "What happened to your hand?"

"I burned it," I said. "Do you have a Band-Aid?"

She pushed back her chair. I watched her struggle to her feet, and followed her down the length of the pool, away from the party, through a sliding-glass door to the master bedroom, which was cool from climate control, and vacuumed, the bed made, expecting guests. Hannah believed she could insert herself into my relationship with Jesse, I figured, as though marrying someone old enough to be our father made her older by association—but I have to admit that, in

The QUEER
FICTION ISSUE

GLASS
by SARAH GERARD

ISSUE NO.
SIXTY-TWO

– – –

retrospect, I am grateful for her intrusion. I decided at the time to play into her caretaking urges. To let her mother me. Yet I was also feeling wicked. The room smelled like a Glade PlugIn. A king-size bed with a sheer white canopy sat on a raised wooden platform in the center. We circled it to reach the bathroom. One wall was covered in mirrors.

"If I have one, it's in here," she said. She pushed a mirror at eye level. It popped open. "How badly does it hurt?"

"Pretty bad."

She extracted a bottle of hydrocodone. "You know, we don't keep in touch as much as we used to."

"You're right."

"I hope you know you can talk to me."

She stood in the doorway. One hand rested on her prodigious hip. She rubbed it.

"Thanks," I said. "You can talk to me too."

She left and I took a shit. I cleaned myself with a baby wipe from the box on the toilet. I rummaged through her cabinets. Viagra. I'd seen Richard look tired standing from a seated position. I wondered how long it would be before Hannah initiated an affair with a fellow elementary school teacher. Xanax. There were maybe twelve bars. I stole six. I replaced the bottle back exactly as it was.

In the bedroom, I stood for a long time before the dresser. A collection of framed photographs sat atop it. I looked into the faces. Richard was fishing on a seawall beside three children. The children were replicated in two other photographs. I slid open the drawer at my hip. There was a leather apparatus inside, not a belt, but also not suspenders. In the center, a brass ring connected four leather straps, which looped around to meet one another in a triangle shape.

Two buckles. Two leg holes. One rubber cock.

Something shattered outside. I exited the room and ran across the flagstones toward the sounds of people shouting. Jesse was among

– – –

them, and Hannah, and now several others, were scrapping on the ground. At the patio table, Richard held his face in his hands. Blood dripped onto his khakis. Beside him, a woman was straddling Jesse's chest, and Jesse was cackling. Someone pulled the woman away by her armpits. Jesse scrambled up from the grass and disappeared around the side of the house. Two people followed. I considered running after them, then turned back to the table to find my bag.

"You need to leave," Hannah said. She was already on the phone. Richard was tilting his head backward.

"I'm just getting my purse."

"I'm calling the police."

"I don't even know what happened."

"Who are you anymore?"

I awoke with my nose oozing pus. It was one in the afternoon, a day later, and Jesse was sleeping or dead on the floor beside the bed, which was sodden in urine: not mine. I crawled to the bathroom and lifted myself onto the sink. I looked at my fucked-up face in the mirror. An abscess had opened up inside my septum and had swallowed one side of the jewelry. I had to turn my nose inside out to find the end of it. The act sent pain shooting into my eyes. I gripped the side of the sink and cried. I dug the ring out with a pair of pliers I found beneath the sink. I've saved the broken ring in a box. I carry it from city to city.

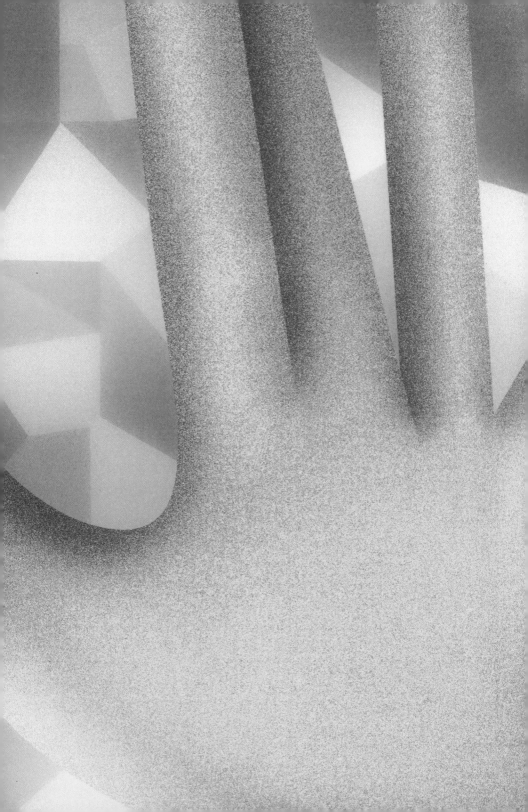

THE
GEODIC BODY
by
BRIDGET
BREWER

—Give her Jesse, the men chanted. Go on, beat the Jesse out of her.

I remember rain. It's hard to understand rain in the prairie.

The whore, pressed against the woodshed, lifted her skirts high above her head—a shield or a surrender: both seemed possible. She wore a ribbon round her neck. Was it to keep her head from falling off, like in the fable? My heel slid in the mud. A man looked down at me.

—You should go home, girl.

His fingers played with a coin.

—I'm not a girl, I said.

The men were taunting her.

—Would you like the Jesse beaten out of you?

After, for years, I believed the whore had been like a nesting

The QUEER
FICTION ISSUE

THE GEODIC BODY
by BRIDGET BREWER

ISSUE NO.
SIXTY-TWO

– – –

doll—that she'd had two people living inside her, one named Jesse, the other with her Christian name, and that these men had wanted to beat Jesse into a separate existence, for sport or out of some kind of divine compulsion. Eventually, I learned that "Jesse" meant "hell." The men meant to give her hell—to beat her so hard that she coughed up her own afterlife.

The whore rolled her eyes.

—Go on then, gentlemen, if you're so jo-fired.

Her skirts did not quiver.

She's unafraid, I thought.

The sky, slavering, pressed down, folded upon the flat land, until the horizon was lost.

Later, the men were tried—a rare moment of justice, a hanging while the sun went down—but the town fixated upon me. Why had a child—dressed only in breeches, no less—watched such a violent affair and not gone for help, or even screamed? And why, in the aftermath, once the men slunk away, had this child come to the body and grabbed a fistful of the bloody earth and eaten it right there?

—Let's hope she don't go mad and make a die of it, said the judge, ruling me innocent. They called me Graveyard from that day on.

So often I dreamed the same dream: A swarm of locusts thick as a mourning sheet, the sky coal-dark, insects skittering some-where—I could hear them eating and shitting out our wheat. I would sink into the pestilential hum, then fall deeper, deeper through time, until I felt my own primordial ooze, became a quivering, half-formed creature still in the womb, a protuberance my mother refused to sing to while her horses froze to death at their hitching posts.

I would awaken, aware. The first cry I made in this life was one of desire, and the last shall be a response to that call.

The QUEER
FICTION ISSUE

McSWEENEY'S
QUARTERLY

ISSUE NO.
SIXTY-TWO

— — —

*   *   *

The town where we lived was built on a riverbank, a small tear in the prairie. People came in wagons, sodbusters settling in homes made of dirt clods, and died with their feet sticking out of the soil. Bounties meant babies. When times were lean, horses were shot for their meat. Flour was rare. Clothes wore out. I'm not saying it was simple. I'm saying there was an order I could not help but break.

For food, I caught ground mice and voles. I caught prairie grouse. I caught passenger pigeons; I roasted locusts; I taught myself the ways of wild hares. I fought grass snakes and won. I followed rattlesnakes to their dens, dark nests that stank sweet, reeked sour, like the hair rimming one's secret holes: I smelled the rattlesnakes and sang as I speared them, a riot of hissing deep down in the earth. I couldn't manage deer, bison, or wolves, but in the end, when we were hungry, my mother coughing up the mess in her chest, it was my catch of rattlesnakes that saved us. I stripped them, fried them with lard in the pan, browned them, turned them over, browned them again.

—What is this, said my mother, revolted, jaundiced, jabbing at the seared white meat, but already I had come to crave the poisonous and subterranean. I filled my mouth with snake flesh, rocking my pelvis against the edge of my chair.

—What is this, my mother would say, looking at me, and for her I had no answer.

One day I looked up from milking the cow. In the distance, against the hills downstream, I could see small movements. The wind bore the smell of campfire from some Native settlement nearby.

The QUEER
FICTION ISSUE

THE GEODIC BODY
by BRIDGET BREWER

ISSUE NO.
SIXTY-TWO

— — —

—Ma, I called. New sodbusters.

Through the window, I heard my mother curse.

I watched the sodbusters approach as I harvested hard knots of potatoes and scattered the feed for the grouse. When, at dusk, they finally arrived, I counted four—one woman, three girls—hemlines limp, blouses sullied, bare feet crusted with blood and caked in mud.

—Where're your shoes? I asked.

None of them answered.

—We've come far today, said the woman, voice worn.

I stood and wiped my palms on my apron. I held out my hand. She took it.

—My mother has made ash cakes, I said. We're out of coffee.

—Thank you, said the woman. A bead of sweat ran down her wide cheek.

Inside, my mother and I sat on the ground while the sodbusters sat on our benches around the fire and ate, sucking to soften the hard, unleavened bread. My mother asked their names and origin. They were a woman called Jane and her daughters, Miriam, Ellen Madora, Vilate. They'd come on foot from a town a few states over, said Jane.

—But that's a month's worth of walking! my mother exclaimed.

And no shoes to do it in, I thought.

—Didn't know Ohio let in folks like you, said my mother.

—They didn't, said Jane, tearing at the burned edge of ash cake.

—Let us hope the lords of Belle's Landing can find it in their hearts to be hospitable, my mother offered.

—Don't set your heart on it, said Jane. They already made me pay my five hundred dollars.

My mother grunted and drank from her tin cup.

Jane inspired a curiosity in me that most people I knew could not. I was old enough that I'd heard stories of people like her, and the roof of my mouth itched with questions.

The QUEER
FICTION ISSUE

McSWEENEY'S
QUARTERLY

ISSUE NO.
SIXTY-TWO

— — —

—Were you slaves before?

Jane watched me.

—Yes, she said. Her daughters stayed silent, unmoving.

—What kind of slaves were you? The field ones or the house ones?

Jane shoveled crumbs of ash cake onto her pink tongue.

—The kind that should have been freed, she said.

—But how did you get five hundred dollars? I said.

A silence I had caused.

—What's your name? she asked me.

—Graveyard, I said, trying it out. My mother kicked me. Jane raised an eyebrow.

—The townsfolk call her that, said my mother. But I gave her a good Christian name.

I gave Jane my good Christian name.

— _____ , Jane repeated.

Then she looked upon me—not at me or through me but upon me, as if she had beheld me for a thousand years before this moment and knew she had at least a thousand years left in which she would have to contend with me, with the likes of me, with the many, many likes of me. Outside, the crickets spoke in a language I could not fathom.

— _____ , she said at last, you'd do better to treat me with courtesy.

I felt my stomach drop down the well of my body.

—I was only asking, I said.

Jane sat silent. The crickets hummed. The cow lowed in the barn. I thought of killdeer eggs, clustered, disguised as stones on the river-bank to hide from the mouths of snakes, who always, always found them anyway. My skin itched, as if trying to shed. I saw myself anew.

—I'm sorry, I said.

Jane nodded.

The ash cakes were finished in silence. Then the family rose, and one by one they walked back out into the thick, warm night.

The QUEER
FICTION ISSUE

THE GEODIC BODY
by BRIDGET BREWER

ISSUE NO.
SIXTY-TWO

— — —

*   *   *

I found a two-headed snake on the red mud riverbank. She writhed and
spit, her rattler raised above the sludge. I could not kill her, though
hunger was in my gut, for I could see she was my twin.

The river turned to creek, turned to trickle, turned dead; all manner
of varmints vanished from the landscape; the wind lashed my face.
The sky and the plains shared a jaundiced yellow. Sod homes were
abandoned. Gusts ripped away the dirt covering the graves and filled
the air with an uncloaked stench. Some tried to ship in hay for their
horses, but the wheels of the caravans could not move for all the dust.
I shrank to a skeletal, unstable stork, sifting through the detritus for
a locust or beetle to chew. My mother dried up, reduced to a sheet of
thin hide curled up on the bed. I would pick up her arm and let it drop
to her side again.

—Mother, I would say. Mother, tell me what to do.

The days washed together. I couldn't tell you what day it was, what
hour, when at last I stood on trembling legs after digging through an
abandoned dugout for food, preparing to crawl home empty-handed
again.

I raised my eyes. A tall rock, an entire ovoid mountain, floated
before me, unanchored.

Only then did I realize how hungry my eyes had been for a break
in the bleak horizon.

The object hovered, somehow both close enough to touch and too
far above even for tiptoes. Was it a rock? That word seemed too simple.
Who had taught me the word *geode*? Had it been the trapper who'd
passed through last winter? I couldn't remember, but it hardly seemed
to matter: the word for this tall body was *geode*, I knew. Its exterior,

The QUEER
FICTION ISSUE

McSWEENEY'S
QUARTERLY

ISSUE NO.
SIXTY-TWO

– – –

though sloping, seemed common and jagged, but, as if sliced by the sword of an archangel, the geode had been halved, its center revealed. What a paradise within! A grotto made of crystals so lush they burst and broke against one another. A fountain, water pouring down, pure and fragrant, to wet the dust at my feet. I fell to my knees. A new lake rose to my waist, entered each of my many pores. I felt my skin gulp the wet, felt pleasure rack my body. I bent my head and I drank. My flesh swelled.

When I'd had my fill, I crawled forward, hands outstretched to the geode.

—Please, I said.

But although I opened my mouth, the heavenly body danced out of my reach.

—Please! I moaned.

The sun vanished behind its great form.

Then I blinked.

When I opened my eyes, the geode had disappeared. In its place were rain clouds.

Weeks of rain flooded the prairie, and now the river ran once more. I stood before its red, muddy waters. On the banks a stone sparkled. I picked it up and suckled, an infant teething its bite. My eyes closed. The stone yielded, and my mouth filled with milk. I knew then that I wanted to be like that stone from here on out—to yield, to feed.

I slipped and slid through the mud, face tipped up, drinking what the sky gave me, and walked toward the hills, the image of Jane and her daughters approaching us those months ago still branded on my memory. I could see a speck in the distance, a possible sod home. I followed the creek. I was right: it led me to her door. The roof hadn't been finished yet. There were signs of collapse. I resolved to help her fix it.

— — —

I knocked on the wood frame and Jane appeared in the doorway.

—I haven't anything, said Jane.

I held out the pink stone to Jane. As it passed from my hand to hers, our fingers brushed.

—What a lovely stone, said Jane.

—Sorry, I said, that I'm like this.

—Most of you are.

—I didn't think of you.

—Most of you don't.

—I will learn why.

—Maybe, said Jane. Maybe not.

My words felt caught in my throat. The hairs on my neck stood up painfully, small knives of flesh. At my back, the rain fell. This was the first honest exchange of my life. I felt raw.

From the corner of the sod house came a small, sweet tune, with a melody that climbed like a ladder. I peered into the dim and saw Ellen Madora, who sat at a busted piano, fingers moving over the keys. She must have dragged it here from what was once the whorehouse, now a boarded-up shack settled against great dunes of dust. Ellen Madora played two keys together, and the harmony cut through the gloom. I wanted to tell someone, anyone, what I'd kept to myself. It tumbled out of me.

—I had a vision.

Jane waited.

—Could I say it?

Ellen Madora played a key that stuck, and the note rang out until she pried it up again.

—I'm in love with a stone, I confessed at last.

—Ah, said Jane. Love can do wonders for someone like you.

—I love a stone, sang Ellen Madora, her notes high and clear.

The QUEER
FICTION ISSUE

McSWEENEY'S
QUARTERLY

ISSUE NO.
SIXTY-TWO

– – –

*   *   *

The sky wept, the prairie flooded, the gnats returned, and with them the birds, the fish, the rabbits, the snakes. The geode had given life back to the land. I sat out in the open, day after day, waiting for its return—but the sky swelled only with thunderclouds. I fell into a time of despondency. My mother found her health restored and, now intent on improving my reputation, mistook my misery for the feminine docility she'd always dreamed I could display. She put me in a mended, ill-fitting dress and sent me on foot to the dance hall, where the other remaining young people flocked to flirt. My hair done up in loops I longed to suck, my back to the corner: I had little interest in the human faces before me. I pressed the pebbles I now kept in my bodice, hoping to be left alone.

—It's not that you're not pretty, said the blacksmith's son as he placed his hand on the small of my back. It's just that you're pretty odd for a girl.

—I'm not a girl, I said, tired. His ears went red.

—What can you mean? he said.

A change of hands, of guard, of post.

—My mother told me I had to dance with you, said the butcher's son. His sleeves, rolled to his forearms, looked starched, pristine.

—Very fine, Mr. Olsen, I recited, and ruined the downbeat with a lock of my knees. I felt him falter. The butcher's son stopped and stiffly bowed.

I stepped outside and found Ellen Madora standing by her lonesome beneath the mesquite tree.

—You don't like dancing much, said Ellen Madora.

Her hair was still neat, no sweat on her brow. I gave her my cup of punch and she drank.

—I don't dance well in this body, I replied.

— — —

—I'm never asked, she said.

We walked together, circling the dance hall, discussing the topics of love and romance. She had never been kissed, she said, having been raised with religious folk who did not approve of their sons kissing freed girls, and now she found herself stuck in a settlement that was not so different, all things considered. I confessed I had never been kissed, either—not even by my mother.

—But why not? asked Ellen Madora. You're pretty enough. You have lovely eyes.

—Never felt interested, I said, thinking of my geode. I suppose now I'll die an old maid, never kissing anyone but the back of my own hand.

She laughed, a small, tinkling laugh that reminded me of her piano. She made me feel bold. With her, I could pretend to know my shape.

—We could learn how to do kissing together.

Ellen Madora tipped her head, the ribbons on her braids fluttering in a sudden gust.

—That might be nice.

So I leaned down and kissed her. Slowly, her mouth opened to me. I smelled warmth wafting up from the folds of her body, from the crook of her collarbone. When I touched her waist, she pressed herself against me. I wanted to lick her teeth, big white granite, so I did, and she shuddered in my arms. We pulled apart. A spider web of spit strung between our lips.

—Is it always like that? she whispered. Her nipples hardened beneath my fingers. A rabbit skittered through the dry weeds, and my heart thumped with it. I shook my head—I had no idea.

—Perhaps... perhaps you're a man, then?

I shook my head again. I didn't know how to say it—that I felt closer to rocks than to any human name. The pebbles in my bodice grew heavier. I thought I knew what she wanted of me.

—I only know how to touch stones, I said at last. I only know how to drink water.

Ellen Madora took my hand and placed it upon her neck. I felt her swallow; I felt her blood move.

—How do you touch your stone that you love? she asked. How do you drink water?

I pressed my thumb firm against the underside of her chin and felt the hardness of her jaw.

—Show me, she pleaded.

The stars burned above us. The music in the dance hall changed tempo, and the people inside hollered with pleasure. Slowly, I reached into my bodice and took out a pebble. She watched me place it on my tongue. My eyelids fluttered as I felt the familiar grit on my teeth, the jagged edges cutting into the roof of my mouth. The milk I tasted tonight was thin and floral. My tongue lolled in its wet.

Ellen Madora held out her hand, so I reached into my bodice again and handed her my second pebble. She moved the pebble into her mouth. It found its way into her cheek, and I giggled: how sweet she looked, like a child eating too much cake!

—Do you taste it? I said.

But Ellen Madora's face fell. She let the stone fall from her mouth back into her palm.

—What? I asked, my own stone dropping wetly from my lips.

—The stone yields nothing for me, said Ellen Madora.

—But if you just suck differently, I said.

Ellen Madora shook her head.

—If I could show you on your finger, I said.

—Graveyard, she said to me, it's not meant for me. I am barred from it.

A bit of water seeped up from the ground between us where our feet had just trod. Ellen Madora bent down and placed her palm on its surface.

The QUEER
FICTION ISSUE

THE GEODIC BODY
by BRIDGET BREWER

ISSUE NO.
SIXTY-TWO

– – –

—You can go back into the dance hall if you'd like, she said.

—I'm sorry, I said, but even I heard the empty ring of all my words.

I bent down alongside her and we gazed at the puddle, our reflections wavering with each breath we let out.

A wolf, made of many wolves, becomes a pack of wolves. A locust, made of many locusts, becomes a swarm of locusts. A pebble, made of many pebbles, becomes a mountain.

—Stop that, said Mother.

I paused, tongue digging into the pink mudstone. The river was lazy, spit's distance from my nose.

—I like it, I said.

—You'll stop with that girl, as well, said Mother.

—I like her, I said.

Her hand came down and found me. Later, I felt tenderness in the heart of my forehead. A bruise blooming for my turpitude. A few weeks after, I went to find Ellen Madora and tell her more about my rocks—but I found their home emptied, the piano still in the corner and missing a few of its keys. And, beneath the endless sea of grass, I felt the earth awaiting my mouth.

I began to feel shame, even as I spent more and more nights with rocks in my mouth. My mother said my eyes were turning black with prairie madness, and that soon I would do something stupid, like try to eat a hill and die choking on dirt. I came to believe her: I needed someone to help me comprehend myself.

When I came into my sixteenth birthday, I went to visit the

whorehouse, which had been rebuilt since the droughts. I stepped inside and was greeted with dim red gaslight. The parlor stank. Blankets covered the windows. Customers drank liquor in tumblers and eyed me, dubious, as the women spun naked around the room. The madam moved about, carrying a tray. I approached her.

—Which are the ones the girls won't touch? I asked as she twirled a customer's moustache.

The madam pointed. A rumpled corner of men undulated, snorted, all eyes.

—I would like them for my own purposes.

The madam frowned.

—I won't pay you, she said.

—No need, I replied.

She squinted, then smiled.

—You're Graveyard.

—Yes.

—Be my guest, she said, and waved her hand.

I approached the corner.

—Gentlemen, I said, I have a proposal.

A pair of eyes opened and closed.

—What have you got down there? they said.

—A banquet hall, I said. I'd like you to fill it.

Another set of eyes opened wide.

—All of us?

—Yes, I said, and began to unlace my bodice. All of you at once. I should like to be filled properly.

A tongue flashed in the dim lamplight.

—A virgin? one of them croaked.

I merely laughed. What could they know of bodies, of geodes, of swallowing death?

—If you guide me, I said. Instead, I shall do my best.

– – –

When I was naked, clothing pooled at my feet, I let them look upon me. The rumpled corner shuddered. I heard belts unbuckling. Hands, hard and cracked, began petting my legs. Someone pinched my nipple.

In this way, I learned of sex with men.

This, too, though pleasurable, did not cure me. And now all I could see when I closed my eyes was my geode, taunting me, ever out of reach.

How many rocks have I swallowed in my lifetime? What alchemy did I perform that filled me with such lust? I said this to the apples in the orchard, and four fell, rotting. I stood naked in the sun, keening, trying to learn to be worthy of petrification. To the west, a dead city; to the east, a sick bowl of dust. I dug for the horizon; I plunged my hands into the red mud of my birth and prayed to be made different upon waking. I awoke in the dark and walked for miles. I could not understand the limits of what I wanted.

—Graveyard.

I looked across the river from where I scrubbed the laundry, snow melting beneath my knees.

—Graveyard, said the oldest of Mitchum's boys. Eat any dead girls lately?

—Just the milliner's pig, I said and scoured my mother's blouse.

—Graveyard, said the oldest boy. Think you can eat this?

I looked up, half hoping he would toss me some candy. His hands twiddled with the front of his trousers, then revealed a small pink finger of flesh that he began tugging: a sad, meager worm in danger of splitting in two. I rolled my eyes. Mitchum's boys hollered.

—Graveyard! said the middle boy. Graveyard, think you can eat this!

He, too, fiddled with the front of his trousers.

—Graveyard! squealed the youngest boy, patting his groin, too young to understand the game afoot but nevertheless eager to inherit the tradition of female harrying.

—Ho, ho, I said. I slapped the fabric onto the rock beside me and placed the blouse in my basket. Then I stood. Why don't you come over here and find out?

Mitchum's boys faltered. I grinned.

—Walk on the water, sons of Mitchum, I called. And let me show you what I can eat.

Their hands went red as the sun fell behind them.

—Whore! yelled the oldest boy.

I thought of the whore, her brave chin.

—Jesse, I said to myself, and carried my basket back up the banks.

They knocked me down into the snow with a blow to the back of my head when I was just beyond the vegetable garden. Mitchum's boys knelt on my limbs. The oldest boy loomed above me, breath acrid.

His hand opened to reveal a dead baby killdeer, naked, beak askew, neck snapped and crooked, the corpse a small knot in his palm.

—Open up, Graveyard, said Mitchum's oldest boy.

In response, I bit flesh from his thumb and swallowed it while he screamed.

I know he hit me, but I cannot remember the pain, nor can I conjure feeling anything else: knuckles, the taste of bird, the crunch of small bones as they forced my jaw to close. I felt none of it. I could think only of the whore, of the bloody dirt sliding down my gullet to

The QUEER
FICTION ISSUE

THE GEODIC BODY
by BRIDGET BREWER

ISSUE NO.
SIXTY-TWO

− − −

crystallize my gut. I became a rock, unflinching, as he hit me. When I opened my eyes some hours later and found the dead bird still stuffed in my mouth, its foot sticking out from between my lips, I swallowed the bird down within me, where I hoped it would be safe, where I hoped it would find a fitting afterlife.

My mother coughed. Her lips left a red continent emblazoned upon the handkerchief. The wind whistled through the dead grass, the wild rabbit carcasses. I could hear the ants dismantling their meager flesh.

—I will ride for the doctor.

—Unlikely, said my mother.

My mother's last words to me were barbed. Even now, I cannot help but feel proud of her.

I sat beside the grave of my mother. I sat beside my mother's grave. The moon rose, its teeth at my neck. I had yet to cover her body. She lay in the dirt, her soft, mousy curls forming a halo around her head. I couldn't look her in the eyes, though I'd left them open. There was still a chance she could wake up and milk the cow—wasn't there? I lowered myself over her head and placed two coins upon her eyes. I'd heard from Ellen Madora that coins helped settle the dead.

All my life we'd lived together, my mother and I, and now I couldn't make myself mourn. I grabbed a fistful of dirt and tried to swallow it, but my grief for her was faraway. I sat on the edge of the grave and dangled my toes against her cold shin. Elsewhere, stars shone.

—I beat the Jesse out of you, Mother, I said.

That was the end of my eulogy.

I heard a great crack then, neither a gunshot nor lightning but something deeper that made the crickets go quiet. I looked down

The QUEER
FICTION ISSUE

McSWEENEY'S
QUARTERLY

ISSUE NO.
SIXTY-TWO

– – –

at myself and found, with shock, that my body had been halved. Viscera unspooled. I looked into the heart of my split and saw a chasm. Winking purple amethyst lined the center of my body. Bile sat sharp at the back of my throat, an acidic joy: for there, at my center, was everything I had ever consumed. On the rungs of my rib cage, the infant killdeer sat frozen in mid-motion, scuffed-up and worse for wear, locked in longing, with its beak agape. The finger flesh of Mitchum's oldest son draped itself elegantly over my liver, like a velvet shawl in a parlor. The semen of the men at the whore-house dripped from the shard-tips of my broken sternum, mingling with the milk of countless stones and Ellen Madora's spit. I gazed in awe. I could trace my contents to each moment I'd swallowed—there, too, was the water I'd drunk when the geode first appeared, and there was the milk of our cow, small lakes and puddles in my intestinal caverns; there were all the insects, snakes, rabbits, deer I'd killed by my own hand, their forms together but still devoid of life. The dirt from the death of the whore. I could still smell her sweet perfume, a copper blood-stink in the air.

What had I imagined I'd been giving them, all these forms gathered in my graveyard? What had I taken away? Here they had been all along, nesting inside me: I had never been alone once in my life; their entombment within me had been complete. I wept with understanding.

Reaching with my right arm into myself, I pulled out the baby killdeer and placed it on the edge of my mother's grave. The crystals cut my thumb, but what are cuts between lovers? I watched as its chest rose and fell, as its eyes blinked, as it raised itself with a small, piercing chirp and fluttered off into the night. I reached into my split and brought the other flesh within me back into the world, one by one. The snakes shook awake, slithered off through the sweetgrass. The insects and rabbits re-formed, scampered. I dug a shallow hole beside my mother's grave and buried the spit of Ellen Madora, the flesh I'd

The QUEER
FICTION ISSUE

THE GEODIC BODY
by BRIDGET BREWER

ISSUE NO.
SIXTY-TWO

– – –

taken from Mitchum's oldest son, the semen, the milk, the gifts I'd been given. I emptied my cavern, at last, of life.

When the burying was done, the two shards of my body considered each other. They touched each other's edges. Had they ever met? They flirted, they pinned each other down in the mud. One of my right hand's fingernails, jagged, caught on a flap of loose left-hand skin and I shouted—the pain became pleasure, and my right side did it again. The wide, terrible sky made space for me and my geodic body as we danced hand in hand in hand in hand, floating above the world as if winged, light, free. My flesh flayed out, my blood and my tears and my milk rained to the ground, and where they fell, wild roses sprang into existence. I shouted and shuddered. Had I ever been so happy? There I slumbered, at rest, at last.

A pebble, made of many pebbles, becomes a mountain. A grave, made of many graves, becomes a graveyard. A wanting, made of many wantings, becomes a transformation. A transformation is a flight from one place to the next.

DEREK ABELLA is a queer Cuban-American illustrator living and working in Brooklyn. His lush, ethereal pieces have been commissioned by a variety of clients, such as the *New York Times*, the *New Yorker*, the *Guardian*, and Red Bull.

AARUSHI AGNI (@aarushifire, she/they) is a writer, comedian, singer-song-writer, screenwriter, artist, educator, and tenderhearted being. She does stand-up and sketch comedy with Overstep Comedy. She received her MFA in writing and activism from Pratt Institute, and her band, Tin Can Diamonds, is streaming everywhere.

KRISTEN N. ARNETT is the *New York Times* best-selling author of the debut novel *Mostly Dead Things* (Tin House, 2019). Her next two books (*Samson* and *With Foxes*) will be published by Riverhead Books.

GABRIELLE BELLOT is a staff writer for *Literary Hub* and a contributing editor at Catapult. Her work has appeared in the *New York Times*, the *New Yorker*, the *Atlantic*, the *Cut*, the *New York Review of Books*, the *Paris Review Daily*, *Guernica*, and elsewhere. She lives in New York. "The Cruel and Astonishing Tale of Imogen Cabral da Gama" is an excerpt from her novel-in-progress.

VENITA BLACKBURN is the author of the story collection *Black Jesus and Other Superheroes*. She is an assistant professor of fiction at Fresno State. Her next collection of stories, *How to Wrestle a Girl*, will be published in the fall of 2021. More information can be found at venitablackburn.com.

BRIDGET BREWER is a writer, educator, and musician based in Austin, Texas. Their work can be found at bridget-brewer06.com.

K-MING CHANG (張欣明) is a Kundiman Fellow and a Lambda Literary Award finalist. She is the author of the debut novel *Bestiary* (One World, 2020). Her poems have been anthologized in *Ink Knows No Borders: Poems of the Immigrant and Refugee Experience*, *Best New Poets 2018*, *Bettering American Poetry*, vol. 3, and *The Pushcart Prize XLIII: Best of the Small Presses*, 2019 edition. More of her work can be found at kmingchang.com.

EMMA COPLEY EISENBERG is a writer of fiction and nonfiction and is based in Philadelphia. She is the author of *The Third Rainbow Girl: The Long Life of a Double Murder in Appalachia* and a novel and story collection forthcoming from Hogarth.

PATTY YUMI COTTRELL is the author of *Sorry to Disrupt the Peace* (McSweeney's) and the winner of a Whiting Award in Fiction and a Barnes & Noble Discover Award. Their work has appeared in publications like *Granta*, the *White Review*, *BuzzFeed*, *Black Warrior Review*, and most recently in *Pets: An Anthology* (New York Tyrant).

ARIEL DAVIS is a multidisciplinary artist whose practice includes illustration, graphic design, and animation. She lives in New York City and has worked for clients such as the *New York Times*, *Pitchfork*, *Wired*, and *MIT Technology Review*.

SARAH GERARD is the author of the essay collection *Sunshine State*, the collaborative art book *Recycle* (with Amy Gall), and the novels *Binary Star* and *True Love*.

RL GOLDBERG is a PhD candidate at Princeton University, where they research, among other things, Heidegger's theorization of "in-ness" and trans narratives from the midcentury United States.

HURMAT KAZMI is a writer from Karachi, Pakistan. they currently live in Iowa City and attend the Iowa Writers' Workshop.

LEE LAI is from Naarm (Melbourne), Australia, and currently makes comics and illustrations in Tio'tia:ke (known as Montreal). She writes and paints comics in short and long-form fiction, and has been featured in the *New Yorker*, the *Lifted Brow*, *Room* magazine, and *Meanjin Quarterly*. Her first graphic novel, *Stone Fruit*, is due to be released by Fantagraphics in 2021 and has been translated into four languages.

CHRISTOPHER JAMES LLEGO is a Filipino American writer. He is a Kundiman Fellow and a 2020 Kundiman Mentorship Fellow. He is a graduate of Cornell University and lives in Brooklyn.

JULI DELGADO LOPERA is an award-winning Colombian writer and historian based in San Francisco. They're the author of the *New York Times*–acclaimed novel *Fiebre Tropical*, published in 2020 by the Feminist Press. Juli is the former executive director of RADAR Productions, a queer literary nonprofit in San Francisco. The piece in this issue is an excerpt from their novel-in-progress, *Papi*.

AMANDA MONTI is a cross-disciplinary poet based in Brooklyn. They are currently making work about spontaneous urban plants and queer romance. Amanda holds an MFA in writing from the Pratt Institute and has recently published a deck of tarot cards.

EILEEN MYLES has published twenty-two books, most recently *For Now*, an essay/talk about writing from Yale Press that is out in September. "Twins" is a chapter from *All My Loves*, a gigantic forthcoming novel by this author.

VI KHI NAO is the author of four poetry collections: *Human Tetris* (11:11 Press, 2019), *Sheep Machine* (Black Sun Lit, 2018), *Umbilical Hospital* (1913 Press, 2017), *The Old Philosopher* (winner of the 2014 Nightboat Books Prize for Poetry), as well as the short-story collection *A Brief Alphabet of Torture* (winner of the 2016 FC2 Ronald Sukenick Innovative Fiction Prize) and the novel *Fish in Exile* (Coffee House Press, 2016). Her work includes poetry, fiction, film, and cross-genre collaborations. She was the fall 2019 Shearing Fellow at the Black Mountain Institute. More info can be found at vikhinao.com.

DENNIS NORRIS II is the recipient of fellowships from the MacDowell Colony, Tin House, VCCA, and Kimbilio. Their work appears or is forthcoming in the *Cut*, *American Short Fiction*, *ZORA*, *SmokeLong Quarterly*, and other publications. They currently serve as senior fiction editor at the *Rumpus* and co-host of the critically acclaimed podcast *Food 4 Thot*.

TIMI ODUESO's short stories have been published or are forthcoming in Nobrow Press's short-story anthology, *TSSF*, *On The Premises*, and *Crossroads*. A 2018–19 Fellow of the Wawa Book Review Young Literary Critics Fellowship, he is the winner of the 2019 Sevhage Literary Prize in creative nonfiction.

DREW PHAM is a queer, trans-femme writer of Vietnamese heritage and an adjunct professor at Brooklyn College. She serves as an editor at the *Wrath-Bearing Tree*, a literary journal focused on societal violence. She is based in Brooklyn.

PAUL DALLA ROSA is a writer based in Melbourne, Australia. His stories have appeared in *Granta*, *Meanjin Quarterly*, and *New York Tyrant*.

KAYLA KUMARI UPADHYAYA is a lesbian writer of essays, short fiction, and pop-culture criticism. Her work has appeared in the *Cut*, the *A.V. Club*, *Vulture*, *Eater NY*, and *Autostraddle*.

ANGIE WANG is a James Beard Award–winning illustrator, cartoonist, and animator. She also cofounded Comic Arts Los Angeles, an independent comics festival.

BRYAN WASHINGTON is the author of *Memorial* and *Lot*. He lives in Houston.

EMERSON WHITNEY is the author of *Heaven* (McSweeney's, 2020) and *Ghost Box* (Timeless Infinite Light, 2014). Emerson teaches in the BFA creative writing program at Goddard College and is a postdoctoral fellow in gender studies at the University of Southern California.

GARRETT YOUNG is an illustrator and cartoonist living and working in Oklahoma City. His work has appeared in anthologies such as *Swampcone Magazine*, *Happiness*, *Gang Bang Bong*, as well as *Businessweek*. He explores surreal, macabre scenes through psychedelia and cultural arcana.

McSWEENEY'S 58: 2040

McSweeney's 58: 2040 A.D. is wholly focused on climate change, with speculative fiction from ten contributors, made in collaboration with the Natural Resources Defense Council. Using fiction—informed here and there by realism and climate science—this issue explores the tangible, day-to-day implications of these cataclysmic scientific projections. Featuring Tommy Orange, Elif Shafak, Luis Alberto Urrea, Asja Bakić, Rachel Heng, and others.

MY FAVORITE GIRLFRIEND
WAS A FRENCH BULLDOG
by Legna Rodríguez Iglesias

My Favorite Girlfriend Was a French Bulldog is a novel told in fifteen stories, linked by the same protagonist, our narrator, who—in her own voice and channeling the voices of others—creates an unsparing, multigenerational portrait of her native Cuba. *My Favorite Girlfriend Was a French Bulldog* marks the emergence of an original and essential new voice.

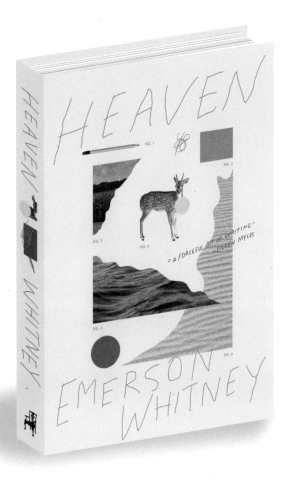

HEAVEN
by Emerson Whitney

An expansive examination of what makes us up, *Heaven* wonders what role our childhood plays in who we are. Can we escape the discussion of causality? Is the story of our body just ours? With extraordinary emotional force, Whitney sways between theory and memory to explore these brazen questions and write this unforgettable book.

ALSO AVAILABLE
FROM McSWEENEY'S

ALL THIS
AND MORE
at
STORE.McSWEENEYS.NET

Founded in 1998, McSweeney's is an independent publisher based in San Francisco. McSweeney's exists to champion ambitious and inspired new writing, and to challenge conventional expectations about where it's found, how it looks, and who participates. We're here to discover things we love, help them find their most resplendent form, and place them into the hands of curious, engaged readers.

THERE ARE SEVERAL WAYS TO SUPPORT MCSWEENEY'S:

Support Us on Patreon
visit *www.patreon.com/mcsweeneysinternettendency*

Subscribe & Shop
visit *store.mcsweeneys.net*

Volunteer & Intern
email *eric@mcsweeneys.net*

Sponsor Books & Quarterlies
email *amanda@mcsweeneys.net*

To learn more, please visit www.mcsweeneys.net/donate
or contact Executive Director Amanda Uhle at
amanda@mcsweeneys.net or 415.642.5609.

McSweeney's Literary Arts Fund is a nonprofit
organization as described by IRS 501(c)(3).
Your support is invaluable to us.